DATE DUE

MAY 0 7 '92

1995

PARENTS AND TEACHERS
OF EXCEPTIONAL STUDENTS

PARENTS AND TEACHERS OF EXCEPTIONAL STUDENTS

■

A HANDBOOK FOR INVOLVEMENT

THOMAS M. SHEA
Southern Illinois University

ANNE M. BAUER
Indiana University Southeast

■

ALLYN AND BACON, INC.
Boston, London, Sydney, Toronto

Series Editor: Jeffery W. Johnston
Production Administrator: Jane J. Schulman
Production Coordinator: Ron Newcomer and Associates
Text Designer: Ron Newcomer
Cover Coordinator: Christy Rosso
Cover Designer: Mary Ann Nute

Library of Congress Cataloging in Publication Data

Shea, Thomas M., 1934–
    Parents and teachers of exceptional students.

    Bibliography: p.
    Includes index.
    1. Exceptional children—Education—Study and teaching
—United States.   2. Parent-teacher relationships—
United States.   3. Exceptional children—United States—
Family relationships.   4. Exceptional children—
Psychology—Teacher training—United States.   I. Bauer,
Anne M.   II. Title.
LC3981.S54   1985   371.9   84–24435
ISBN 0–205–08327–7

Printed in the United States of America

10 9 8 7 6 5 4 3 2 1   90 89 88 87 86 85

To our parents and families:

Dolores, Kevin, and Keith
and
William, Eleanor, Christian, Joan, and Paul

CONTENTS

PREFACE

■ Educators are seeing parents return to classrooms and schools as advocates for their children and their neighbors' children. Since the early 1950s, Americans have demonstrated increasing concern for the rights of all citizens. One part of this movement, backed by legislative mandates and court decisions, is greater concern for exceptional children's rights.

The society as a whole now is more aware of the difficulties confronting contemporary parents in raising their exceptional children, as well as the problems and conflicts these children face in their effort to function fully and successfully in a complex, ever-changing society. As a result, a variety of parent education and training programs are available to help parents of exceptional children. Schools, hospitals, churches, colleges, as well as local, state, and national public and private organizations all offer parenting programs and parent information services. These programs take many forms:

■ *Child development training.* These programs instruct parents in the principles and practices of both normal and exceptional child development. Parents learn about children's physical, intellectual, social and emotional development.

■ *Parenting education.* Secondary schools and continuing education programs offer parent education courses that tend to emphasize normal child development and consumer education, with some attention to the exceptionalities.

■ *Training in behavior management, socialization, and interpersonal communication.* Parent education and training in behavioral and communication topics increased dramatically in the 1970s, giving rise to a considerable body of literature available to the general public. To date, courses in these subjects are largely continuing education offerings.

■ *Support and counseling services.* Counseling programs help parents become more effective in their relationships and consequently become more effective parents. Many private and public mental health and social service agencies offer individual and group therapy and counseling programs to parents.

■ *Information services.* Public and private, local, state, and national organizations provide information to parents on an extensive range of parenting problems and societal concerns, including divorce, hospitalization, death, family mobility, drugs, sex, television, war, alcohol, delinquency, and exceptionality.

■ *Service delivery systems.* Much of the current parent training and education literature for professionals in special education, education, mental health, and the social services discusses how to organize effective and efficient parent-teacher action that will lead to effective parent education and training program.

This text is in the final category of parent services. Its goal is to increase the probability that parents and teachers will work effectively together to benefit the exceptional children for whom they share responsibility. The book is a desk reference for special education classrooms, resource, itinerant, and crisis teachers; school psychologists, counselors, nurses, and social workers; administrators; and other professionals serving exceptional children and their parents. It is also a textbook for college students in special education, preschool, elementary, and secondary education; or in courses on parent-teacher relations and exceptional children. It presents a model and broad range of parent-teacher activities that provide a framework for developing parent-teacher programs. A goal of the model is to provide enough flexibility for parents and teachers to design programs responsive to their needs, the exceptional children's needs, and the educational environment.

The first section sets the stage for parent involvement by discussing parents' and children's experiences of exceptionality and outlining a parent involvement model. Chapter One explains the social dynamics affecting parents, teachers, and children, emphasizing that parenting is an art and that exceptional children are, first and foremost children, with needs and desires common to all children. The chapter highlights the impact of societal change on parenting from the 1930s to the 1980s to bring home these themes.

Chapter Two focuses on the "exceptional" in exceptional children and parents. It discusses the role of the exceptional child's parents, the parents' reactions to the birth and diagnosis of a child with an exceptionality, the coping behaviors parents use to adjust to their new role, and the impact of an exceptional child on the family. Given the complexity of these factors, the chapter also explores why some parents and teachers do not participate in cooperative activities.

Chapter Three discusses the need for and desirability of parent-teacher involvement and its advantages for exceptional children, parents, teachers, schools, and communities. It emphasizes the rights and responsibilities of exceptional children and their parents as key factors governing parents' and teachers' approach to cooperative programs.

Chapter Four describes a detailed model that can help teachers think about and plan for involvement programs. It defines the model's purpose, limitations, and process and provides several forms that can guide the writing of individualized programs for parents. The chapter discusses guidelines for interpersonal communication that are critical to effective use of the model.

The second section of the book augments the model by presenting activities that can smooth the way for parent participation. Chapter Five discusses approaches to written and phone communication, including daily and periodic report cards, newsletters, notes, notices, and telephone contacts. It also introduces several innovative activities, such as task analysis report cards, passports for positive parent-teacher communication, and learning charts.

Chapter Six discusses the parent-teacher conference as a key part of the communication process. The discussion highlights progress report, problem-solving, and behavior management training conferences, with special attention to the individualized education program conference and home visits. It also explores two special issues of conferencing—including the child and dealing with parents' negative reactions.

Chapters Seven and Eight focus on parent-teacher group activities. Chapter Seven establishes a framework and offers general guidelines for large and small group parent-teacher activities. Chapter Eight looks at specific types of groups, including informational, communication, problem-solving, discussion, and training groups.

Chapter Nine considers the parent as an important resource in the classroom and school, at home, and in the community. It discusses parents' potential contributions as paraprofessionals, instructors, committee members, volunteers, home-based teachers, and home study supervisors. It also looks at resource centers, teaching packages, and training techniques that can help parents perform these roles effectively. Chapter Ten applies the material in the preceding chapters in an extensive illustration of how to apply the parent-teacher involvement model in a special education setting.

Each chapter ends with exercises and topics for discussion that reinforce the chapter concepts and provide practice in the techniques described. Extensive reference lists lead readers to other sources that can broaden their understanding of the chapter content.

The book includes five appendixes. Appendix A reviews several practical assessment instruments for use during the parent-teacher assessment phase of the parent-teacher involvement model. Appendix B presents cases for study and role playing for students who do not have access to exceptional children and their parents in the course of their study. Appendix C supplies a resource list of support and informational organizations for parents and teachers. Appendix D provides worksheets and forms introduced in the text, and Appendix E presents the same forms in Spanish in recognition of the unique problems confronting bilingual parents and children in a predominantly English-speaking society.

We hope this handbook will help teachers become true partners with parents in educating exceptional children. Many people have contributed to the development of the text. We appreciate the assistance of Dr. Rosemary Egan, our students, many parents, and numerous friends and colleagues who have participated in our work in many ways.

Thank you to Jeffery Johnston, Sue Canavan, and Jane Schulman of Allyn and Bacon for their support, guidance, and assistance in producing the final manuscript. Special thanks also to Jean Wildhaber, who cheerfully typed and retyped the manuscript.

Finally, we thank Dolores, Kevin, and Keith Shea and Bill and Eleanor Bauer for their patience and encouragement.

PARENTS AND TEACHERS
OF EXCEPTIONAL STUDENTS

A MODEL FOR PARENT-TEACHER INVOLVEMENT

■

■ Chapters One through Four offer an introduction to parent-teacher collaboration in behalf of exceptional children. Chapter One serves as an overview of the art of parenting for all children. Effects of social change occurring between 1930 and the present on parenting is discussed. Throughout this chapter, exceptional children are described as first and foremost children with similar needs and desires as nonexceptional children.

Chapter Two analyzes what is special about parents and families of exceptional children. The effects of this specialness on parents, families, and teachers are assessed. Parent needs for professional support are described.

Chapter Three provides perspectives on parent-teacher involvement. Guidelines for fostering home and school cooperation are provided. The rights and responsibilities of parents of exceptional children are reviewed.

Chapter Four concludes this section with a presentation of the model for parent-teacher involvement, its purposes, limitations, processes, and procedures. Specific information is provided on communication, interviewing techniques, and competencies for parent-teacher involvement. The section concludes with a description of the use of professionals and paraprofessionals in the parent-involvement process.

CHAPTER ONE

PARENTING

■ Parenting is a complex, dynamic process that affects both parent and child. A parent develops and uses the knowledge and skills required to plan for children, give birth to them, and/or rear and care for them (Morrison 1978).

In general, one or more adults are primarily responsible for a child's basic care, direction, support, protection, and guidance. Most people play a parenting role, either directly or indirectly, in their lifetime. A parent may be a child's biological parent, foster parent, stepparent, aunt, uncle, older sibling, relative, or parent surrogate. Parents are many ages, single or married, male or female.

Parenting is the most essential and enduring profession acknowledged by society, but it is one for which most participants are inadequately prepared. For better or worse, we become parents and parent surrogates responsible for raising children to live in society.

This text, devoted to parent-teacher involvement in teaching exceptional children, opens with a general discussion of parenting for two reasons. First, exceptional children and their parents are first and foremost children and parents; the factors influencing them are the same that influence all children and parents. Second, exceptional children and their parents participate in the same parenting process experienced by all parents and children. Parenting an exceptional child is unique in degree and intensity rather than in kind. Like all children, exceptional children need love, care, guidance, support, protection, and direction. Efforts to meet exceptional children's special needs must not ignore these basic human needs.

SOCIAL CHANGE AND PARENTING

Child rearing takes place in a social context. The society influences parents' behavior, children's behavior, and the overall parenting process. Thus, parents must essentially learn to manipulate the environment for their children's benefit, protecting them from social forces that conflict with their parenting philosophy and objectives.

Fromm's statement about loving applies also to parenting: "If love is a capacity of the mature, productive character, it follows that the capacity to love in an individual living in any given culture depends on the influence this culture has on the character of the average person" (1956, 70). Many parents raise their children following the social conventions of their generation. They remain out of touch with the present. Effective parents view the society as it is, not as it was when they were children, nor as the ideal society they wish it could be.

The past two generations have seen significant social changes that directly influence the parenting process. Table 1-1 highlights social changes between the 1930s and the 1980s that have affected parenting. As the following discussion of these changes points out, despite some people's plea for a return to the good old days, parents must recognize that today's children and adolescents, normal and exceptional, are growing up in a world very different from that of their parents.

The Family

In the 1930s, children lived in extended families that usually included a mother, a father, and two or more brothers or sisters. Single-parent families were rare. Frequently, aunts, uncles, cousins, married siblings, and grandparents lived in the home and actively participated in family life. These adults gave the child's parents advice and guidance (Croft 1979; Morrison 1978).

In the 1980s, the most common living unit is the *neolocal nuclear family,* a social unit existing apart from parents, grandparents, and relatives (Toffler 1970; Morrison 1978). The neolocal nuclear family does

TABLE 1-1 *Social Changes*

Factors	1930s	1980s
Family	Extended, traditional nuclear	Neolocal nuclear
Neighborhood	Personal, cohesive	Impersonal, multicultural
Neighbors	Concerned, responsible, active	Concerned, defensive, passive or indirectly active
Companions/friends	Close, cohesive, socially and emotionally supportive	Often distant or unavailable, nonexistent for many needing social and emotional support
School	Small, in the neighborhood, personal	Large, outside the neighborhood, impersonal
Teachers	Accepted as friends, neighbors, community leaders	Perceived as strangers, professional, specialists
Knowledge	Limited, manageable within existing standards of behavior and application	Exploding, unmanageable within existing standards of behavior and application
Church	Influential	Relatively uninfluential
Standards/values	Rigid, widely accepted, emphasizing the normal	Relative, fragmented, emphasizing the bizarre and unacceptable
Work	Simple, personal, available, sufficient to produce needed goods, supportive of artisans	Mechanized, automated, specialized, unavailable to many, unsupportive of artisans
Material goods	Limited, emphasizing necessities for living	Available to majority, emphasizing luxuries
Mobility	Limited for most people	Nearly unlimited
Communication/ transportation	Limited, slow, inefficient	Nearly unlimited, rapid, efficient
National and world events	Not widely followed or understood	Extensively followed and understood worldwide

not depend on the knowledge, skills, and support system traditionally provided by the parents' families.

The once typical family of working husband, full-time wife-homemaker, and two children now occurs in only 7 percent of families with married couples (Scott and Wishy 1982). The husband is the family's sole earner in only 26 percent of married-couple families. These statistics reflect a significant change in the division of labor by sex roles within the family. Today, couples jointly, even though unequally, share responsibility for family duties (Caplow, Bahr, Chadwick, Hill, and Williamson 1982). Fathers spend more time with their children (Caplow et al. 1982). The birth rate has followed a general downward direction: Women now marry later in life and have fewer children. Thus, they are more employable and have greater work experience. In turn, their economic independence makes women more likely to seek divorce if their marriages come under stress (Scott and Wishy 1982). Mothers now more frequently reenter the labor force when their children enter a day care facility or school.

People unable to unwilling to live as a nuclear family often choose other living and parenting arrangements, which are increasingly available and acceptable in contemporary society (Talbot 1976):

■ *Androgynous household.* The key characteristic of this living arrangement is a blurring or merging of the traditional masculine role of breadwinner and the conventional feminine role of household manager and caretaker. Parents share work, housekeeping, and child-raising duties and responsibilities. The mother and father may stagger their work schedules to be available at home at different times during the day.

■ *Communes, collectives, and cooperatives.* In this modern parenting unit, two or more couples and their children live as a group in a house, on a farm, or in a small community. The members share work, household, and parenting duties and responsibilities. Children grow up with an ever-enlarging circle of "semi-siblings" (Toffler 1970).

■ *One- and single-parent households.* One-parent and single-parent households are valid choices for many adults today. The parents in these households are alone for a number of reasons: They are divorced, a spouse has died, they have adopted a child, or, for single women, they have decided to have a child on their own (Croft 1979). One out of eight children now lives in a single-parent home, and the number of one-parent households has increased 100 percent since 1970 (Sheils, Weathers, Howard, and Givens 1983). Moreover, more and more unmarried men are seeking responsibility for raising their children (Toffler 1970).

Since 1970, family households have grown by only 19 percent, while nonfamily households have increased 89 percent, now representing more than one-fourth the total. However, nine out of ten people continue to live in households as family members (Sheils et al. 1983).

Neighborhoods, Neighbors, and Friends

Communities in the 1930s, even in large cities, were limited geographic areas populated by families with common racial, ethnic, and religious characteristics (McAfee and Vergason 1979). Small towns as much as large cities contained ghettos populated by racial, ethnic, or religious groups. These communities were highly cohesive; citizens depended on each other for their economic well-being and social lives. As a result, children in the 1930s often viewed neighbors almost as family. In turn, neighbors did not hesitate to tell parents about a child's transgressions.

Modern neighborhoods differ in that they are conglomerates of families and individuals with dissimilar racial, ethnic, social, and religious backgrounds. Contemporary neighborhoods change constantly as families come and go. With this increased mobility, people have few opportunities to develop common standards of behavior for the neighborhood. They often become confused because accepted norms of behavior in their new neighborhood differ from those of their old neighborhood.

Thus, though 1980s parents care as much about their children's welfare as did 1930s parents, they may hesitate to speak out when their children or neighbors' children transgress. Today's parents are more likely to turn to community authorities—the police, courts, and schools—to deal with children's deviant behavior. Many simply avoid any action in fear of confrontation with neighbors and authorities.

Schools and Teachers

Fifty years ago, education was highly personalized. School was nearby, and children seldom left the neighborhood to attend school (McAfee and Vergason 1979). Teachers were members of the community. They knew children and their parents personally. They cared about students as individuals, not simply as readers, writers, spellers, and mathematicians. When teachers reprimanded and praised children, they usually did so in concert with the parents' wishes. Teachers were a significant force in a child's life.

All students received a general program of instruction emphasizing basic reading, writing, and arithmetic skills, with some attention to physical science, history, and civics. Formal education was designed to develop children into good citizens and productive adult workers. Toffler (1970) suggested that public education generally reflected the world into which children would graduate in its structure of jobs, roles, and institutions.

Part-time employment was a significant part of a child's education in the 1930s. A broad range of jobs were available to the young, such as delivering newspapers and mail, stocking shelves, mowing lawns, gardening, or washing dishes. Parents and teachers felt that these work opportunities provided excellent training and discipline.

Education has become increasingly impersonal in recent decades (McAfee and Vergason 1979), although the school remains the only social institution to which, at least theoretically, every child and parent is connected for a span of years.

Contemporary educators are organized professionals who strive for their personal and professional welfare as well as that of the children in their charge. They are frequently not members of the community in which they work. In addition, schools in the 1980s are more likely to be outside students' neighborhoods, requiring busing of children to and from school. Given these facts, parents' associations with teachers and other educational personnel tend to be infrequent and formal.

The knowledge explosion of the past several decades has led educators to place greater emphasis on developing children's cognitive abilities. They design instructional programs for the accumulation of specific knowledge and skills more than for critical thinking and problem-solving.

Churches, Standards, and Values

Churches were primary arbiters of moral and social behaviors in the 1930s. Lessons were clear and precise. The society at large rarely debated standards and values because codes of conduct and their supporting values were nearly universally accepted within the community (Croft 1979). People had little difficulty judging an act or an idea as good or bad, acceptable or unacceptable.

The church in 1980s society has less impact. Established churches have lost much of their credibility for many people. Many churches have been slow to articulate definitive positions on national and international problems, such as the Vietnam War, the Watergate scandal, racial integration, equal rights for women, the exploitation of natural resources, or nuclear power. Churches themselves are in the midst of change, with many of their long-standing principles and procedures called into question by their members.

In contemporary society, parents and children have few universally recognized and accepted personal and social values and standards to turn to. Standards of conduct vary greatly from community to community and within a community over time. Public debate about the proper stand on many issues, such as abortion, punishment of criminals, pornography, and equal rights, is constant and inconclusive.

Work and Material Goods

Work was physically demanding in the 1930s. Many artisans produced such essential goods as shoes, clothing, furniture, and household, farm, and manufacturing products. Moreover, people obtained satisfaction and received recognition in their community for providing needed goods and services.

Most 1930s families had enough money to satisfy their basic food, clothing, shelter, and transportation needs (Morrison 1978). However, the Great Depression brought with it considerable poverty, and little government money was available to assist the needy. Families obtained additional material goods through personal ingenuity and effort—by raising a few chickens or a cow in the back yard, for example, or planting a vegetable garden or obtaining a second job. People kept their possessions as long as they could, reusing them and repairing them as necessary.

Today, material goods and services are abundant in the United States. The population is conditioned to purchase goods and services simply for the pleasure of buying (Morrison 1978) and lives in a "throwaway" society of paper towels, tissues, and nonreturnable soft drink bottles (Toffler 1970). Purchasing is often unrelated to need: luxury purchases and entertainment consume a large portion of families' financial resources. Yet in the middle of this abundance are many individuals and families who live in poverty.

Work in the 1980s is highly mechanized, automated, and specialized. Few workers participate in the total production process of goods. The proportion of the work force in professional occupations has tripled in the past two generations. Craftspeople, who accounted for 21 percent of the male work force in 1920, made up only 9 percent in 1970. The proportion of women in the work force has also increased dramatically (Scott and Wishy 1982).

Mobility, Knowledge of the World, and Change

In the 1930s, people had limited mobility. A seven- or eight-mile car or bus trip to shop, see a movie, or attend a ballgame was a long journey for most people. If people left the community, they did so to seek employment or educational opportunities.

Similarly, people's knowledge of the world outside their immediate neighborhoods, towns, or cities was limited in the 1930s. Because communication and transportation were relatively primitive, events in distant cities and states did not seem personally significant. Although people were aware of major news events in Europe, reports from Asia and South America were practically nonexistent.

Change occurred slowly in the 1930s and had limited immediate impact on the average person. Because living conditions remained generally stable, formal and informal rules governing reactions to change evolved and were accepted at the time or shortly after the discovery of new knowledge, techniques, and products (McAfee and Vergason 1979).

Today, many of the forces for stability in the 1930s no longer apply. Mobility has increased manyfold during the past two generations, for example. Short-term mobility allows people to commute many miles each day for work, shopping, and entertainment. It exposes family members to a variety of people, places, and things. Children see a variety of life-styles and meet people from many ethnic, racial, religious, and cultural groups (McAfee and Vergason 1979; Croft 1979).

Long-term mobility allows families to move from one area to another several times during the life of a family unit. The average length of residence in one place in U.S. cities is less than four years (Toffler 1970). Family moves are often the result of work relocations. Long-term mobility reduces the family's opportunities to receive support from parents, other relatives, and friends. Children must repeatedly adapt to new neighborhoods, schools, homes, and companions during their formative years.

Today, thanks to highly efficient communication and transportation systems, the average person's knowledge of world and national events is potentially limitless. Newspaper and magazine articles and radio and television reports explore our inner space, daily life events, and the earth's outer space. Daily, people encounter the serious and the absurd, the loving and the savage. Parents have limited control over the information put before their children.

The pace of change has increased significantly in the past half century. Today, the process of change occurs with great rapidity and, at times, appears uncontrolled. A change often occurs before the society can develop the supporting values, standards, and behavioral norms to govern its effects. A few such changes are nuclear energy, exotic weaponry, abortion, and the prenatal detection of birth defects.

Social Problems

The dramatic differences between the 1930s and 1980s, in part, reflect society's efforts to realize the fundamental principles of U.S. democracy. The United States has taken great strides in this direction, demonstrating concern for equal rights and opportunities for all citizens, increased educational opportunities, the equitable application of law, and other democratic principles (Morrison 1978). Supporting these changes have been a knowledge explosion and technological advances in communication, transportation, and production.

However, along with these changes have come certain social problems that influence parenting in modern society. Aloneness and personal isolation are perhaps at the root of many of these problems, for contemporary society has seen interpersonal relations break down. As schools, neighborhoods, workplaces, churches, and recreational institutions have become more impersonal, many people have become alienated from society. This problem is exacerbated by increasing mobility, reliance on technology and automation to solve human problems and to do work, and the fragmentation of personal and social standards of behavior.

Alienation can take many forms, and parents try to be aware of these problems, understand them, and guide their children in confronting them. For example, tobacco, alcoholic beverages, and narcotics are readily available to children and youth in contemporary U.S. society, and many young people are harmed by indiscriminate, excessive use of these substances.

Parents find it necessary to help their children interpret the mass media for personal and societal advantage. Parents also try to help their children chart a course through the diversity of opinion about birth control techniques and their availability to young people, the morality and legal implications of abortion, child abuse and neglect, pornography, and other volatile issues. Parents are naturally concerned about the problems of illegitimate birth, teenage pregnancy, and venereal disease as well.

Children and parents must also cope with the high crime rate in the United States. The past decades have seen dramatic increases in juvenile delinquency, white collar crime, homicide, larceny, and rape. Political malfeasance and assassination, bribery in business and industry, tax fraud, and welfare cheating are other realities of the 1980s.

While preparing their children to function in a complex world, parents can also help them build on the strengths of society. Children today have, within prescribed limits, a right to actualize their potential, express their individuality, exercise political freedom, make personal decisions, live in relative comfort and safety, love and help others, work and be productive, and procreate. Parents can be their exceptional or nonexceptional children's greatest supporters in recognizing this potential.

THE ART OF PARENTING

Parenting is a dynamic process. Parents perpetually adapt their parenting to fit their children's emerging needs and interests, to meet their own needs and reflect new learning, and to respond to the ever-changing influence of society.

Parents guide their children's efforts to maintain the often precarious balance between love and hate, acceptance and rejection, work and idleness, kindness and cruelty, constructiveness and destructiveness, honesty and dishonesty, learning and ignorance, openness and prejudice, and self-discipline and self-indulgence.

Research has shown certain components of parenting to be responsive to scientific analysis, but helping a child develop and maintain a positive balance is ultimately an art. It requires knowledge, skill, understanding, and dedication equal to or exceeding that required of sculptors, composers, painters, poets, and other artists.

Just as artists aim for ideals in their art, parents try to attain certain standards of effective child rearing. They aim for objectivity, trying to see their children, themselves, and society as they are, not as they wish them to be. They accept themselves, children, and others as individuals capable of positive action and error. Like artists, they possess the "feel of childhood," which goes beyond scientific understanding of children (Dodson 1970). Parents have faith in themselves and are firm in their personal convictions. They believe in the goodness and potential of their children. They have the courage to stand up for those social values and standards important to them and know when to dismiss those of little or no consequence. Above all, they act on their children's behalf.

Like artists, parents are self-disciplined in their personal lives and support their children's efforts to attain self-discipline. They concentrate on the art of parenting, devoting time and energy to analyzing their functions and responsibilities.

Parents are patient, accepting that mistakes do occur and that a child's attainment of maturity is a slow, difficult process. They consider raising their children sufficiently important to make personal sacrifices to attain their goals. At times, parenting takes precedence over personal, social, and occupational goals.

Modern parents are above all versatile, able to play numerous roles and juggle many responsibilities (Table 1-2). Indeed, the breadth of their responsibilities makes it clear that they cannot personally meet all their children's needs. Parents must depend on others outside the family to assist with the responsibilities of parenting. Important allies in parents' efforts to raise their children are the teachers.

No parent is perfect, but many parents are successful. Perhaps a successful parent is "one who knows a good many of the right things to do in raising a child, and who *more than half the time* does the right thing instead of the wrong" (Homan 1977, 8). Effective practice of the art of parenting is an ideal toward which parents strive throughout their parenting years.

CHILDREN'S NEEDS

Human needs have remained constant for innumerable generations. Children and parents all have physical and psychosocial needs, and all apply the same human faculties in efforts to meet their needs. Contem-

TABLE 1-2 *Parents' Roles in Contemporary Society*

Arbitrator	Healer (doctor, nurse)
Babysitter	Homemaker (cook, maid)
Caregiver	Housewife
Chauffeur	Income provider
Community worker	Janitor
Companion	Lawmaker/Judge
Consoler	Learner
Counselor	Listener
Dietitian	Lover
Disciplinarian	Mother
Economist (shopper, budget maker)	Nurse
Entertainer	Peacemaker
Father	Playmate
Financier (budget, bank account)	Psychologist
Friend	Seamstress/Tailor
Groundskeeper (landscaper, gardener)	Security provider (guard)
Guardian	Teacher
Plumber/Electrician	Volunteer

Source: Morrison 1978, 31.

porary parents spend less time and energy meeting their children's physical needs than did parents of previous generations, but they invest more time and energy in meeting their children's psychosocial needs.

Talbot and the participants in the Harvard Interfaculty Seminar suggested that contemporary children have the following basic psychosocial needs:

1. Being needed and wanted

2. Being attended to, cared for and protected

3. Being valued, cherished, accepted and given a sense of belonging

4. Being guided, educated, stimulated toward social capability and subject to limits of socially acceptable behavior

5. Being given opportunities to gain satisfaction in life through useful work and creative and recreational activities. (1976, 6)

According to Homan (1977), effective parenting is the process of "responding responsibly" to a child's expressed and unexpressed needs for love, behavior management leading to self-discipline, emotional security, intellectual stimulation, freedom to explore, feedback on efforts, joy of living, and physical care, nourishment, and safety. Of course, parents will emphasize different needs for different children, at different times during a child's formative years, and in keeping with changing circumstances.

Love

All humans need to love and be loved. Research has shown that infants deprived of love do not thrive (Spitz 1946). A child's very survival depends on giving and receiving love.

To receive love from others, children must learn to love others and to be lovable. They must develop the capacity to give themselves to others. All human beings will eventually respond to love once they recognize it as genuine (Powell 1972).

Parenting begins with love. Parents and children can never share too much love (Homan 1977). Parents' task is to form a loving tie with their children that enables the children to approach the world positively (Brooks 1981).

The love between parent and child is unique. Parental love goes beyond sentiment; it is a responsible response to need. This responding won't solve all a child's problems, but it is a prerequisite for all other successes (Beck 1977).

Fromm described love as "an *attitude,* an *orientation of character* which determines the relatedness of a person to the world as a whole" (1956, 38). It is the individual's total response, as a person, to his or her world and the people in it. Moreover, love is the capacity to share oneself and all one's possessions with others simply because one wishes to do so, not for personal gain or recognition.

Love is learned (Fromm 1956; Powell 1972; Buscaglia 1972). Children are not born lovers. They learn to love by repeating acts of love until these acts become habitual and generalize to all facets of life. As in learning any complex human behavior, learning love requires concentration, practice, understanding, and insight.

Teaching love is demanding. Effective parents strive for self-discipline and concentrate on getting across a message of love to their children. Each act of love takes a child closer to realizing the "love orientation" that Fromm called the essence of love. Parental love demands patience with oneself and with children. The loving parent recognizes that all humans are fallible beings capable of errors or regressing under stress.

Motherly love is the uncritical, unconditional affirmation of the child's life and total acceptance, even when the child's behavior is undesirable. The parent accepts total responsibility for the child's life and strives to care for his or her every need. Motherly love is essential during the child's infancy and childhood (Homan 1977).

Perhaps the greatest deterrents to love between parent and child are overindulgence, domination, disinterest, and unwillingness to be an adequate behavior model. Loving parents respond to their children as individuals capable of making decisions and judgments in accordance with their maturational level and life experiences. Parents who truly love their children do not treat them as pets or prized possessions who cannot make their own decisions.

Loving parents avoid dominating their children. They encourage them to make decisions, take actions, and succeed and fail as a result of personal effort. Of course, parents cannot allow children to make decisions inappropriate for their level of maturity, nor should they allow children to fail repeatedly in their efforts. Children prohibited from expressing themselves or taking responsibility for their actions often have difficulty learning to love.

Loving parents are sincerely and overtly interested in their children, and their children are aware of their significance to their parents. Children first learn to love by imitating a loving model. In this way, they learn acceptable and unacceptable attitudes, skills, knowledge, and behavior.

Ideally, mature, loving parents have the following qualities:

1. They perceive themselves as loving and lovable.

2. They seek growth in knowledge and understanding of themselves, their children, and their environment.

3. They respond appropriately to their children's expressed and unexpressed needs and desires.

4. They see their children as they are and respect their children's humanness.

5. They participate actively in their children's lives and foster their well-being and growth.

Though no parent is likely to meet this ideal, loving parents strive for these qualities throughout their parenting years. Children themselves do not need perfect parents as long as they experience love and sincerity in their parents' efforts.

Behavior Management and Discipline

Parents devote great amounts of energy to guiding their children's behavior. Behavior management is the subject of constant discussion, trial-and-error experimentation, and concern.

- How can we make Paul stop fighting with his brother?

- How can we make Bobby learn to think for himself?

- Should we punish Jean when she doesn't complete her work?

- Should we ignore Marian's interruptions?

- Are we harming or helping Donny when we send him to his room?

Behavior management is parents' acting to help their children develop self-fulfilling, productive, and socially acceptable behaviors (Shea 1978).

Behavior management is a complex process that takes into account the child and the purpose of his or her behavior, parents and the reason they want to change the child's behavior, and the setting and conditions affecting the behavior. It requires planning and objectivity, and it must be individualized to be effective.

Before imposing discipline, parents should attempt to ascertain the cause of the child's behavior. Homan (1977) suggested that parents make two basic assumptions about the cause of children's behavior. First, children want to do what is right given the circumstances and the people with whom they find themselves. Second, from children's unique perspective, they are taking the best possible action.

Part of behavior management is establishing behavioral limits in keeping with a child's developmental level and emerging needs. Parents develop such limits to ensure that children will not harm themselves, other people, or property (Brooks 1981; Dodson 1970).

Different situations require varying degrees of strictness and structure. However, consistency from situation to situation is important, for it helps children develop trust in the predictability of their environment.

We (parents and teachers) should keep clearly in mind what the goals of discipline are. They are not to develop an automaton responding mechanically to our commands, but a child who has gradually learned to internalize controls while feeling free to express herself. A child whose discipline is too strict will feel inhibited in her attempts to express herself for fear of reprisal. On the other hand, a child who has had no limits set on her behavior may feel basically anxious about her own omnipotence and may express her need for controls by escalating her (unacceptable) behavior in attempts to have limits set for her. (Harmon and Yarrow 1977, 395)

Self-discipline is the goal of all behavior management: to allow children to gain control over their behavior in varied circumstances involving many individuals and groups. Self-control develops over many years and includes many developmental phases. During this process, children naturally progress and regress. A child may appear to be in excellent control of his or her behavior one day and out of control the next day. Parents can measure progress in self-discipline—maturing, learning, and growing—by the slowly increasing lengths of time between unacceptable behaviors.

The word *discipline* derives from *disciple,* a follower of a master's teaching. Thus it conveys the idea of learning from a person the child wants to emulate. The most effective discipline grows out of mutual respect and understanding between parent and child. It is voluntary and cooperative, not simply an authority figure's imposition of limits on another person.

Generally, benign, positive management techniques are desirable. Harsh, punitive techniques may distort the child's self-image and perception of the environment and may increase existing conflicts.

Homan (1977) offers parents four guidelines for managing their children's behavior. First, parents must establish themselves as authority figures with their children. They should communicate that they know and understand more than their children do and that their life experiences qualify them to establish limits. As authority figures, parents must be reliable, dependable, and unafraid to act.

Second, parents should be consistent in their acts of love and discipline. Children are confused by inconsistency and prefer to know the limits on their behavior and the consequences of exceeding those limits. Parents' words and actions must be congruent. Third, parents should never derogate their children's worth and right to love and respect. When discipline is necessary, parents should criticize and correct behaviors without attacking the child as a person.

Finally, parents should avoid premature and unnecessary explanations of their discipline. When an explanation is necessary, parents should use concepts and words the child can understand. When an explanation is impossible, the parent must set and enforce appropriate limits on behavior.

Emotional Security

Children need a sense of belonging, emotional security, to develop into mature adults (Bessell and Kelly 1977), and parents have the major responsibility for filling this need. Effective parents communicate, directly and indirectly, to their children that they are acceptable, accepted, and safe. Children must know their parents want them and need them. They must feel they are loved because of who they *are,* not because of what they do or contribute. Children lacking a sense of belonging become anxious about their continued existence, which they express through tension, apprehensiveness, nervousness, uneasiness, and indecisiveness.

Children develop their sense of belonging through thousands of parent actions that say, "I love you. You are the most important person in the world to me. Your needs, desires, and interests are uppermost in my mind every day." In this manner, children learn that they are valued, cherished, and accepted. They know their parents will protect them, physically and psychologically, from personal errors and the errors and aggression of others.

A child must be free of the fear of abandonment as well (Bessell and Kelly 1977). Children whose parents shun them or act as if they are superfluous feel insecure. They live in fear that their needs and desires will be neglected or overshadowed by those of their parents.

Perhaps equally detrimental to a child's feeling of emotional security is overindulgence. Parents who respond to all their children's desires rob them of a realistic understanding of the world and deny them opportunities to mature and function independently.

Family turmoil and parent conflict are harmful to children's feelings of security. Young people exposed to frequent disagreements, arguing, and fighting in their family learn to be cautious and careful for fear they may lose their parents.

Social Experience

Children are social beings who naturally seek companionship and strongly desire the acceptance and approval of others. From infancy to maturity, children benefit from exposure to a broad spectrum of social experiences. Parents can help them learn to evaluate their social experiences objectively (Bessel and Kelly 1977).

During the childhood years, children should participate in a variety of family-centered activities, such as parties and family gatherings, visits to relatives and friends, showings of selected television programs and movies, sports events, community and church group activities, errands to the supermarket and shopping center, and so on. Parents can plan outings, excursions, and vacations to expose their children to people of various cultural, ethnic, religious, and racial backgrounds.

Parents should also regularly discuss important spiritual, educational, cultural, and historical topics with their children, helping them interpret and evaluate these experiences. However, parents must aim for honest, unbiased evaluations and be willing to listen to and consider their children's perceptions.

As children mature, they seek companionship and experiences outside the home and family. In school, they mingle with children and adults with many different physical characteristics, personal abilities, attitudes, values, interests, and social backgrounds.

During the school years, parents must draw back somewhat from direct supervision of their children's social lives and depend more on other adults, especially teachers, to guide them and their children. However, parents retain the responsibility to know their children's whereabouts, companions, and activities.

By the time children reach adolescence and young adulthood, they have internalized the best of their parents' values and standards. At this point they become independent decision makers actively shaping their own lives.

Intellectual Development

Parents have responsibility for their children's intellectual development from infancy to adulthood. Parents first provide their infants with a stimulating environment—a bright and cheerful nursery with attractive furnishings, toys, and pictures that the baby can see, hear, feel, and manipulate. In the early years, the parent is a "loving play partner," sensitive to the child's cues (Gross 1981). As children mature, their parents encourage them to join them in exploring the home, neighborhood, and other places of interest. Parents are teachers, helping children identify what they see, hear, taste, smell, and touch.

Young children need play materials that encourage creativity. They enjoy playing with household items such as pots, pans, brushes, brooms, cans, boxes, spoons, and beaters, for example. During the preschool years, parents can offer their children opportunities to develop proficiency with school-related tools, such as crayons, pencils, pens, paper, paints, blocks, puzzles, scissors, and simple construction and kitchen tools.

As children grow older, they benefit from picture books and easy-reading books. These are personal possessions for the children to keep in their toy chests or bookcases. Puzzles and educational games also stimulate children's early learning.

Language skills are critical to success in school and the community. Children learn speech by hearing language used appropriately, and they need opportunities to practice proper usage. Frequent parent-child conversations, discussions, and word games stimulate children's language skills.

Another important parent responsibility is to help develop pre-reading skills. Reading to children, encouraging them to listen to and discuss stories, gives them an excellent start. Time devoted to studying and discussing the pictures, words, colors, shapes, sizes, and visual configurations in printed material fosters reading skills.

When children reach school age, parents begin to share with teachers the responsibility for their children's intellectual development. Parents who show their interest in their children's school activities, and who assist with home assignments when appropriate, help foster their children's love of learning. The parents have an obligation to provide an intellectually stimulating home environment as well, making available reading materials and educational games, encouraging individual and family projects in animal care, rock collecting, stamp collecting, baking, carpentry, and so on. Family vacations and weekend outings provide excellent opportunities to stimulate interest in learning. Family discussions can become a routine part of any new or unusual activity.

Parents should encourage junior and senior high school children to participate in intellectually stimulating school, church, and community activities, such as dramatics, language clubs, sports, science fairs, essay contests, or debate clubs.

The more parents show interest in their children's environment, are stimulated by new ideas, events, and problems, and participate in serious discussions, the more likely their children will model their behavior.

Freedom to Explore

From the day of birth, children need freedom to explore themselves and their environment. Parents can encourage and assist their children in this area of development by providing limits within which they are free to explore and develop their abilities (Brooks 1981).

When their children are infants, parents physically help them explore. Mother and father carry the young child about the nursery, home, yard, drawing attention to objects and happenings. They encourage their children to use their senses of vision, hearing, taste, touch, and smell.

Even when infants are confined to their crib, playpen, or nursery, they can explore toys, mobiles, pictures, and furnishings in their immediate surroundings. In fact, infants and toddlers need little encouragement to explore their environment. On occasion, toddlers explore too much, too quickly, too carelessly, and in the wrong places at the wrong time. When necessary, parents must restrict or supervise children's explorations.

Although severe restriction of children's freedom to explore is unwise, it is equally unwise to remove all objects or secure all areas of the home that pose potential dangers. As children explore, they learn which objects and areas are dangerous and therefore not available for exploration (electric cords and outlets, stoves, fireplaces, stairways, power tools, and appliances). They learn that they must ask permission or have supervision to explore certain objects and areas governed by other family members (kitchen, workshop, parents' sewing basket or toolboxes, and brother's and sister's rooms and toys). Children also learn that their personal possessions and toys are theirs to explore freely.

As children mature and enter school, parents continue to encourage them to explore their immediate surroundings and to extend their experiences through discussing them with others, reading books and magazines, and viewing plays, movies, and television programs.

In encouraging their children to explore throughout their growing years parents can follow these guidelines:

1. Encourage measured and systematic exploration. Children do not benefit from exploring topics beyond their comprehension nor can they learn effectively if they explore so many areas that they explore nothing in depth.

2. Encourage children to explore themselves as unique individuals with special abilities, experiences, and interests. Allow them to devote time to quiet consideration of themselves and their world.

3. Protect children from physical and psychological dangers as they explore.

Feedback

Children develop and modify their self-image as a result of feedback from others. Parents provide children encouragement and feedback as they develop their psychomotor abilities to crawl, walk, climb, run, play ball, write, and so on. They offer feedback on cognitive skills, such as language, memory, comprehension, problem solving, reading, spelling, and arithmetic. And they reinforce children's affective learning, such as obedience; thoughtfulness; social and interpersonal skills; home, school, and play behaviors; and values and standards.

Frequent feedback is necessary when a child is learning a new behavior or skill. Once the behavior becomes habitual, parents can reduce the frequency of feedback.

During infancy and early childhood, their parents' pleasure is children's primary reinforcement. Therefore, parents must show their pleasure or displeasure with the child's actions in a manner the child understands. In the early years, a hug, a kiss, a smile, a toss in the air, a drawing displayed on the refrigerator door, a cookie, and so on are all very rewarding to children. A frown, the removal of an object, a restriction on freedom, or a sharp word are usually sufficient negative feedback. A young child should receive feedback as soon as possible after the behavior occurs so that the connection between his or her behavior and the parent's response is clear.

Joy of Living

Living should be a joy for every child. Children's lives should be exciting, interesting, and satisfying. Parents can raise their children to feel the joy of living rather than to view life as a trial to be endured with caution, fear, and suffering.

For an infant, joy is a smile from a parent, a tussle with a father, a peekaboo game with a grandparent, or a spoonful of favorite food. Joy in childhood is a visit to the zoo, a red balloon on the end of a string, a ride in the family car, a whirl on a merry-go-round, a visit to Santa Claus, or a make-believe tea party. Joy is the new, the unusual, the exciting, and the adventurous.

During the early school years, joy is a family outing, excursions to interesting places, family vacations, family projects around the house, and physical activities. Joy is exploring the neighborhood with a friend, participating in Scouts, 4-H, and Little League. Joy is going to the playground, exploring nearby woods, and participating in after-school games.

In the preteen and early teen years, joy is a pajama party, a phone conversation with a friend, a shopping trip, a ballgame, a hobby, a family gathering, a bike ride, and a chance to do real work.

In the adolescent years, joy is participating in a school club or team, receiving recognition for efforts and accomplishments from people important to you, and exploring the arts, crafts, and music. Joy is a best friend with whom to share life's secrets and a group of friends to "hang out" with. Joy is having important responsibilities, finding a part-time job, driving the family car, selecting and buying clothes, dating, and making important personal decisions. To teenagers, joy is being treated as equals by adults and having parents who try to understand their points of view, who listen, and who express confidence in them.

For all young people, joy is a good joke, an unusual happening, and a good laugh. Children learn that there is a time to laugh and a time to cry and that both are acceptable human behaviors. They learn to laugh with others, not at others. They learn never to take satisfaction in others' failures, faults, personality traits, physical features, and handicaps.

If children are to develop joy in life, parents must refrain from demanding unwanted and undesirable participation, ill-advised competition, and unattainable levels of performance. Moreover, each parent must model the joy of living for his or her child. The parent who sees life as a dark and dreary winter day will raise a child who sees life similarly. The parent who radiates a joy of life and sees beauty in the world will raise a child who shares this view.

Physical Care, Nourishment, and Safety

The child's physical care, nourishment, and safety are basic parental responsibilities. Children's physical well-being is not only important in itself but also has a major impact on all other aspects of their psycho-social development. Chronically ill, undernourished, or abused children have difficulty functioning effectively. Moreover, their pain, discomfort, and insecurity create a distorted perception of reality and a negative self-concept. Children whose basic needs go unmet view themselves as unwanted, unloved, and worthless, and they see their parents and the world as uncaring.

Care for children's physical well-being begins even before birth. The mother's prenatal care, health, diet, emotional state, and social habits all affect the baby's development, as do her use of alcoholic beverages, tobacco, and drugs. Research has shown that the mother's level of anxiety, stress, and frustration during pregnancy affect the baby's health as well.

After their baby's birth, the parents provide the food, shelter, clothing, and care most appropriate to his or her needs. Most parents in the United States have access to the housing, money, insurance, and transportation they need to care properly for their children. Unfortunately, however, this ability to provide is not universal in the United States and certainly not in the world.

Many children suffer physical and emotional neglect because their parents cannot obtain the basic necessities of life. Some parents are ignorant about what their children need. Still other parents, because of the immobilizing effects of personal and social-emotional handicaps and pathologies, cannot respond to their children's needs.

Parents are responsible for protecting growing children from illnesses and infectious diseases as much as possible. Children need a clean, healthful home in which disease cannot germinate or spread, and they need access to corrective and preventive health care services.

A well-balanced diet is necessary fuel for children's active daily lives. Parents provide healthy food to protect the child from malnutrition (a lack of proper nutrients) and obesity (excessive body fat resulting from nutritional imbalance).

Parents provide a safe environment for their children as well to avoid childhood accidents and injuries that could have a life-long effect. Bumps, cuts, and bruises are a normal part of childhood. However, parents should eliminate as many potential hazards as possible in their homes and teach children to avoid those that cannot be eliminated. If a child is too immature to understand the dangers of certain items and situations, parents must secure them. Safety includes protecting children from their natural curiosity by securing medicines, cleaning materials, and dangerous tools and equipment.

All children need a safe place in which to play, eat, sleep, and care for their body functions. Moreover, parent responsibility extends to teaching children self-care skills, such as toileting, bathing, washing before meals, brushing teeth, keeping their clothing and room reasonably clean, and wearing proper clothing. Parents teach children to care for themselves and to seek care when they are ill or injured.

SUMMARY

This introductory chapter provides a general overview of the art of parenting *all* children, exceptional and nonexceptional. The discussion establishes premises that lay the groundwork for the parent-teacher involvement model and activities presented in the remainder of the book.

A variety of social changes have changed parenting between the 1930s and 1980s. The chapter highlights changes in family structure, neighborhoods, schools, churches, work places, overall mobility, and social tensions. The discussion emphasizes that parenting is an art—complex, dynamic process—and describes an ideal of effective parenting. It discusses the basic human needs of *all* children to be loved, secure, and guided toward a satisfying life and spells out parents' duties and responsibilities in each category of children's needs.

Chapter Two considers the role of the parent of an exceptional child and describes parent reactions to the birth and diagnosis of an exceptional child. It describes the defense mechanisms and coping behaviors typical of parents first confronted with a diagnosis of exceptionality, assesses the effects of the exceptional child on family functioning, and discusses why some parents and families of exceptional children do not participate in parent-teacher involvement programs.

EXERCISES AND DISCUSSION TOPICS

1. Discuss the following statement: "Parenting an exceptional child is unique in degree and intensity rather than in kind." Do you agree? Why or why not?

2. Using the social change factors presented in Table 1-1, compare the society of your childhood to the present. Can you add other social change factors or social problems that have occurred in your lifetime?

3. Trace one or more of the social change factors in Table 1-1 through your childhood, your parents' childhood, and your grandparents' childhood. Library research or interviews with your parents, grandparents, or people of similar ages may assist you in this exercise.

4. Research one of the specific social problems discussed in this chapter (pp. 10–11). What information and assistance is available to help contemporary parents understand and cope with the problem? Assess the quality and quantity of the resources you find. Discuss your findings in a formal class presentation or write a report.

5. Research the definition of "art." Discuss or write a report on parenting as an art, describing the ways you think parenting is similar and dissimilar to other arts. In your report, contrast the ideal and the reality of the art of parenting.

6. Research and discuss one of the psychosocial needs of all children discussed in this chapter (pp. 12–22). Define the need, describe how parents can respond to it, compare its importance in a child's life to that of the other psychosocial needs discussed.

7. This text is for people interested in parent-teacher involvement to benefit exceptional children. Explain why this chapter, applicable to all exceptional and nonexceptional children and their parents, opens the book.

8. Compare the philosophy and parenting methods presented in two or three articles or books of your choice on contemporary parenting.

REFERENCES

Beck, J. 1977. Looking ahead to parenthood. *Parent's Magazine Expecting* 10:(1), 13–14, 46, 48, 50.

Bessell, H., and T. P. Kelly. 1977. *The parent book.* Sacramento, Calif.: Jalmar Press.

Brooks, J. B. 1981. *The process of parenting.* Palo Alto, Calif.: Mayfield.

Buscaglia, L. F. 1972. *Love.* Thorofare, N.J.: Charles B. Stack.

Caplow, T., H. Bahr, B. A. Chadwick, R. Hill, and M. G. Williamson. 1982. *Middletown families: Fifty years of change and continuity.* Minneapolis: University of Minnesota Press.

Croft, D. J. 1979. *Parents and teachers: A resource book for home, school, and community relations.* Belmont, Calif.: Wadsworth.

Dodson, F. 1970. *How to parent.* New York: Signet.

Fromm, E. 1956. *The art of loving.* New York: Harper and Row.

Gross, D. W. 1981. The changing needs of children. In *The pleasure of their company,* ed. The Bank Street College of Education. Radnor, Pa.: Chilton Book Co.

Harmon, R. J., and R. Yarrow. 1977. Personality formation. In *The parenting advisor,* ed. F. Caplan, Princton Center for Infancy. Garden City, N.Y.: Anchor Press/Doubleday.

Homan, W. E. 1977. *Child sense: A guide to loving, level-headed parenthood.* New York: Basic Books.

McAfee, J. K., and G. A. Vergason. 1979. Parent involvement in the process of special education: Establishing the new partnership. *Focus on Exceptional Children* 11(2):1–15.

Morrison, G. S. 1978. *Parent involvement in the home, school, and community.* Columbus, Ohio: Charles E. Merrill.

Powell, J. 1972. *Why am I afraid to love?* Niles, Ill.: Argus Communications.

Scott, D. W., and B. Wishy. 1982. *America's families: A documentary history.* New York: Harper and Row.

Shea, T. M. 1978. *Teaching children and youth with behavior disorders.* St. Louis: C. V. Mosby.

Sheils, M., D. Weathers, L. Howard, and R. Givens. 1983. A portrait of America. *Newsweek* January 17, 20–33.

Spitz, R. A. 1946. Anaclitic depression. *Psychodynamic Study of the Child* 2:313–42.

Talbot, N. B. 1976. *Raising children in modern America: What parents and society should be doing for their children.* Boston: Little, Brown.

Toffler, A. 1970. *Future shock.* New York: Bantam Books.

Winick, M. 1970. Fetal malnutrition and growth processes. *Hospital Practice* 5(5):33–41.

CHAPTER TWO

PARENTS, FAMILIES, AND EXCEPTIONAL CHILDREN

■ Chapter One pointed out that exceptional children are first and foremost children, with similar needs and desires as nonexceptional children. This chapter analyzes what is special about exceptional children and assesses the effects of their specialness on their relationships with their parents, other family members, teachers, and others. Parents face the most dramatic adjustment to their children's exceptionality, and the coping behaviors they develop affect the family as a social system.

In a study of the first year and a half of parenthood, Waisbren (1980) found that parents of exceptional children reported physical health, social activities, activities with the baby, marital relationships, and plans for the future that were strikingly similar to reports by parents of nonexceptional children. In both groups, parents reported difficulties sleeping and relaxing, and both cited changes in their marriages toward increased intimacy and increased tension.

Daily interaction with children, exceptional or nonexceptional, is also essentially the same. In a study of mentally handicapped children, parents' attitudes toward daily interaction with their child were within the range reported by parents of nonexceptional children (Rees, Strom, and Wurster 1982). Clark and Clark (1980), writing as parents of an exceptional child, stated that all members of their family were special, including their exceptional child, and that this attitude helped their exceptional child fit into the family without great difficulty.

Just as parenting a nonexceptional child has crisis points—such as the birth of a sibliing, school entry, or adolescence—so does parenting an exceptional child. Parents of exceptional children may experience crises as their child matures, producing value conflicts over such issues as institutionalization (Schild 1982; Hoff 1978). A child's failure to succeed in a normal classroom or development of behavior problems unique to the exceptionality causes stress, as does others' rejection of the exceptional child (Hoff 1978; Searl 1978). Parents report an increase in stress as their exceptional child approaches puberty or his or her twenty-first birthday (Wikler et al. 1981).

Most parents at times become exhausted, anxious, and overwhelmed. However, these feelings may be more frequent and intense for parents of exceptional children (Sonnenschein 1981). Moroney (1981) indicated that families with exceptional children are more likely to have financial burdens, interrupted sleep, social isolation, restricted recreational activities, behavior management problems, limitations in shopping and carrying out other normal household routines, and pessimistic feelings about the future than are families without exceptional children.

Greer (1975) suggested that contemporary social attitudes toward marriage and childbirth increase the problems confronting parents of exceptional children. Current myths view marriage as an eternally blissful union of two adults, who in turn produce physically and mentally perfect children. The classification of more than 15 percent of the school-age population as exceptional calls these myths into question. With the birth or diagnosis of an exceptional child, parents often cannot respond appropriately to either society's expectations or their resulting expectations of themselves as parents.

Parents may feel that a normal, well-behaved child symbolizes their membership in good standing in society (Kozloff 1979). Conversely, they may feel that an exceptional child calls into question their capacity as parents or even members of that society. Society expects good parents to do all they can to help their children (Fairfield 1983). Thus, parents of an exceptional child may try to be "superparents," devoting all their energy to their child so that society cannot condemn them as "superbad" parents (Goldstein 1975).

Parents become aware of their child's exceptionality at birth or shortly thereafter, during the preschool years, or after the child enters school. If they recognize their child's exceptionality before school entry, they have time to adjust to the child's condition and can accept the need for special education and related services to encourage their child's development. If they become aware upon or after school entry, they may need time to adjust to the diagnosis, thereby delaying implementation of the needed services (Barsch 1969).

PARENTS' EMOTIONAL ADJUSTMENT

No matter when parents become aware of their child's exceptionality, they are inevitably shocked (Love 1970) and painfully surprised (Barsch 1968). They must suddenly adjust to a new role as the parents of an exceptional child, and they must adjust their self-image to cope with new responsibilities and functions (Meadow and Meadow 1971; Buscaglia 1971).

The transition to any new role requires socialization and learning new ways of behaving. Socialization, as a parent of the exceptional child, requires mastery of two types of tasks: instrumental or technical, and expressive or emotional. Though these two aspects are interwoven, Meadow and Meadow distinguish them in this way:

> Examples of instrumental aspects of the role include learning ways to help a cerebral palsied child to use his muscles (Schiller 1961) or learning how to help a deaf child use and regulate a hearing aid. Expressive aspects of this role include learning to cope with feelings of guilt, shame, and sorrow; learning to cope with responses of pity, rejection, and avoidance from neighbors (Begab 1956; Roos 1963); learning to cope with responses of grief and denial from relatives; learning to cope with the temptation either to overprotect or to underprotect the child; and learning to cope with the emotional problems which may develop in relation to the disability. (1971, 21–22)

This chapter discusses the expressive aspects of parenting an exceptional child. Chapters Five through Ten discuss the instrumental skills parents need to further their children's education.

Initial Crisis Reactions

Human beings react dramatically to a crisis (Webster 1977), whether it is the death of a loved one, a serious traffic accident, a natural disaster, a lost job, a divorce and separation, or a child's failure in school. The birth or diagnosis of an exceptional child is a crisis for the vast majority of parents (Hoff 1978); most are likely to confront psychological, physical, and material difficulties (Seligman 1979). Though experts disagree considerably on parents' adjustment process, they generally agree that no single reaction pattern is common to all parents. As in any crisis, parents' reactions, and the sequence in which they occur, in large part depend on their personal characteristics, life experiences, education and training, expectations, cultural background, and personal, social, and economic resources (Chinn, Winn, and Walters 1978; Hosey, personal communication, 1983). Moreover, parents' reactions may vary according to the degree of their child's handicap and the importance they place on having a normal child (Hoff 1978).

Webster (1977) suggested that the parents of exceptional children experience more crises than other parents over a long period, for they must find appropriate medical and dental care, therapeutic services, education and training programs, social acceptance for the child, residential care, and recreational services at every stage of their child's development. Teachers, as human beings who have experienced crises, although perhaps not as severe as the birth or diagnosis of an exceptional child, should be able to empathize with parents facing the crisis of exceptionality. Effective teachers recognize that parents of exceptional children are not necessarily "problem parents" but are simply normal people reacting naturally to a crisis—a trauma. Like most people in a crisis, parents may temporarily misperceive reality, be unable to act, or experience confusing emotions and thoughts. Yet people in crisis are basically normal, capable of helping themselves, and capable of further growth with assistance (Hoff 1978).

Indeed, becoming a parent of any child calls for a role change that subjects new parents to many unique stresses that may constitute a crisis. The birth of an exceptional child adds a situational crisis, one that results from an unanticipated, traumatic event beyond parents' control (Hoff 1978).

McDowell (1976) suggested that parents progress through six emotional stages upon discovering their child's exceptionality: disbelief, guilt, rejection, shame, denial, and a feeling of helplessness. The last phase, a feeling of helplessness, frequently leads parents to action, at which point they often seek professional help.

Hosey (1973) described her reactions upon discovering that her son, Stephen, was profoundly retarded, cerebral palsied, and epileptic. Stephen, with visual and auditory perceptual handicaps, does not walk, talk, or comprehend speech.

> I had spent many hours fighting panic—swinging upward when I got the details of a test result, and then down again when I made myself face the facts, as I had begun to face them the day I first called the pediatrician. . . .
>
> . . . But I will always remember my feelings of numb despair. I didn't cry or give much external sign of my inner hysteria but I felt that I would never be able to adjust to this situation.
>
> The shock of the birth of a child like this doesn't come all at once. It's worse in some ways than the death of a child because you gradually realize that this child is never going to live in the fullest sense of the word. . . .

It was difficult for us to absorb the first shock, which is truly physical as well as mental. We were numb, we could scarcely walk about and do our normal day's work, or talk to other people. . . .

. . . The shock consisted of knowing that we had a child who would never grow up. . . .

. . . I feel strongly that no couple, no matter what their age or experience, can make a wise or even a fully conscious decision at a moment like this. I feel that unless a decision is absolutely imperative because of life or death alternatives, it should be postponed. (1973, 15–16).

Though reactions to the birth or diagnosis of an exceptional child vary from parent to parent and from family to family, people seem to share common elements. Frequently, parents' initial feelings are shock and numbness. Parents may experience periods of panic, anxiety, and helplessness, as well as periods of indifference and anger, at which time parents face nearly overwhelming depression, apathy, and bitterness. As parents' negative feelings decrease, they begin to plan for their child.

Defensive Responses

After the initial crisis, parents use a variety of defensive responses to cope with the continuing reality of their child's exceptionality. These responses, and the accompanying family turmoil, are common during any adjustment and do not necessarily indicate instability in the family or parents (Seligman and Seligman 1980).

Parents' defensive responses are highly individual, varying in intensity, duration, and frequency over time. Parents use those defenses they need to sustain themselves during different phases of their adjustment, seldom adopting all the defensive responses reviewed in this section. To work effectively with parents of exceptional children, teachers must understand parents' coping mechanisms and the diverse and individual needs underlying their use (Seligman and Seligman 1980; Gallagher, Beckman, and Cross 1983).

Mourning and Sorrow. Parents feel extreme unhappiness upon facing their child's exceptionality. They may perceive their changed circumstances as so severe that they lose their joy or reason for living. They may find it impossible to smile, laugh, or participate actively in life's common pleasures. Enjoying themselves may cause guilt.

In its extreme, this unhappiness resembles mourning the death of a loved one; in essence, parents mourn the death of the normal child they anticipated (Hoff 1978). As in mourning, parents may express despair and show typical grief reactions, such as weeping, sighing, withdrawal, diminished energy levels, and so on. Mourning may also include increased irritability, loss of appetite, insomnia, and anger (Prescott and Iselin 1978).

Searl (1978) indicated that parents' feeling of sorrow never entirely disappears but stays on as part of their emotional life. Parents report chronic sorrow, and experience periodic crisis during the child's development rather than time-bound sorrow (Wikler et al. 1981). Parents and professionals can view this sorrow as a natural and understandable response and should not deny its existence. Professionals can help parents learn to cope with it, understanding that sadness need not preclude satisfaction and joy in the child's achievements.

Denial. Another typical defensive response is to deny a child's exceptionality; parents may wrongly reason that denying the exceptionality will make it go away so that they need not deal with it. Such denial is also a natural response to the crisis—the urge to avoid a painful reality.

Parents' denial of their children's exceptionality may take several forms: seeking opinions from several specialists in an effort to find a more acceptable diagnosis; participating in new, unusual, or unproved treatments; overprotecting and sheltering the child; or establishing unattainable expectations for the child (Prescott and Iselin 1978). Frequently, denial inhibits efforts to provide needed services for the child. Professionals can help parents recognize their denial and understand the reality of their situation.

Most important, professionals should not assume that parents' difficulty accepting their children's exceptionality is unhealthy but should recognize it is a natural first reaction to distressing news. Effective teachers learn to distinguish between parents' natural instinct to deny the diagnosis and a more worrisome long-term denial (Seligman and Seligman 1980).

Avoidance and Rejection. For some parents, the diagnosis of exceptionality is so traumatic that they avoid contact with their child, finding themselves unable to feed, clothe, or play with the child. In the extreme, parents may deny that the child is theirs, accusing the hospital staff of confusing their child with someone else's.

In severe cases of nonacceptance, parents may criticize, ridicule, blame, or unfavorably compare their child to others. They may physically and psychologically neglect their children, abuse them, or even abandon them.

Prescott and Iselin (1978) suggested that parents avoid and reject their exceptional children in three ways: First, they may set unrealistic goals for the child, making them either overly ambitious or not ambitious enough. Second, they may escape by abandoning the child. Finally, they may act or talk in ways inappropriate for the circumstances of their child's birth or diagnosis.

Guilt. Because of society's expectations, their own expectations, the reality of the child's exceptionality, or the uncertain etiology of the exceptionality, parents may believe the exceptionality is their fault. They may feel guilt and shame, assuming responsibility for the condition, and search for the cause of the exceptionality. Some parents become convinced that they did something wrong (Sonnenschein 1981) and scrutinize their pasts for an event or genetic influence on which to affix blame. In some cases, parents may see the exceptionality as punishment for a past sin or a character flaw (Prescott and Iselin 1978).

Teachers may err if they assume that parents feel guilty about their exceptional child, however. In a 1963 study, Roith found that some professionals construed any parental action as guilt produced. If parents asked for reports on their child's condition, some professionals assumed they were projecting their guilt onto the doctor; if the parents didn't ask, they assumed the parents were reacting to their guilt by "forgetting" the child. However, when asked directly if they felt guilty about their child's exceptionality, 94 percent of Roth's sample of mothers reported that they did not.

Anger and Hostility. Parents of exceptional children may feel hostile and, on occasions, express overt anger toward others (Gordon 1976). The target of parents' anger may be a doctor, nurse, social worker, teacher, relative, neighbor, or a person who simply glances at or asks questions about the child. Or they may express anger at themselves, their spouse, or God in an effort to assign blame for their difficulty. Parents become angry at the drastic changes the child forces in their self-perceptions and their life-style. They resent the time, energy, social, and financial burdens imposed on them. They may become bitter when they see the child as interfering with personal, family, and social goals (Love 1970).

Self-Doubt. Feelings of self-doubt, inferiority, or inadequacy are common among parents of exceptional children. Parents may question their worth as people and as parents because they have produced an imperfect child. Roos (1978), among others, discussed his feeling of insignificance as the parent of an exceptional child. As human beings, searching for meaning through their roles of mother or father, parents may lose out on social reinforcement for their parenting role. With no social rewards for parenting their exceptional children, parents may begin to feel insignificant.

Chinn (1979) indicated that because some minority parents see education as "a way out" for their children and a way to improve the family's socioeconomic standing, they may see their children's exceptionality as a serious barrier to achieving their goals. As a result, their self-concepts suffer in the face of their child's inability to better the family's lot.

Parents may express their self-doubt as feelings of helplessness. Parents who feel inferior and inadequate may become overly dependent on others, helpless to make even minor decisions about their children.

Sonnenschein (1981) indicated that parents, already suffering from a loss of self-esteem, may suffer even further self-doubt when they need to seek help in coping with their children's problem. Effective teachers are careful not to suggest that they are stronger and better able to cope with life's problems than are the parents.

Withdrawal and Depression. Parents may react to their child's exceptionality by withdrawing, almost as if they hope that sufficient thought and time away from the problem will yield a solution. In some cases, withdrawal leads to depression, requiring professional intervention to help parents return to normal functioning.

Embarrassment and Social Isolation. Some parents are embarrassed by their exceptional children and become uncomfortable when people look, comment, or ask questions about the child. In the extreme, parents' embarrassment may lead them to isolate themselves socially and to avoid going out for shopping, walking, visits, or entertainment.

Turnbull and Blancher-Dixon (1980) suggested that parents of *mainstreamed* exceptional children face a daily reminder of the differences between their child and the normal children with whom they attend school. Thus, parents with children in mainstream schools may feel that they share the perceived stigma of their child's exceptionality, are not accepted by other parents, or have nothing in common with the parents of nonexceptional children. Professionals can help such parents recognize others' comments and questions as the common expressions of concern and curiosity they are.

Fear, Confusion, and Frustration. People fear the unknown, whether it be entering a hospital for exploratory surgery, beginning a new career, or moving to a new community. For parents, most of whom know little or nothing about exceptionalities, the diagnosis of an exceptional child may be frightening. They may be fearful and confused about the cause of their child's exceptionality, its normal course, its treatment, and its present and future effects. These feelings stem largely from emotional turmoil and a lack of factual information and professional guidance. The misinformation and incomplete information presented by the mass media and popular literature only add to their fears.

In addition, throughout the exceptional child's developmental years and beyond, parents are frustrated by their inability to obtain needed services. Their community may lack services altogether, may fail to provide a full range of services, or may offer only highly specialized service agencies. Parents often encounter insensitive and inadequately trained professionals who are unable or unwilling to empathize with their problems.

Whereas parents of normal children look forward to the future, parents of exceptional children may look to the future with apprehension, anticipating school problems, unemployment, and constant supervision for their child. As a result, they may become entrenched in a "past orientation" (Roos 1978), a tendency to think of the child in terms of the less threatening early childhood rather than the uncertain future. They fear for the child's welfare (Hoff 1978).

Indeed, parents of an exceptional child devote a major part of their lives to locating diagnostic and treatment services, completing forms, reading reports, transporting their child, participating in program development efforts, and volunteering time and money to programs and organizations devoted to the welfare of exceptional people. Most of all, they spend an inordinate portion of their life waiting.

All the defensive responses reviewed here are the natural consequence of the traumatic experience parents suffer when they learn of their child's exceptionality. Professionals are most effective when they see these emotional reactions as normal under the circumstances and recognize that they are not under parents' conscious control. Above all, professionals can help parents by seeing them as individuals and avoiding assumptions about their responses or false readings of their words and actions.

> It is a tremendous blow to realize your child has a handicap. It can seem as if all your hopes and dreams have been ruined. Some people never recover from the unhappiness that results. Parents need and are entitled to a period of adjustment to their problems, which might include rejecting the child or each other, withdrawal, irrationality, uncontrollable anger, or depression. There is a certain art to understanding ourselves well enough to wind these emotions down and slowly build the determination to help the child with a handicap grow. (Gordon 1976, 19)

Coping Behaviors

After a period of coming to terms with their feelings about parenting an exceptional child, parents begin to "think and behave constructively thereby facilitating development of the child's human potential. When the parents are no longer focusing on the disability, but rather on their child as a person adaptive and capable of compensating, a new, more flexible, and nourishing relationship develops" (Prescott and Iselin 1978, 177). This new relationship helps parents confront the realities of their situation.

Fairfield (1983) warned teachers to differentiate between parents' genuine coping and apparent coping. Parents who are "doing well," "coping," or "being brave"—that is, appearing calm, courageous, and controlled—may in fact have been discouraged from expressing their negative feelings and may be experiencing great difficulty. Fairfield recommended that professionals encourage parents to talk about their early feelings about their exceptional child to determine whether their behavior is genuine or a facade.

Acceptance. Generally, self-acceptance as parents of an exceptional child is difficult for most people, and parents may feel considerable frustration and self-doubt. Parents can, however, emerge from the crisis more mature, stronger, wiser, and more compassionate, with an enhanced sense of their value to society (Chinn, Winn, and Walters 1978).

According to one study, mothers who develop healthy self-acceptance generally have two major sources of strength: existing ego strength and self-confidence and a commitment to a set of supporting values, such as strong religious beliefs (Gallagher, Cross, and Scharfman 1981).

Minority families may show a different pattern of acceptance. Rather than experiencing shock, disbelief, and sorrow, parents may feel protective and accepting of their exceptional children; the strong kinship bonds of certain cultures allow families to absorb the exceptional child without reservation. However, in all families, acceptance requires a conscious decision to love the child and to do everything possible for the child (Clark and Clark 1980).

Love and Hope. As their crisis reactions lessen and parents become more accepting, they see more reasons to feel good about themselves and their special child (Marcus 1977). Berry (1981) described successful exceptional parents as those who can enjoy their exceptional children while feeling good about themselves. At such times, parents' sense of satisfaction and willingness to make adjustments for their children's sake is strong enough to overcome negative feelings (Searl 1978).

"To love a thing in the deepest sense is to want it to *live fully,* and to want to live fully oneself in relationship to it" (Murphy 1981, 169). As parents' love for their special child grows, they become more fully aware of the child's expressed and unexpressed needs and desires. They learn to appreciate and share their children's pride in their efforts and achievements. In turn, parents grow in self-love, learning to see themselves, their children, and reality clearly and objectively. Parent and child develop a giving and sharing relationship, a love without which neither can fully live.

With mature love comes joy. Parents and children learn to take joy in their mutual love and in their shared and independent accomplishments. Their rewards are the same as any child's or parent's—joy in a first smile, a hug, a kiss, a new word, a first step, the first day of school, a new skill, and so on. With their joy for living, they face each morning with interest and enthusiasm, viewing each day as a challenge.

Parents develop faith that they, with others, can and will help their special child reach his or her fullest potential. They become confident that they will locate the professionals, services, facilities, and other support systems they need to further their child's development. As this conviction grows, parents' negative feelings, disappointments, and periodic regressions dissipate. They learn to overcome their occasional feelings of anger, frustration, and discouragement.

In the same way, parents come to see their children as people willing to and capable of adapting and compensating. They value their exceptional children's willingness to work toward their goals. They believe in their children's ability to overcome barriers (Marcus 1977).

Now the parents can begin to hope for a better future for their child and for themselves. This hope is a realistic one, "the imagining of *real* things, the imagining of things that really have the possibility of coming true" (Murphy 1981, 84). They dare to hope that their child will learn the skills to become independent or semi-independent, depending on the nature of the exceptionality. They dare to hope that they will find or develop needed schools, professionals, and treatments. For Murphy, this reality-based hope has three components:

> First, one must be able to take the view that the problem can be solved—if this possibility cannot be recognized, it is unlikely that one would take action. Second, one must believe that appropriately effective ways exist for achieving that which is desired. Third, one must feel that there is at least one other who is not only interested but has some capacity to participate helpfully in effecting the desired change. (1981, 85–86)

Empathetic and knowledgeable professionals can play an indespensable role in fostering parents' realistic hopes. Counselors, psychologists, physicians, teachers, and social workers can first help the parents see that their problems can be solved and then explore alternative solutions with them. Perhaps most important, professionals can communicate to parents their desire to participate actively in the problem-solving process.

Once parents accept their child's exceptionality and recognize the real problems confronting them, they become open to suggestions, actively seeking out helpful professionals and treatments. With empathetic professionals to turn to, parents can more fully express their anxiety, hurt, anger, and frustration.

Parents who have struggled successfully with the personal and practical problems raised by their child's exceptionality become an excellent resource for other exceptional children, parents, and families. Parents are empathetic. They not only know the facts of exceptionality but they also know how it feels. They have walked the road new parents of exceptional children must walk. Because they have succeeded, they reach out to counsel others, often participating in counseling groups, service organizations, schools, treatment programs, and other programs.

EFFECTS ON THE FAMILY

Exceptional children do not live in a vacuum. They touch the lives and color the futures of their parents, brothers and sisters, other relatives, neighbors, classmates, teachers, and others. Estimates suggest that exceptional children directly affect the lives of 20 percent or more of the U.S. population.

The family is essentially a microsociety or small social system. As such, it develops norms, values, and expectations for its members and establishes rules and procedures to maintain and perpetuate itself. Each family develops a style based on its background, the self-concept of its founders, and the relationships among its members. The family's style begins to take shape as husband and wife establish their marital relationship and then evolves as they decide who is responsible for what functions, determine how and when to perform these functions, and develop patterns of interpersonal interaction and communication within the family and with individuals and groups outside the family (Chinn, Winn, and Walters 1978).

The family's purposes are to procreate and raise children, to socialize children and oversee their education, to maintain and protect its members, to provide social status for its members in the larger society, and to gratify personal needs (Vander Zanden 1970). These purposes vary over time from society to society, subculture to subculture, and generation to generation.

Family structures vary greatly in contemporary society. However, the most common structure remains the nuclear family—two married adults and their offspring in one household. Other family structures include the extended family, the single-parent family, and the multiparent family. The family's structure formalizes the relationships among its members, helping to define roles and functions, the division of labor, acceptable social behavior, and patterns of interpersonal interaction.

Although few laws enter the sphere of family functioning, societies mandate certain rules governing the care, nurturance, and health of family members. Thus, all modern societies have laws on child abuse and neglect, education, and labor. The family itself seeks to control behavior, develop values and standards, and instill customs, folkways, and mores.

The family is the primary training ground for children, where they develop their personalities and learn to relate to others and the environment. Thus, family relationships are models for the children's relations to the world, and the family's attitudes toward its children shape their attitudes toward themselves. Clearly, parents play a crucial role whether the children are normal or exceptional. Moreover, the principles of family interaction are the same in both instances; only the conditions differ. The exceptional child, whose physical or mental status differs in some way from the expected norm, introduces an extra factor into the family-child relationship that may disrupt interactions or be detrimental to the child's personality development (Ross 1964).

A family's style remains relatively consistent over time though events both within and outside the family—such as the death or departure of an old member, the addition of a new member, economic and natural disasters, or the diagnosis of an exceptional child—will call for adjustments. According to Chinn, Winn, and Walters (1978), families adopt either *open* or *closed* styles of functioning. The "open" style places the growth of individual members and the family unit first, accepting individuality and differences among the members as normal and beneficial to the family. The closed family seeks to maintain the status quo, suppressing individuality and differences among family members and viewing deviations from the expected ways of functioning as a potential threat to the family's continued existence.

The birth of a child creates stress in that it calls for family members to adjust their role commitments (Rossi 1975). A family's adjustment to the birth or diagnosis of an exceptional child will reflect its habitual response to stress (Cohen 1962), taking into account family style, the nature of the event, the resources of the family, and the family's perception of the event (Chinn, Winn, and Walters 1978). According to Chinn and colleagues, an open family will probably adjust to the birth of the exceptional child relatively easily, given that the family will probably already have accepted individuality and differences among its members. The closed family, with its relatively rigid rules, standards, and norms, will be threatened by the different member, perceiving the exceptional child's birth or diagnosis as a crisis.

In a study of the families of trainable mentally handicapped children, Mink, Nihira, and Meyers (1983) found five family styles. The first style was the cohesive, harmonious family. Religion played an important part in these families, and the exceptional child had little influence on the marriage, precipitating few stressful life events. The family was stable, and its children had high self-esteem.

The second family style was control oriented and somewhat non-harmonious. Unlike mothers in the first type of family, a high percentage of the mothers of these families worked. Parents used physical punishment to discipline children, and the children were low in adaptive behavior. The third family style was below average in openness and unharmonious. These families had less harmonious residential environment and lower achievement orientation than families representing other styles. They had many stressful life events, and the exceptional child negatively affected the family functioning.

The fourth family style was child oriented and expressive. These families showed concern for the child's well-being and scored high in pride, affection, warmth, and nonuse of physical punishment. The fifth family style, characteristic of disadvantaged families with low morale, offered little stimulation and experienced many stressful life events.

Of course, families already expecting the birth or diagnosis of an exceptional child will respond less intensely than those that do not even consider the remote possibility of the birth of an exceptional child. The nature and degree of the exceptionality also makes a difference. Farber (1975) suggested that the amount of time and energy the exceptional child demands is important: the more severe and complex the exceptionality, the more significant its impact on the family.

The extent of family resources affects the family's functioning (Farber 1975). Families with an abundance of personal, social, political, and financial resources are better able to adjust to the problem because they can enlist those resources to obtain needed services. The family with few resources is less able to manipulate the larger society to serve the child and cannot afford to redirect its limited personal and financial resources to alleviate the problem (Abrams and Kaslow 1977).

If a family perceives the exceptionality as negative or symbolic of its unworthiness and inadequacy, its capacity to function decreases. The family that perceives the exceptionality as a naturally occurring event tends to consolidate its resources and proceed to solve its problem. Marion (1980, citing Marion and McCaslin 1979) suggested that before Public Law 94-142, the culturally diverse parent reacted primarily with "feelings of protection and acceptance of the handicapped child. . . ." After passage of the law, "the greatest reaction expressed by parents of culturally diverse handicapped children has been one of anger and dismay at the policy of overinclusion of their children in classes for the mentally retarded and emotionally disturbed" (617).

Professionals need not assume distress in a family because of an exceptional child. Korn, Chess, and Fernandez (1978) reported that 75 percent of their sample of families with exceptional children felt that the child did not impair marital quality or family patterns. Dunlap and Hollingsworth (1977) also found that a large number of parents felt that the exceptional child has little effect on their families. The parents in their study stated that their problems were most likely to be practical ones, such as meeting time, money, and physical demands. However, parents did report in one study that the exceptional child restricted their activities as a family unit (Blackard and Barsh 1982).

Blackard and Barsh also found that in general professionals magnified the impact of the exceptional child on the aspects of family functioning they studied. Though few parents reported changes in the family resulting from the exceptionality, professionals overestimated changes in marital relationships, changes in family goals, restrictions of family activities, effects on siblings, financial costs, and amount of community rejection. These findings showed that families respond in a variety of ways and that professionals cannot assume a negative impact.

Abrams and Kaslow (1977) stated that a family may contribute, either directly or indirectly, to a child's psychologically caused severe learning disabilities as well as other exceptionalities related to environmental and interpersonal factors. For example, family disorganization, which can cause high levels of anxiety and feelings of insecurity, may impede the child's ability to learn. Or exceptional children may react defensively toward their families' concerns and efforts to help, thereby disrupting the family and in turn further reducing the children's ability to function.

Vogel and Bell (1980) cited several family factors that may affect the child's learning:

1. Tension and conflict in the home that inhibits the child's concentration

2. Parents' and other family members' values and attitudes toward the child and his or her exceptionality

3. Financial and emotional stress in the family caused by the exceptionality

4. Criticism and antagonism toward the child or casting the child as family scapegoat.

Abrams and Kaslow (1977) stated that family factors affecting a child's learning disability can be treated, and they suggested a continuum of possible treatments: educational intervention for the child only via tutoring and remedial education; individual therapy to help the child improve personal coping skills, or a combination of individual therapy and educational tutoring; parent group counseling; concurrent child and parent therapy with different therapists or the same therapist; and conjoint family therapy involving child, parents, and siblings.

STIGMA AND PARENTS OF EXCEPTIONAL CHILDREN

One persistent problem for parents of exceptional children involves stigma, an attribute that is deeply discrediting (Goffman 1963). This stigma spreads from the handicapped child to his parents and family. Though the negative impact of having an exceptional child on society's perceptions of the family have decreased, stamina on the part of parents is still required if they are to maintain a positive attitude (Boggs 1978).

Parents and families of exceptional children suffer from stigmatization, society's reaction to members who are different and do not conform to the usual expectations of society (Darling 1979). Not only are exceptional individuals stigmatized because they are not normal, but they are denied the opportunity to be normal by the very society that stigmatizes them. Parents and families of exceptional children suffer from "stigma transference"—guilt by association (Darling 1979).

Parents of exceptional children may be worried about the dangers of exposure to stigma. People may hesitate to become close to the family of an exceptional child fearing that they too may share in the stigma. Darling and Darling (1982, 41) maintained that "a great number of the problems faced by parents of congenitally handicapped children are a direct result of an inadequately structured society."

In describing the impact and stigma on a family with an exceptional child, Darling and Darling proposed a four-phase family experience. Initially, the family "finds out," and is faced with too early decision making, professional denial, and they are suspicious of the information they are receiving. To address these suspicions they begin during the second stage to seek help. Parents must contend with problems produced not only by having an exceptional child, but by the reaction (or lack of reaction) of others. They enter the medical referral structure and seek treatment. After exhausting the medical structure, they seek help through education and other services.

Throughout these help-seeking periods, Darling and Darling (1982) indicated that families are faced with financial problems, a need for physical and emotional relief, and a need for practical solutions to their problems. Solutions are sought through the use of special equipment, behavior management training, legal advice, and other services.

After completing the help-seeking phase, Darling and Darling described a quest among parents and families of exceptional individuals to normalize their existence. During this phase, parents become less involved in parents' associations, and perceive themselves first and foremost as parents than as parents of exceptional children. However, this normalization may be threatened from time to time by changes in the social structure.

Some parents and families, however, are unable to establish normal routines. These parents, usually with more severely handicapped exceptional children, become more involved in organized programs as their children become older, entering a *crusadership* mode. These parents and families strive to achieve normalization by increasing public awareness, promoting legislation, and challenging systems they perceive as unfair.

Parents and families of exceptional children develop techniques for managing people's impressions of their children. They may "lower" their child's ages, or avoid certain situations by limiting the time their child spends outside the home. Parents consistently report that they do not appreciate the "pseudo-concern" they encounter when in the community with their children (Darling 1979). Others are willing to explain openly their child's problem.

A final demonstration of the stigma encountered by parents and families of exceptional children is described by Darling (1979) as *parental entrepreneurship,* the development of the social role of *exceptional parent.* Though they experience societal stigma, parents feel they maintain a positive definition of their children. The parents may fill an entrepreneurial role of promoting their child's cause. The parent entrepreneur is a product of a community that does not provide the services needed for the exceptional child and family. Parents become information seekers and crusaders in an attempt to fit into a society in which parents are perceived as good if they do their best to help their children progress as fully as possible (Darling 1979).

PARENTS' NEEDS FOR PROFESSIONAL SUPPORT

In addition to common parent concerns about their children's social development, physical health, emotional stability, educational and vocational preparation, and capacity for independent functioning in the community, parents of exceptional children have several additional concerns:

1. The effect of their attitudes and feelings toward exceptionality on their child's self-acceptance and acceptance by others

2. The availability and quality of specialized treatments and habilitation services

3. The availability of specialized education and training programs

4. The effects of the exceptional child on family members and on the group as a whole

5. Prospects for the child's and the parents' future.

These concerns vary in intensity from family to family and within a particular family over time. Moreover, as discussed in the preceding sections, the specific effects the exceptional child will have on the family depends on the family's style, size, composition, resources, as well as the exceptional child's characteristics and other factors. Hammer recognized six periods of stress in the lives of families with exceptional children:

1. At birth or upon suspicion of the handicap

2. At time of diagnosis and treatment of the handicapping condition

3. As the child nears age of school placement

4. As the child nears puberty

5. As the child nears the age of vocational planning

6. As parents age and the child may outlive them. (Hammer 1972, 10; Marion 1981, 17)

During these periods, parents need understanding and support, coupled with information and facts. They need to participate actively in planning habilitation for their child and to understand their role in furthering their child's development. Parents also need to maintain their identities as competent individuals and as parents and participating members of the community. And they need to understand their role in developing positive and realistic expectations for their child (Hammer 1972; in Marion 1981).

Parents' primary need, however, is to communicate as equals with empathetic and knowledgeable professionals (Chinn, Winn, and Walters 1978). Professionals can help parents learn about and understand their child's exceptionality, provide needed social-emotional support, and serve as a resource for information on the etiology of the exceptionality, as well as its medical, educational, and social ramifications.

If treatment is not readily available for the exceptional child, professionals can help parents obtain it. When the child's condition requires long-term planning and treatment, professionals can participate in the planning process and help obtain services (Chinn, Winn, and Walters 1978).

According to one parent of an exceptional child, "The greatest single need of parents of mentally retarded children is constructive professional counselling at various stages in the child's life which will enable the parents to find the answers to their own individual problems to a reasonably satisfactory degree" (Murray 1959, 1084). Murray suggested six basic areas in which parents benefit from professional help:

1. Accepting that the child is exceptional

2. Handling the lifelong financial problems accompanying the birth and diagnosis of an exceptional child

3. Coping with the emotional tensions of living with an exceptional child

4. Confronting and resolving the theological issues raised by the tragedy of exceptionality

5. Facing and preparing for lifetime care for the child, even after the parents' death

6. Handling the frustrations of receiving inept, inaccurate, or ill-timed advice from insensitive or poorly trained professionals.

Parents of culturally diverse exceptional children may have unique concerns arising from a negative view of special education (Marion 1980). Marion suggested that parents of culturally diverse exceptional children often distrust testing as potentially biased, a fear that may cause friction in their dealings with professionals. They may also be concerned about criteria for including or excluding their children in special education programs. Like all parents, these parents want accurate information, but they may not take advantage of established information systems or organizations. Written material, a source of information for many nonminority parents, may not be in the appropriate language.

Parents of culturally diverse exceptional children often demonstrate a need to belong (Marion 1980), but they may hesitate to join child advocacy organizations because they are typically run by white middle-class people with whom minority parents do not identify. Consequently, teachers can meet the needs of minority parents by developing parent groups specifically designed for them. Teachers are also in a position to help minority parents wishing to speak up for their children's needs—by accompanying them to meetings of existing organizations, for example.

Without doubt, life for the parents of an exceptional child is difficult. They must weather the tornado of the initial crisis of diagnosis and then the periodic storms of obtaining treatment, education, vocational training, and other services throughout the child's life. Professionals who understand parents' needs in these difficult circumstances can play an important role in securing the best possible future for each child.

THE UNINVOLVED PARENT

Although many parents recognize a need for and welcome professional support, some parents, and some teachers, do not actively cooperate in the education of the exceptional children for whom they are responsible. As a consequence, both may lose the assistance of their most valuable ally.

Morrison (1978) suggested two reasons for the ineffectiveness of some parent-teacher programs:

- A lack of real effort on the part of most schools to implement an effective community involvement program

- A lack of enthusiasm on the part of teachers and other educators to make parent programs work, perhaps because of fear of "outside influences" in the classroom.

Generally, failures reflect both parents' and teachers' inability to see the benefits of collaboration (see Chapter Three).

Parents give many reasons for their lack of involvement, some more valid than others. Teachers who want to develop meaningful parent-teacher involvement programs benefit from listening to these reasons in any case. Many parents remember unsatisfactory experiences with school personnel, during their years as students and as parents, and they remain uninvolved to avoid repeating these unhappy and embarrassing experiences. Other parents perceive teachers as ineffective in their work with exceptional children. They may distrust teachers who constantly seek their assistance in managing their children's behavior or teaching them, thinking that the teachers want them to do their jobs for them.

Some parents may suffer from incapacitating personal, marital, and social problems that interfere with their ability to benefit from parent-teacher activities. Though they may participate to some degree, their personal problems are likely to take precedence over school involvement. In such cases, it is more appropriate for teachers to refer parents to appropriate professionals and service agencies.

And finally, several situational factors may influence parents' level of involvement (MacMillan and Turnbull 1983). The more severe the child's disability, the greater the demands on the parents; for some parents, the school day is their only respite so they seek to stay uninvolved from it. Family factors, such as whether the family is a one-parent family, the availability of family support, whether both parents work, and the availability of child care, may discourage involvement as well.

Lee (1980) cited several failings of parent-teacher programs that many parents see as insurmountable barriers to their participation in conferences, workshops, meetings, and other activities:

1. *Inconvenient meeting times and locations.* Some parents are simply too busy raising their children, caring for their homes, and providing for their families to attend parent-teacher activities. Parents of young children may be unable to attend meetings without employing a baby-sitter, which they may be unwilling or unable to do. A few parents do not own an automobile and cannot afford bus or taxi fare. And some parents believe they do not have proper clothes for school meetings.

2. *Inadequate parent input during program planning.* If not involved in initial planning, parents feel that programs will not respond to their needs. They resent others' telling them what they and their exceptional child needs.

3. *Unwarranted assumptions about parents' skills.* Many parents of today's school children do not speak English; others do not have the reading, writing, or verbal skills to participate successfully in some of the activities. Programming often ignores special cultural considerations as well.

4. *Inadequate feedback and follow-up services for parents.* Parents often become "lost in the system," treated as passive recipients. If they miss an activity, no one appears to notice or makes an effort to update them.

5. *Parent feelings of inadequacy.* Parents may feel threatened by professionals in charge of parent programs or by the program setting itself. They may feel dominated by the professional and worry about saying something stupid or doing something improper. The teacher's use of professional jargon and complicated technical terms may reinforce these feelings of inadequacy.

6. *Inability to implement suggestions.* Some parents do not have the time or skills to carry out suggestions made at meetings.

7. *Parent-teacher competition.* Many parents perceive programs as competition for their child's attention. They may be uneasy hearing that their child behaves one way for the teacher and another way at home and feel threatened that their child likes the teacher more than he or she likes them.

8. *Parent exhaustion.* Some parents are exhausted from previous unsuccessful attempts at parent-teacher involvement. They have become guarded and less willing to commit themselves to another program.

9. *Unresponsiveness.* The program may not respond to the parents' social-emotional needs nor to their need for knowledge and skill.

Teachers frequently live, work, and play in a different level of society from the parents they work with. As professionals working with parents from all levels of society, teachers must make every attempt to understand each parent and his or her life circumstances.

The parents of culturally diverse exceptional children may have several reasons for choosing noninvolvement. They may be indifferent to education because they feel the school system reneged on its promise to help them become someone (Chinn 1979). Minority parents' involvement with schools, including their experiences with special education, has not always been pleasant (Marion 1981).

Those minority parents who participate in parent-teacher involvement activities may do so with suspicion. They may believe stereotypical views of special education as a "dumping ground" for those unable to learn and for "troublemakers" (Marion 1981). They may believe that teachers perceive minority children as inferior.

Teachers, too, offer many excuses for not participating in parent-teacher activities:

1. Parents do not wish to become involved in the education of their exceptional children. They think their children's education is the responsibility of the school and teachers.

2. Most, if not all, parents lack the training to understand the educational process. The teacher would have to spend too much time training parents in the basics of education before an effective parent-teacher involvement program would be possible.

3. Parents are unwilling to accept that their child is exceptional and in need of special education services. Until they accept the facts, teachers' efforts to involve them are a waste of time.

4. Parents are hesitant to allow school personnel even to assess their child. How can teachers expect to involve them in other activities?

5. Parents refuse to attend parent-teacher conferences and individualized education program meetings. They will not permit home visits. Teachers cannot force themselves on parents. If parents are afraid of the teacher and school, no one can change their attitude.

6. Parents do not speak the teacher's language—namely, English. Teachers are not multilingual nor should they be.

7. Parents do not live like teachers live. They live in substandard housing, eat strange foods, and participate in unusual activities. Teachers cannot understand them or their culture.

8. Teachers are trained to educate children, not counsel parents. They simply do not have the skills to work effectively with parents.

Teachers also may oversimplify the issue by equating parent involvement in educational programs with parent involvement with the exceptional child (MacMillan and Turnbull 1983). Parents' decision not to be involved in their child's educational program does not mean they are also uninvolved with the child at home. MacMillan and Turnbull maintained that parents have the right to choose not to be involved in educational programming when they feel noninvolvement is beneficial to them, their child, or the family. Indeed, parents forced into involvement against their better judgment may become frustrated, be absent from work or from their families for extended times, have decreased free time, or become an inordinate drain on school staff. Decisions about the degree of involvement should grow out of individual preferences rather than generalized expectations.

Parent involvement in their exceptional child's educational program may be a benefit to some parents and a detriment to others (Turnbull and Turnbull 1982). Because not all parents are suited to be advocates, the Turnbulls pointed out the need to individualize programs for parents as well as for their exceptional children. Parents' needs, abilities, and preferences and families' expectations are important considerations. Professionals must allow parents to remain uninvolved in educational activities if they so choose.

SUMMARY

This chapter discusses the impact of the birth or diagnosis of an exceptional child on his or her parents and family, focusing primarily on the expressive aspects of parents' adjustment. (Later chapters discuss some instrumental, or practical, aspects.) Parents first react to the birth or diagnosis with shock. They experience a crisis, during which they progress through disbelief, guilt, rejection, shame, denial, and a feeling of helplessness. In an effort to avoid being emotionally overwhelmed by their predicament, parents adopt one or more (usually several) defensive responses, such as mourning, denial, guilt, anger, and self-doubt. As the crisis reactions lessen, parents begin to cope with the practical problems and emotional confusion introduced by their exceptional child.

Although some generalizations are possible, parents' reactions are highly individualized; they progress at their own rate and in their own way. Moreover, their adjustments may continue to some degree throughout their lives.

The child's impact on the family unit also varies considerably, reflecting family style, purpose, structure, rules, methods of operation, values, and expectations. In addition, the impact of the exceptional child on minority or culturally diverse parents and families is frequently different than its impact on majority culture parents and families.

The chapter concludes with a review of the many reasons parents and teachers offer for noninvolvement in cooperative educational activities to benefit the exceptional child. Parents may avoid involvement because of past bad experiences in the school system or a belief that the school has total responsibility for educating their children. In turn, teachers may feel the educational process is too complex for parents to understand or be unwilling to adapt their approach to accommodate parents with different backgrounds.

Chapter Three assesses the need for and advantages of parent-teacher involvement, highlighting advantages for the child, parent, teacher, school, and community. It discusses several general guidelines for effective parent involvement and reviews exceptional children's and parents' rights and responsibilities.

EXERCISES AND DISCUSSION TOPICS

1. Discuss the following statement: "Marriage is the mating of two adults who live in an eternally blissful union, which produces physically and mentally perfect children." Is this statement generally true? false? Are views of marriage and parenthood changing as time passes? Discuss this statement with your contemporaries, your parents, and your grandparents.

2. Socialization as the parent of an exceptional child occurs through performance of instrumental, or technical tasks and expressive, or emotional tasks. Interview the parent of an exceptional child or read several articles or books written by parents of exceptional children. Using the information you gather, classify the various aspects of the parental role as either instrumental or expressive. Define these aspects for at least two types of exceptionality.

3. Interview the parent of an exceptional child, and discuss his or her first reaction to discovering his or her child's exceptionality.

4. Using McDowell's phases of the crisis reaction—disbelief, guilt, rejection, shame, denial, and a feeling of helplessness—analyze a crisis you have confronted. Did you react as McDowell outlined? If you reacted differently, why?

5. Divide your study group or class into smaller groups, and have each group interview parents of an exceptional child. Compare notes on the defensive responses and coping mechanisms parents used to adjust to their child's exceptionality. How did the group findings differ and why?

6. Discuss the following statement: "The greatest single need of parents . . . is constructive professional counseling . . . which will enable the parents to find the answers to their own individual problems to a reasonably satisfactory degree" (Murray 1959).

7. Analyze your family. Is it open or closed? What are its purposes, structure, rules, methods of operation, norms, values, and expectations for its members? How do you think your family would respond to the birth or diagnosis of an exceptional child?

8. Discuss the following statement: "Some parents are very involved with their exceptional child, but they do not participate in formal parent-teacher activities."

9. What are special education teachers' responsibilities to culturally diverse and minority families? How can they meet these responsibilities?

REFERENCES

Abrams, J. C., and F. Kaslow. 1977. Family systems and the learning disabled child: Intervention and treatment. *Journal of Learning Disabilities* 10 (2):86–90.

Barsch, R. H. 1968. *The parent of the handicapped child.* Springfield, Ill.: C. C. Thomas.

Barsch, R. H. 1969. *The parent-teacher partnership.* Reston, Va.: The Council for Exceptional Children.

Begab, M. J. 1956. Factors in counseling parents of retarded children. *American Journal of Mental Deficiency* 60:515–24.

Berry, J. O. 1981. The art of coping and hoping. *The Exceptional Parent* 11 (4):35.

Blackard, M. K., and E. T. Barsh. 1982. Parents' and professionals' perceptions of the handicapped child's impact on the family. *The Journal of the Association for the Severely Handicapped* 7 (2):62–69.

Boggs, E. M. 1978. Who is putting whose head in the sand or in the clouds as the case may be? In *Parents speak out,* eds. A. P. Turnbull and H. R. Turnbull, III. Columbus, Ohio: Merrill.

Buscaglia, L. F. 1971. Parents' need to know: Parents and teachers work together. In *The child with learning disabilities: His right to learn,* ed. J. I. Arena. Pittsburgh: Association for Children with Learning Disabilities.

Chinn, P. C. 1979. The exceptional minority child: Issues and some answers. *Exceptional Children* 45 (7):532–36.

Chinn, P. C., J. Winn, and R. H. Walters. 1978. *Two-way talking with parents of special children: A process of positive communication.* St. Louis: C. V. Mosby.

Clark, S. P., and H. W. Clark. 1980. Parenting a special needs child: Private and public concerns. *The Pointer* 25 (1):5–7.

Cohen, P. C. 1962. The impact of the handicapped child on the family. *Social Casework* 43 (3):137–42.

Darling, R. B. 1979. *Families against society.* Beverly Hills, Calif.: Sage.

Darling, R. B., and J. Darling. 1982. *Children who are different.* St. Louis: C. V. Mosby.

Dunlap, W. R., and J. S. Hollingsworth. 1977. How does a handicapped child affect the family? Implications for practitioners. *Family Coordinator* July, 286–93.

Fairfield, B. 1983. Parents coping with genetically handicapped children: Use of early recollections. *Exceptional Children* 49 (5):411–15.

Farber, B. 1975. Family adaptations to severely mentally retarded children. In *The mentally retarded and society,* eds. M. J. Begab and S. A. Richardson. Baltimore: University Park Press.

Gallagher, J. J., P. Beckman, and A. H. Cross. 1983. Families of handicapped children: Sources of stress and its amelioration. *Exceptional Children* 50 (1):10–18.

Gallagher, J. J., A. Cross, and W. Scharfman. 1981. Parental adaptations to a young handicapped child: The father's role. *Journal of the Division of Early Childhood* 3:3–14.

Goffman, E. 1963. *Stigma.* Englewood Cliffs, N.J.: Prentice-Hall.

Goldstein, S. 1975. The brain-damaged parent (a parody on special services). *Exceptional Children* 41 (8):563–64.

Gordon, S. 1976. A parent's concerns. *The Exceptional Parent* 6 (3):19–22.

Greer, B. G. 1975. On being the parent of a handicapped child. *Exceptional Children* 41 (8):519.

Hammer, E. 1972. Families of deaf-blind children: Case studies of stress. Paper presented at the First Regional American Orthopsychiatric Association Conference, Dallas, Texas, 1972.

Hoff, L. E. 1978. *People in crisis.* Menlo Park, Calif.: Addison-Wesley.

Hosey, C. 1973. Yes, our son is still with us. *Children Today* 2 (6):14–17, 36.

Korn, S. J., S. Chess, and P. Fernandez. 1978. The impact of children's physical handicaps on marital quality and family interaction. In *Child influences on marital and family interaction,* eds. R. M. Lerner and G. B. Spanier. New York: Academic Press.

Kozloff, M. A. 1979. *A program for families of children with learning and behavior problems.* New York: John Wiley & Sons.

Lee, B. 1980. Materials developed for parent involvement. Springdale School, Special School District of St. Louis County, Mo.

Love, H. D. 1970. *Parental attitudes toward exceptional children.* Springfield, Ill.: C. C. Thomas.

McDowell, R. L. 1976. Parent counseling: The state of the art. *Journal of Learning Disabilities* 9 (10):614–19.

MacMillan, D. L., and A. P. Turnbull. 1983. Parent involvement with special education: Respecting individual differences. *Education and Training of the Mentally Retarded* 18:4–9.

Marcus, L. M. 1977. Patterns of coping in families of psychotic children. *American Journal of Orthopsychiatry* 47 (3):388–99.

Marion, R. L. 1980. Communicating with parents of culturally diverse exceptional children. *Exceptional Children* 46 (8):616–23.

Marion, R. L. 1981. *Educators, parents and exceptional children.* Rockville, Md.: Aspen Systems Corporation.

Marion, R. L., and T. McCaslin. 1979. Parent counseling of minority parents in a genetic setting. Unpublished manuscript. Austin, Tex.: University of Texas.

Meadow, K. P., and L. Meadow. 1971. Changing role perceptions for parents of handicapped children. *Exceptional Children* 38 (1):21–27.

Mink, I. T., K. Nihira, and C. E. Meyers. 1983. Taxonomy of family life styles. *American Journal of Mental Deficiency* 87 (5):484–97.

Moroney, R. M. 1981. Public school policy: Impact on families with handicapped children. In *Understanding and working with parents of children with special needs,* ed. J. L. Paul. New York: Holt, Rinehart and Winston.

Morrison, G. S. 1978. *Parent involvement in the home, school, and community.* Columbus, Ohio: Charles E. Merrill.

Murphy, A. T. 1981. *Special children, special parents: Personal issues with handicapped children.* Englewood Cliffs, N.J.: Prentice-Hall.

Murray, M. A. 1959. Needs of parents of mentally retarded children. *American Journal of Mental Deficiency* 63:1078–88.

Prescott, M. R., and K. L. W. Iselin. 1978. Counseling parents of a disabled child. *Elementary School Guidance and Counseling* 12:170–77.

Rees, R. J., R. D. Strom, and S. Wurster. 1982. A profile of childrearing characteristics for parents of exceptional intellectual and handicapped children. *Australia and New Zealand Journal of Developmental Disabilities* 8 (4):183–96.

Roith, A. J. 1963. The myth of parental attitudes. *Journal of Mental Subnormality* 9:51–54.

Roos, P. 1963. Psychological counseling with parents of retarded children. *Mental Retardation* 1:345–50.

Roos, P. 1978. Parents of mentally retarded children—Misunderstood and mistreated. In *Parents speak out,* eds. A. P. Turnbull and H. R. Turnbull. Columbus, Ohio: Charles E. Merrill.

Ross, A. O. 1964. *The exceptional child in the family: Helping parents of exceptional children.* New York: Grune and Stratton.

Rossi, A. S. 1975. Transition to parenthood. In *Selected studies in marriage and the family,* eds. F. Winch and G. B. Spanier. New York: Holt, Rinehart and Winston.

Schild, S. 1982. Beyond the diagnosis: Issues in recurrent counseling of parents of the mentally retarded. *Social Work in Health Care* 8 (1):81–93.

Schiller, E. J. 1961. Creative habilitation of parents of the cerebral-palsied child. *Journal of Rehabilitation* 27 (6):14–15, 39, 42.

Searl, S. J., Jr. 1978. Stages of parent reaction. *Exceptional Parent* 8 (2):F27–F29.

Seligman, M. 1979. *Strategies for helping parents of exceptional children.* New York: Free Press.

Seligman, M., and P. Seligman. 1980. The professional's dilemma: Learning to work with parents. *The Exceptional Parent* 10 (5):S11–S13.

Sonnenschein, P. 1981. Parents and professionals: An uneasy relationship. *Teaching Exceptional Children* 14 (2):62–65.

Turnbull, A., and J. Blancher-Dixon. 1980. Preschool mainstreaming: Impact on parents. In *New directions for exceptional children, I,* ed. J. Gallagher. San Francisco: Jossey-Bass.

Turnbull, A. P., and H. R. Turnbull. 1982. Parental involvement in the education of handicapped children: A critique. *Mental Retardation* 20 (3):115–22.

Vander Zanden, J. W. 1970. *Sociology: A systematic approach.* 2d ed. New York: The Ronald Press.

Vogel, E. F., and N. W. Bell. 1960. The emotionally disturbed child as the family scapegoat. In *A modern introduction to the family,* eds. N. W. Bell and E. F. Vogel. Glencoe, Ill.: The Free Press.

Waisbren, S. E. 1980. Parental reactions after the birth of a developmentally disabled child. *American Journal of Mental Deficiency* 84 (4):345–51.

Webster, E. J. 1977. *Counseling with parents of handicapped children: Guidelines for improving communication.* New York: Grune and Stratton.

Wikler, L., M. Wasow, and E. Hatfield. 1981. Chronic sorrow revisited: Parent vs. professional depiction of the adjustment of parents of mentally retarded children. *American Journal of Orthopsychiatry* 51 (1):63–70.

PERSPECTIVES ON PARENT-TEACHER INVOLVEMENT

■ The success of the U.S. educational system may have unwittingly alienated many parents and teachers from each other. In recent decades, the quantity and complexity of knowledge has surged dramatically, making it difficult for many parents to master the information or skills they need to help their children succeed in school and function successfully in modern society.

As a result, professional educators have inherited the major responsibility for transmitting knowledge from generation to generation. Today's teachers are experts in specialized fields and in instructional techniques. However, their increased effectiveness and efficiency have essentially excluded many parents from playing a meaningful role in the formal education of their children.

Parents and teachers agree that more coordinated efforts will benefit both children and society, but they often diverge when they discuss how to accomplish this goal. What are parents' and teachers' proper roles and functions in raising children? What should children learn to function successfully? Who should teach what? When should parents or teachers introduce new topics, and how should they present controversial issues? Attempting to answer such questions is confusing for both parents and teachers. Sex education is an excellent example: Is sex education appropriate in the schools? Who should teach it? When? How? Should exceptional children receive sex education?

Every day another so-called parenting expert appears on the horizon to advise on these and other questions. The popular press and mass media bombard parents with parenting information and misinformation on everything from their child's diet to lighting fixtures in the home, disciplinary methods, or listening techniques. Often this information is contradictory.

Oversimplification of parenting advice is another problem for contemporary parents: Various formulas hold that parents must actively listen to the child, conduct frequent family councils, ignore unacceptable behavior, reward acceptable behavior, and so on if they are to be good parents. The experts' messages are clear: "Follow my formulations, and your child will mature." In fact, however, much parenting advice fails to look at the total process of parenting and encourages parents to seek a foolproof method.

As previously stated in this text, successful parenting is an art. It necessitates that parents devote time, energy, and thought to the analysis, evaluation, and integration of many factors into the whole of their unique parenting perspective and methods. Parents' efforts are facilitated through collaboration with others, such as teachers, who know the child and the parents' situation. Teachers can assist parents in interpreting the seemingly contradictory information parents receive.

This chapter discusses the value of parent education and parent-teacher involvement in educating exceptional children. It offers guidelines for parents and teachers wishing to foster home-school cooperation and summarizes the advantages of this cooperation for exceptional children, parents, teachers, schools, and communities. The chapter also reviews parents' rights and responsibilities—an important issue for parents and teachers who in effect act as child advocates.

THE NEED FOR PARENT INVOLVEMENT

A minority of special education teachers and other professionals remain skeptical about the need for and desirability of school-sponsored parent education and training programs. However, experience and research suggest that parent programs are not only needed and desirable but essential in developing effective programs for exceptional children.

Parents of exceptional children are effective change agents in their children's lives. Recognizing the responsibility they share with teachers for their children's social and academic learning, parents are moving, physically and intellectually, into the U.S. educational system (Clements and Alexander 1975). The question, then, is not whether parent education is important but how to conduct effective parent involvement programs that will benefit exceptional children, parents, and teachers.

Clements and Alexander argued that the front-line practitioner, the special teacher, is primarily responsible for parent services. Simpson (1982) suggested that just as mainstream teachers must learn new skills to deal with exceptional children, teachers of exceptional children must expand their skills to work with parents. He maintained that expecting anyone other than school personnel to meet the parents' education and training needs is unrealistic, and he encouraged teachers to develop appropriate programs for the parents of the exceptional children in their charge.

Gardner (1974) and Karnes and Zehrbach (1972) maintained that joint home-school endeavors serve exceptional children better than school endeavors alone. However, they argued that the teacher must help parents become full partners in the collaboration. Gardner outlined the problem in this way:

> Many parents do need assistance in recognizing that what they are doing may create additional problems for the child. Many could benefit from guidance in modifying the manner in which they interact with or respond to their children. They do not need the teacher to place blame on them or to lecture them on what they have done wrong or how they have created the child's problems. They do require information, guidance, and support. They need information about how specific and general problems can be approached and how their day to day interactions with their child can contribute to the child's development. They do not need generalities about being a good parent. They do need specific, concrete, and practical suggestions about how they can best promote optimal adjustment for their child. (1974, 316)

It is Karnes and Zehrbach's (1972) belief that services for exceptional individuals can be substantially improved if parents are meaningfully involved in the program. They suggested that teachers should be continuously seeking new and improved ways of involving parents in an educative process.

Devereux (1956, 363) took this perspective one step further, suggesting that some parents need as much therapy and guidance as their children: "The most tragic difficulty of work with disturbed children is hard to define without sounding almost grotesque. Briefly stated, one usually has to treat or educate the wrong person".

Indeed, many of the most effective programs for exceptional children consider a parent program essential. At Rutland Center, which serves preschool to fourteen-year-old children with severe emotional or behavioral problems, Wood (1975) and her collaborators offer parents information about the needs of the exceptional child and practical assistance in meeting the child's needs. The center actively involves parents in their children's rehabilitation.

The staff of Pathfinder School, an early education center for three–seven-year-old brain-injured children and their families, also views parents as partners in educating handicapped students. According to Susser (1974), success in the classroom will last only if school and home cooperate in twenty-four-hour-a-day follow-through and share a consistent approach.

For their part, parents of exceptional children are painfully aware of their needs for education and training. In *Heartaches and Handicaps: An Irreverent Survival Manual for Parents,* Stigen (1976) wrote of her unceasing need for assistance with her special child. She discussed (with both humor and anguish) the inadequacy of the guidance and supportive services she received from hospitals, schools, clinics, and other service agencies.

Kratoville (1975a, 1975b) and Jogis (1975), both parents of exceptional children, wrote about their need for sensitive practical assistance in acting as their children's prime therapists. They described their frustration when professionals in schools, clinics, and community agencies failed to offer assistance and understanding, and they pointed to a need for better professional training and greater sensitivity.

Rockwell and Grafford made the following statement about educating preschool children, which is equally applicable to educating exceptional children:

> Parents and schools need to be involved with each other because they have a *common element—children*. To the young child, home and school are two of the most important areas in which he functions. He spends a majority of his time in these areas. In order to assist the child and to provide the most effective learning environment, both school and home must be in cooperation—pulling together to benefit the child. Lack of cooperation and understanding between the two forces most instrumental in a young child's development can only serve to foster frustration and anxiety. . . . When parents participate, the child knows his parents care enough about him to become involved. . . . School should unite parent and child, not isolate them from each other. (1977, 2)

Sayler stated that "the school and the home need each other" (1971, 7). They have a common goal, helping children grow. If conflict exists between home and school, children may become confused and anxious and less able to learn. Indeed, "extensive research demonstrates unequivocally that children learn more, adjust better, and progress faster when parent training is effected" (Clements and Alexander 1975, 7).

ATTITUDES TOWARD PARENT INVOLVEMENT

Teachers do not universally agree on parent education and training:

> Attitudes toward parental involvement in the education and so-
> cialization of their children, while nearly always officially af-
> firmative and encouraged by school personnel and special
> education in particular, in reality run the gamut from total dis-
> association to active participation and commitment required of
> parents for their children to continue to receive educational and
> therapeutic services. (Clements and Alexander 1975, 1)

In an article advocating parent participation in the special education of their child, Kelly (1973) discussed teachers' two major objections to parent involvement. First, some teachers argue that the modern educational process is so complex that parents cannot participate meaningfully without considerable education and training. Second, some teachers suggest that parental indifference and mismanagement of their child makes parents unable and unwilling to accept a meaningful role in their children's education.

Simpson (1982) suggested two other reasons educators have made few efforts to involve parents in the educational process: Some incorrectly believe that educational decisions are solely their domain, not to be shared with parents. Other professionals consider parents the cause of many of their children's problems and in need of help themselves.

In a detailed discussion of parent involvement, McAfee and Vergason (1979) noted several deficiencies and problems in current educational practice that provide additional insight into professionals' attitudes. According to the researchers, parent involvement programs do not recognize parents as the most important influence on their children's development. In addition, such programs frequently ignore the fact that disenfranchised parents will not be motivated to support the educational system and in fact may work against it.

McAfee and Vergason also suggested that current programs mistakenly assume that teaching parents about their child's education ensures parent support and participation in it. In fact, means are lacking to enforce mutual agreements arrived at by parents and teachers. Moreover, many programs fail to emphasize that many people—not teachers alone nor parents alone—are responsible for children's educational achievement. Finally, parent programs make the mistake of trying to dictate parent responsibility rather than developing it over time for the benefit of the child, parent, and teacher.

Given these flaws in existing efforts to involve parents, McAfee and Vergason made three recommendations for future programs:

1. Parents and teachers should structure a contract, unwritten or written, to ensure that each contributes equally toward common goals.

2. Parents must assume some responsibility for the education of their children.

3. Parents and teachers must seek ways to regain community support for the educational system.

Findings by Yoshida, Fenton, Kaufman, and Maxwell (1978) support other researchers' work on professionals' views of parent involvement. In 1976, they surveyed 1,526 placement and program planning team members in Connecticut on their view of parents' appropriate role on their children's educational planning team. Analysis of 1,372 questionnaires from administrators and supportive and instructional personnel indicated that over half the respondents selected only two appropriate activities for parents: presenting information relevant to the case and gathering information relevant to the case. In some areas in which legal and legislative initiatives have increased parent participation (such as reviewing the student's educational progress, evaluating the appropriateness of the student's program, judging programming alternatives, and finalizing decisions), affirmative responses were few. The researchers concluded that the professional members of the planning team expected parents to provide information but not to participate in decision making about their exceptional child's program. In turn, they suggested that the professionals' attitudes help determine the actual role parents assume during team meetings.

In contrast, Lusthaus, Lusthaus, and Gibbs surveyed parents to determine their perceptions of their current and desired roles in decision making for their exceptional children's education. Researchers asked parents to indicate their current and desired levels of participation in several decision-making areas: no involvement, giving and receiving information, and having control over decisions.

> Parents in this study stated that the role they play vis-à-vis their schools is one of information giving and receiving. They also said that, in general, this is the role they wish to play. A few notable exceptions are apparent. Parents want more than an informational role in three decision areas: the kinds of information kept on their children; medical services for their children; and transfer of their children to other schools. Their desire for decisional control in these three areas may indicate the beginning of a change in the way parents see themselves and their role. As they achieve greater participation in planning for their children and greater understanding of the educational system, they may want their foremost role to change to one of making and monitoring decisions. (1981, 257)

The work cited in this chapter leads to several conclusions about parent involvement in their exceptional children's education:

1. A need exists for educating and training parents of exceptional children.

2. Parent programs are desirable because they both respond to parents' needs and affect the children's program positively.

3. The teacher, a specialist in instructional processes and behavior management, is the logical professional to coordinate parent programs. Only the teacher can approximate the parents' intimate knowledge and understanding of the exceptional child.

4. The approaches used in the home and in the school must be consistent.

5. Parent programs are most effective when they are practical, concrete, specific, and, above all, meaningful to the parents.

6. Teachers need training to assume parent education and training responsibilities.

7. Parent education and training will improve parents' ability to make and monitor decisions affecting their exceptional children.

BENEFITS OF PARENT-TEACHER COOPERATION

Despite some resistance in the professional community, the advantages of parent-teacher cooperation appear to outweigh the problems. Many writers have documented these advantages, which accrue to the school and community as well as to parents, teachers, and exceptional children. This section offers a sampling of these writers' views.

Advantages for the Child

■ Parent-teacher cooperation has a positive effect on children's academic achievement (Kroth and Scholl 1978; Lillie 1974), increasing their chances of success in school. Parent involvement significantly increases the number of people available to foster the child's development, and the availability of more individualized instruction increases the time the child can devote to learning.

■ As parents' training changes their behavior toward the child, the child's behavior may also change positively (Patterson and Gullion 1969; Kelly 1973). Children learn from their parents and siblings in the home. Parents can be trained to instruct their children effectively in parent-teacher involvement programs (Patterson and Gullion 1969, Benson and Ross 1972; Karnes and Zehrbach 1972; Lillie 1974).

◼ When parents and teachers use similar instructional techniques, they increase the probability that the child will generalize the knowledge and skills learned at home or school to other environments (Hymes 1974; Lillie 1974).

◼ Parent training early in the child's life enables parents to teach at home the prerequisite and readiness skills needed for school success (Lillie 1974; Cooke and Cooke 1974; Shearer 1974).

◼ Parents and teachers who systematically work together on specific behaviors and tasks increase the probability that the child will learn them. Close cooperation is particularly important if the child is severely or profoundly handicapped (Kozloff 1973).

◼ Consistent parent and teacher expectations of the child have a positive effect on learning and behavior (Hymes 1974; Blackard 1976). This consistency protects the child from anxiety, confusion, and frustration. It also reduces the probability the child will play parents and teacher against each other and become caught in the middle of a conflict.

◼ Consistency helps the child develop personal values and standards and build a sense of wholeness or unity with life (Auerbach 1968; Ross 1964).

◼ Active parent interest and involvement can boost the child's self-image, which in turn increases feelings of security at home and in school (Auerbach 1968; Susser 1974). Children are proud to have parents involved in their education.

◼ Frequent communication between parents and teachers is more likely to promote positive discussions of the child than sporadic parent-teacher interactions reserved for crises and problems (Feldman, Byalick, and Rosedale 1975).

◼ Parent-teacher communication increases the child's awareness of his or her duties and responsibilities at home, school, and in the community (Auerbach 1968).

◼ When parents and teachers are cooperative, friendly, and respectful of one another, the child learns that positive communication is an accepted way to solve problems and avoid conflicts (Karnes and Zehrbach 1972).

◼ With teachers and parents in frequent contact, the child need not experience the anxiety of carrying messages of unknown content back and forth (Croft 1979).

◼ Parents and teachers working together are less likely to use the child as a scapegoat when frustrated (Susser 1974; Auerbach 1968).

◼ Parent-teacher cooperation allows 24-hour-a-day, 365-day-a-year opportunities for the child to develop. This total program is essential if severely handicapped children are to progress (Barsch 1969; Susser 1974).

Support for the Parents

■ Involvement in their child's education helps parents fulfill their social and ethical duties to help the child develop as fully as possible (Kelly 1973; Warfield 1975).

■ Working with teachers helps parents change their behavior, if necessary, improving the educational value of the family environment. Ideally, these changes open parents to new ideas and activities to share with their child (Calvert 1971; O'Connell 1975; Murphy 1981).

■ With close association, parents perceive teachers as allies in the effort to raise the child (Hymes 1974; Feldman, Byalick, and Rosedale 1975).

■ Parent education increases the parents' competence as the child's primary teachers in the home. Parents learn effective instructional and behavior management techniques and productive communications skills (Warfield 1975; Wood 1975; Moersch 1978).

■ Involvement with understanding teachers and other parents improves parents' self-worth and self-satisfaction (Feldman, Byalick, and Rosedale 1975; Greer 1975; Murphy 1981).

■ Parent involvement may reduce personal and family problems related to the exceptional child's difficulties (Ross 1964).

■ Parents receive social and emotional support from other parents with similar child-raising problems. Through association with other parents, they discover that their problems are neither unique nor insoluble. In addition, they learn to support other parents (Lillie 1974).

■ Parents receive factual information on the child's exceptionality, its prognosis, and related topics (Karnes and Zehrbach 1972; Cooke and Cooke 1974).

■ Parents become familiar with the purposes and operation of clinic, school, and classroom. Their improved understanding of the school's problems decreases parents' negative perceptions of the school and fosters positive and helpful attitudes toward school personnel and other professionals in their community (DeFranco 1973).

■ Parents develop understanding of the responsibilities of the many professionals and paraprofessionals working with their child (Warfield 1975).

■ Through association with teachers and other parents, parents develop a greater appreciation for their child and his or her strengths and weaknesses (Auerbach 1968).

- Parents come to view teachers as a readily available source of help as new problems emerge during the exceptional child's years in school (Susser 1974).

Advantages for the Teacher

- Parent involvement increases teachers' understanding of the exceptional child and the child's life circumstances. Teachers obtain important information on the child's personal history, current problems, and family and home situation (Marion 1981).

- Teachers learn to see the parents as individuals worthy of respect and understanding. They are also better able to support the parents' efforts at home and thus improve the child's school experience as well (Bailard and Strang 1964; Susser 1974).

- Through association with parents, teachers receive reinforcement for their efforts, which can improve their self-image and sense of professional identity (Sayler 1971).

- Parent involvement increases the chances for teachers' work with the child to succeed. Teachers can share instructional responsibility with parents and increase opportunities for individualized instruction. Teachers benefit from increased consistency between home and school (Sayler 1971; Hayden 1974).

- Parent involvement fosters positive parent-teacher communication and reduces negative communication and miscommunication. A positive relationship allows the teacher to discuss the child openly and honestly with the parents. As a consequence, the teacher becomes a knowledgeable and helpful ally (Susser 1974).

Payoffs for the School and Community

- The school and community gain recognition for program excellence. Satisfied parents promote positive community relations and increase community pride (Hayden 1974; Hymes 1974).

- Development of a positive, trusting parent-school relationship reduces the probabilities of protests, lawsuits, and general mistrust of the schools (Liddle, Rockwell, and Sacadat 1967; Fanning 1977).

- Parents can serve as effective lobbyists for the school, supporting efforts to obtain the funds, personnel, and facilities needed to improve services (Benson and Ross 1972; Hymes 1974; Fanning 1977; Klein and Schleifer 1976).

- Parents, by supplementing the teaching team, can support the school's efforts to provide individualized programs.

- ■ Parent involvement increases the schools' accountability to the exceptional child (Turnbull, Turnbull, and Wheat 1982).

- ■ Parents can contribute useful ideas for developing and improving the special education and general school program (Hayden 1974; Fanning 1977).

- ■ Parents can promote cooperation between the school and community agencies and the general public in developing programs for exceptional children (Sayler 1971). Parents can make available to exceptional children a variety of untapped community resources, such as the YMCA, YWCA, Boy Scouts and Girl Scouts, and recreation facilities.

THE EFFECTIVE PARTNERSHIP

"Cooperation, communication, respect and appreciation are what all adults hope for and want from each other as they work together to meet the needs of children with disabilities" (Klein and Schleifer 1976, 10). An effective parent-teacher partnership requires trust, commitment, work, appreciation, and communication. The partners are equals working together to set goals, find solutions, and carry out and evaluate these solutions (Rutherford and Edgar 1979).

Parents and teacher must rely on each other's character, ability, and strengths, and they must trust each other. Each must show confidence that the other will do his or her best for the child and the partnership (Stewart 1978). If parents and teachers mistrust each other, the tension in the relationship may well affect the exceptional child, with the danger that the child will become a pawn in a nonproductive game between parents and professionals.

In an effective partnership, both parties commit themselves to the purpose of the partnership—that is, to help the exceptional child develop and to support each other's work. Each accepts responsibility for bringing about mutually agreed on plans and actions. Each understands that working together is more effective than working alone. Each is aware of how much there is to learn and appreciates the complexity and significance of the educational process.

As they plan and take action, parents and teachers increasingly become involved in the difficult work of helping the child and maintaining the partnership. They must have the capacity and will to spend the necessary time and energy to make the partnership work. As their relationship develops, they learn to appreciate each other's needs and hopes, and they learn to reinforce each other's efforts and successes.

Communication is the key to developing and maintaining an effective partnership. Parents and professionals must actively listen to each other (Lichter 1976) and understand that trust, respect, appreciation, and collaboration depend on honest communication. Communication dispels mistrust.

Though it is difficult to specify those personal qualities most needed for parents and teachers to work together effectively, several traits and practical skills are common among parents and teachers active in successful parent-teacher programs. The remainder of this section highlights these qualities. (Additional qualities, such as curiosity, willingness to learn, persistence, flexibility, and a sense of humor are important supplements to the qualities discussed here.)

Self-Awareness

Effective teachers have taken the time to examine why they work with exceptional children and their parents and how their work fits into their life-style (Shea 1978). They have determined to the best of their ability the extent to which they are motivated by self-interest, a need to help others, or a combination of these motives. Teachers, like parents, are subject to denial and guilt, possibly feeling that they have contributed to the child's or parents' problems (Seligman and Seligman 1980). Thus, effective teachers will explore for negative emotions such as guilt, fear, sympathy or pity, and a need to control others and the extent to which they are balanced by acceptance, empathy, concern, and a deep desire to help others. They will also be aware of their expectations of children from different cultures and be alert to variations in the instructional activities (Henderson 1980). From this kind of awareness, the teacher learns self-acceptance.

Parents can also benefit from exploring their motives, perhaps working with a professional counselor to sort out their feelings about their children's exceptionality. Often they will need time to regain their emotional equilibrium, their sense of self, and their commitment to their special child.

As they grow in self-insight and self-acceptance, and as they acquire skills and experience, parents and teachers gain self-confidence, which in turn breeds acceptance of each other as partners in helping the exceptional child. Self-confident teachers avoid tugs-of-war with parents and other teachers over the child's educational program (Murray 1959). They accept themselves as they are while seeking to improve personally and professionally. They are realistically confident in themselves and their abilities but are not so overconfident as to be naive. They do not have an unrealistic "I can do anything" attitude and are honest with themselves, parents, and other teachers about their professional strengths and weaknesses.

Expertise

Effective teachers are knowledgeable and skilled in the disciplines of child development, exceptionality, behavior management, instructional methodology, counseling, therapy, parenting, and parent education. They know the limits of their knowledge and skills and conscientiously seek to expand them (Lynch 1978).

Parents must also be knowledgeable, making a concerted effort to learn all they can about their child and his or her exceptionality. They need information on the origin of the exceptionality, its probable course with and without treatment, and its effects on the child's learning and behavior. They must learn about the impact of the exceptionality on the child's present and future and investigate available medical, social, and education programs (Schleifer et al. 1978).

Control of Emotions

Effective teachers recognize and control their emotions. They cope with the anxiety that frequently accompanies difficult tasks, new settings, or new students and their parents. Moreover, they exercise strict control over negative emotions that may arise during intensive interactions with others.

Although insensitive, incompetent professionals or a dearth of needed services may be extremely taxing, prudent parents also control their emotions. They recognize that anger can accomplish little of lasting value (Odle, Greer, and Anderson 1976).

Compassion

Effective teachers are compassionate and empathetic. They communicate their empathy to the parent who is hurting, sad, confused, or frustrated. They possess an understanding heart and can communicate their understanding and willingness to help. They project a deep concern for the parent, child, and problem. The effective teacher distinguishes between empathy and sympathy; teachers who consistently experience sympathy and pity may not be well-suited to work with exceptional children (Seligman and Seligman 1980).

Parents and teachers must understand that their partners are human beings with strengths, weaknesses, abilities, and emotions. Parents must recognize teachers' limits in knowledge and skills. Parents, too, must be empathetic toward teachers, who can become as frustrated as parents by their inability to provide needed services (Lynch 1978).

Sensitivity to parents is another important quality. Hilliard (1980) suggested that insensitivity, particularly to a parent's cultural differences, will produce professional errors. A sensitive teacher will be open and receptive to the cultural contributions each child and parent can make (Chinn 1980).

Patience and Acceptance

Effective teachers are patient with themselves, parents, and other teachers. They recognize that all parties may make errors and become discouraged. They understand that the seriousness and chronic nature of a child's exceptionality makes instant solutions impossible. Teachers' acceptance of parents as legitimate partners is essential to assure positive parent involvement (Simpson 1982).

Parents in turn need patience. They learn that helping exceptional children is not an exact science and that teachers face many real limits on their ability to bring about change.

Moreover, effective teachers and parents accept others as they are, with all their strengths and weaknesses, perfections and imperfections. And they accept people of every race, color, creed, and handicap (Buscaglia 1971; Goolsby 1976).

Honesty

Harmon and Gregory remarked, "Why is anything as simple and straightforward as honesty so terribly difficult to sustain in our day-to-day human experience?" (1974, 11). Articles by parents and professionals repeatedly emphasize the professional's responsibility to communicate honestly with parents. Even when the truth hurts, parents want to know the true status of their child's progress. They do not want to hear "Don't worry" or "It will be all right" when they know otherwise (Murray 1959). Professionals owe parents their most honest and complete judgments, including truth about the unanswerable. In fact, Shigley (1980) suggested that dishonesty delays parents' adjustment process. Sensitive teachers will nonetheless present the truth with kindness and consideration and will not indulge in bluntness and brutality in the name of honesty.

Parents benefit from honesty when they communicate with others about themselves and their child. They have the responsibility to let the teacher know when they do not understand something, do not agree with a proposed treatment, or lack the time and energy to participate in an activity. If they are honest with themselves, they can accept that they cannot be all things to their child (Taccarino 1976).

Advocacy

Wolfensberger (1978) identified three criteria for effective advocacy. First, advocates possess a special commitment to advance the cause of another person. Second, advocates expend their own time, effort, and other resources. Finally, advocates are free of conflicts of interest and independent of the outcomes they seek.

Effective teachers are advocates for parents and children. They have an idealistic vision of what could be if all individuals and agencies exert maximum effort to help the exceptional child. Moreover, they are willing to take risks to serve the child and parent (Goolsby 1976).

Parents serve as advocates not only for their child and for themselves but also for other parents and exceptional children. They know their child's legal rights and their rights as their child's principle advocate. They are aware of the federal and state laws and regulations protecting the child and providing needed services. Armed with a thorough knowledge of their rights, parents must then know when to negotiate and compromise in planning and implementing services.

PARENTS' RIGHTS AND RESPONSIBILITIES

Parents are the first and most essential teachers of their children. As such, they have ethical and legal rights to participate actively in their children's formal education. Nonetheless, many parents feel they have been denied meaningful participation in their children's educational programs. Rowell (1981) stated that all parents have the rights to know, to understand, and to share in all decisions that affect their children's education. Because parents are their children's principle advocates—that is, act on the child's behalf—they in effect must exercise their exceptional children's rights for them.

Recent federal and state legislation and several court cases are having and will continue to have a significant impact on parents' role in educating their children. These laws and judicial decisions have already significantly influenced the practices and procedures of special and regular education programs and related service programs.

One of the most important court cases affecting the education of exceptional children was *Pennsylvania Association for Retarded Children v. the Commonwealth of Pennsylvania* in 1971. A consent agreement between the two parties granted all mentally retarded children full access to free public education. This consent agreement and similar suits have influenced educational services for the mentally retarded and other exceptional students throughout the United States.

In 1972, *Mills v. Washington, D.C., Board of Education* affirmed the right of all handicapped children to a publicly supported education, including appropriate alternatives for those unable to attend regular classes or schools. In addition, the decision required school systems to guarantee exceptional students the constitutional protections of due process and equal protection under the law.

These decisions prompted several legislative initiatives by the U.S. Congress during the 1970s. Public Law 93-112, Title V, Section 504 (The Rehabilitation Act of 1973), established equal rights for all handicapped people. The *Federal Register* expressed the hope that this regulation would "usher in a new era of equality for handicapped individuals in which unfair barriers to self-sufficiency and decent treatment will begin to fall before the force of law" (4 May 1977, 22677).

Several other provisions of Public Law 93-112 are particularly important. Section 501 forbids federal departments and agencies to discriminate in employment based on handicapping conditions. Section 502 calls for eliminating architectural, transportation, and attitudinal barriers confronting people with handicapping conditions. Section 503 prohibits federal contractors and subcontractors from discriminating against people with handicapping conditions in employment and promotion practices.

Public Law 93-380 (Education Amendments Law of 1974) is a major step toward realizing and protecting the educational rights established in the Rehabilitation Act of 1973. Among its major provisions:

1. Expenditure of federal monies to provide full service to handicapped children.

2. Development of state plans to implement Public Law 93-380, including procedural safeguards for the "identification, evaluation, and educational placement of handicapped children." These safeguards include: (a) prior notice to parents or parent surrogates when the educational agency proposes a change in the child's educational placement, (b) the opportunity for parents to have an impartial due process hearing, (c) the right of parents to examine their child's school records, and (d) the right of parents to present an independent evaluation of their child's needs and progress at a due process hearing.

3. Placement of the exceptional child in the least restrictive educational setting capable of meeting his or her needs.

4. Use of a parent surrogate as an advocate when the child's parents are unknown or unavailable.

The Buckley Amendment to Public Law 93-380 protects the rights and privacy of all students and parents. This legislation states that schools cannot release information or a child's records without parent consent. The amendment establishes parents' right of access to their child's school records and their right to challenge information in the records they deem inaccurate or inappropriate (Fanning 1977; Pasanella and Volkmor 1977).

The legislation reviewed in the preceding section establishes national policy governing the federal, state, and local rules and regulations for educational service programs for exceptional children and their parents. Public Law 94-142—known as the Education of All Handicapped Children Act of 1975—made these policies operational, mandating a *free, appropriate public education for all handicapped children.* Congress's intent in passing this law was to provide all exceptional children with an education appropriate to their needs, whatever the nature of their exceptionality. Moreover, the public school system is to provide this free, appropriate education.

This act will significantly affect the structure and operation of the U.S. educational system, from preschool to postgraduate levels, for many years to come. It will reshape both regular and special education services and affect both exceptional and nonexceptional students.

Abeson and Weintraub (1977) highlight the following provisions of Public Law 94-142 as most important to the parents of exceptional children:

1. Each child requiring special education and related services is to have an *individualized education program* (IEP) written in response to his or her specific educational needs.

2. Parents are to participate in the development, approval, and evaluation of their children's IEP. As partners with professionals in their children's education, parents have other important responsibilities and functions: to participate in assessments of their children's progress, to contribute to placement decisions, and to participate in program evaluations. In addition, parents can participate directly in the child's educational program through instruction.

3. Regular and special education teachers are to be full participating members of the IEP decision-making team. As the professionals primarily responsible for delivering services to handicapped children, teachers have a full and active role in IEP development, implementation, and evaluation.

4. Exceptional children are to be served in "the least restrictive environment" necessary to meet their unique educational needs—that is, in an educational setting as close to a normal school placement as feasible that does not sacrifice responsiveness to the child's needs. The special education setting meets the needs raised by the child's exceptionality; the regular class and school setting meets the child's normal childhood and educational needs.

The following section of the law is important to teachers, allied professionals, and parents interested in parent-teacher programs.

> The term "related services" means transportation and such developmental, corrective, and other supportive services as are required to assist a handicapped child to benefit from special education, and includes speech pathology and audiology, psychological services, physical and occupational therapy, recreation, early identification and assessment of disabilities in children, counseling services, and medical services for diagnostic or evaluation purposes. The term also includes school health services, social work services in school, and parent counseling and training. (*Federal Register,* 23 August 1977, 42479)

Thus, "parent counseling and training" qualify as related educational services under Public Law 94-142.

Other important provisions of the law call for federal funds to state and local education agencies for early identification and screening programs, reaffirm earlier legislation guaranteeing the accessibility and confidentiality of a child's school record, mandate nondiscriminatory testing, and require "due process" procedures to protect the exceptional child's rights when parents and educational agencies disagree on the child's educational program. Due process protects exceptional children from misclassification, inappropriate labeling, and education unequal to that offered the nonhandicapped (Stewart 1978). Either the educational agency or the parents may request a due process hearing to impartially resolve disagreements.

A key provision of P.L. 94-142 is the individualized education program (IEP) to be written for each child who is declared eligible for special education. The law specifically requires the direct participation of parents, teachers, and when appropriate, the exceptional child in the IEP development process. In addition, P.L. 94-142 mandated that a child be integrated into the regular school programs for education activities unless such integration is detrimental to the child's overall educational progress.

Analysis of the description of the IEP in P.L. 94-142 suggests the following minimum requirements under the law:

1. The child's educational performance must be assessed and resultant data included in the written IEP.

2. The results of the assessment must be translated into annual goals and short-term instructional objectives to form the base on which the child's educational program is designed.

3. The educational program must be written and implemented in response to the child's individual needs as stated in the annual goals and short-term instructional objectives.

4. Objective procedures must be designed and implemented to evaluate the effectiveness of the program implemented in response to the child's individual needs.

The Individualized Education Program provisions of Public Law 94-142 require that parents and educators cooperatively develop and provide educational and related services in response to the needs of each exceptional child. The effectiveness of the education and related service program must be objectively evaluated. The IEP meeting is discussed in detail in Chapter Six of this text.

In addition to the rights afforded parents through Public Law 94-142, parents also possess certain rights as human beings concerned about their children. Within broad limits, they have the rights and obligations to decide all questions affecting their family (Schopler, Reichler, and Lansing 1980).

Buscaglia (1975) identified those rights due the parents and family of the disabled, including the following rights applicable to parent-teacher involvement:

1. The right to helpful, relevant, and specific information about their role in meeting their child's special needs

2. The right to information about the educational opportunities for their child and the requirements for admission to formal schooling

3. The right to information about community resources for meeting their family's intellectual, emotional, and financial needs

4. The right to hope, reassurance, and human consideration as they meet the challenges of parenting an exceptional child

5. The right to value their child's potential over his or her imperfection

6. The right to good reading material to help them acquire important information

7. The right to interact with other parents of exceptional children

8. The right to actualize their personal rights as growing, unique individuals apart from their children.

Parents and teachers alike must be well-versed in the legislation reviewed in this section, and in their human rights, if they are to function effectively as advocates for exceptional children. Teachers can help parents learn their rights and responsibilities and can act competently and ethically when they know their own legal roles.

SUMMARY

This chapter considers the need for and advantages of parent-teacher involvement in the education of exceptional children. The discussion demonstrates that though some professionals resist parent involvement, most parents and educators recognize that services for exceptional children improve with parent-teacher cooperation. The chapter points out specific benefits for all groups affected by the parent-teacher relationship—the children, the parents, the teachers, the school, and the community.

Next, the discussion focuses on the necessary components of effective parent-teacher collaboration to help the exceptional child. Personal characteristics most likely to foster parent-teacher communication and cooperation include self-insight, self-acceptance, and self-confidence; knowledge about exceptionality; emotional control; compassion, empathy, and sensitivity; the ability to communicate support and provide feedback on others' efforts; patience and acceptance of others; honesty; and advocacy.

The chapter concludes with a brief review of recent judicial decisions and legislative mandates affecting exceptional children, parents, and teachers. Parents and teachers, as advocates for exceptional children, must be knowledgeable about these laws and regulations governing special education.

EXERCISES AND DISCUSSION TOPICS

1. In interviews with the parents of an exceptional child and a special education teacher, explore their positive and negative perceptions of the need for and desirability of parent-teacher involvement.

2. Select one of the guidelines cited in the section entitled "The Effective Partnership." Conduct a group discussion or write a brief paper relating this guideline to a personal experience with a teacher, colleague, parent, or student.

3. The term *partnership* appears throughout this chapter and elsewhere in the text. Write a paper or deliver an oral presentation on the meaning of this term in the education of exceptional children.

4. Spend some time contemplating the concept of self-insight. Answer the following questions:

∎ What is self-insight?

∎ How does an individual develop self-insight?

∎ Why did I enter (or why do I plan to enter) a helping profession?

∎ Why do I work (or wish to work) with exceptional children?

∎ Why do I work (or wish to work) with the parents of exceptional children?

5. Why is it difficult to honestly report negative (or potentially negative) information to the parent of an exceptional child? Interview an administrator, psychologist, social worker, or special teacher about the difficulties of honest, yet sensitive, communication of negative information.

6. Write a brief paper on the advantages and disadvantages of parent-teacher involvement for the child, parent, teacher, school, or community.

7. Write a paper on the legal rights of exceptional children, parents, and teachers in your state, commonwealth, or province.

8. Using Wolfensberger's criteria for an advocate, answer the following question: Can parents and teachers of exceptional children be effective advocates? Defend your position.

REFERENCES

Abeson, A., and F. Weintraub. 1977. Understanding the individualized education program. In *A primer on individualized education programs for handicapped children,* ed. S. Torres. Reston, Va.: The Foundation for Exceptional Children.

Auerbach, A. B. 1968. *Parents learn through discussion: Principles and practices of parent group education.* New York: John Wiley.

Bailard, V., and R. Strang. 1964. *Parent-teacher conferences.* New York: McGraw-Hill.

Barsch. R. H. 1969. *The parent-teacher partnership.* Reston, Va.: The Council for Exceptional Children.

Benson, J., and L. Ross. 1972. Teaching parents to teach their children. *Teaching Exceptional Children* 5 (1):30–35.

Blackard, K. 1976. *Introduction to the family training program: Working paper.* Seattle: Experimental Education Unit, University of Washington.

Buscaglia, L., ed. 1975. *The disabled and their parents: A counseling challenge.* Thorofare, N.J.: Charles B. Slack.

Calvert, D. 1971. Dimensions of family involvement in early childhood education. *Exceptional Children* 37 (9):655–59.

Chinn, P. 1980. The exceptional minority child: Issues and some answers. *Exceptional Children* 46 (8):598–605.

Clements, J. E., and R. N. Alexander. 1975. Parent training: Bringing it all back home. *Focus on Exceptional Children* 7 (5):1–12.

Cooke, S., and T. Cooke. 1974. Parent training for early education of the handicapped. *Reading Improvement.* 11 (3):62–64.

Croft, D. J. 1979. *Parents and teachers: A resource book for home, school, and community relations.* Belmont, Calif.: Wadsworth.

DeFranco, E. B. 1973. For parents only. *Parent-Teacher's Association Magazine* 68 (1):8–9.

Devereux, G. 1956. *Therapeutic education: Its theoretical bases and practice.* New York: Harper and Row.

Fanning, P. 1977. The new relationship between parents and schools. *Focus on Exceptional Children* 9 (5):1–10.

Feldman, M. A., R. Byalick, and M. P. Rosedale. 1975. Parents and professionals: A partnership in special education. *Exceptional Children* 41 (8):551–54.

Federal Register. 1977 (May 4). Part 4, 42 (86).

Federal Register. 1977 (August 23). Part 2, 42 (163).

Gardner, W. I. 1974. *Children with learning and behavior problems: A behavior management approach.* Boston: Allyn and Bacon.

Goolsby, E. L. 1976. Facilitation of family-professional interaction. *Rehabilitation Literature* 37 (11, 12):332–34.

Greer, B. G. 1975. On being the parent of a handicapped child. *Exceptional Children* 41 (8):519.

Harmon, M., and T. Gregory. 1974. *Teaching is.* . . . Chicago: Science Research Associates.

Hayden, A. H. 1974. A center based parent training model. In *Training parents to teach: Four models, first chance for children,* Vol. 3, ed. J. Grim. Chapel Hill, N.C.: Technical Assistance Development System, North Carolina University.

Henderson, R. W. 1980. Social and emotional needs of culturally diverse children. *Exceptional Children* 25 (1):8–11.

Hilliard, A. G., III. 1980. Cultural diversity and special education. *Exceptional Children* 46 (8):584–88.

Hymes, J. L., Jr. 1974. *Effective home-school relations.* Sierra Madre, Calif.: Southern California Association for the Education of Young Children.

Jogis, J. L. 1975. To be spoken sadly. In *The disabled and their parents: A counseling challenge,* ed. L. Buscaglia. Thorofare, N.J.: Charles B. Stack.

Karnes, M. B., and R. R. Zehrbach. 1972. Flexibility in getting parents involved in the school. *Teaching Exceptional Children* 5 (1):6–19.

Kelly, E. J. 1973. Parental roles in special educational programming: A brief for involvement. *The Journal of Special Education* 7 (4):357–64.

Klein, S. D., and M. J. Schleifer. 1976. Editorial: Parents and educators—Bases of effective relationships. *The Exceptional Parent* 6 (4):10.

Kozloff, M. A. 1973. *Reaching the autistic child: A parent training program.* Champaign, Ill.: Research Press.

Kratoville, B. L. 1975a. What parents feel. In *The disabled and their parents: A counseling challenge,* ed. L. Buscaglia. Thorofare, N.J.: Charles B. Stack.

Kratoville, B. L. 1975b. What parents need to hear. In *The disabled and their parents: A counseling challenge,* ed. L. Buscaglia. Thorofare, N.J.: Charles B. Stack.

Kroth, R. L., and G. T. Scholl. 1978. *Getting schools involved with parents.* Arlington, Va.: Council for Exceptional Children.

Lichter, P. 1976. Communicating with parents: It begins with listening. *Teaching Exceptional Children* 8 (2):66–71.

Liddle, G. P., R. E. Rockwell, and E. Sacadat. 1967. *Education Improvement for the Disadvantaged in an Elementary Setting.* Springfield, Ill.: Charles C. Thomas.

Lillie, D. L. 1974. Dimensions in parent programs: An overview. In *Training parents to teach: Four models, first chance for children,* Vol. 3, ed. J. Grim, 1–9. Chapel Hill, N.C.: Technical Assistance Development System, North Carolina University.

Lusthaus, C. S., E. W. Lusthaus, and H. Gibbs. 1981. Parents' role in the decision process. *Exceptional Children* 48 (3):256–57.

Lynch, E. W. 1978. The home-school partnership. In *Parents on the team,* ed. L. Brown and M. S. Moersch, 21–24. Ann Arbor, Mich.: University of Michigan Press.

McAfee, J. K., and G. A. Vergason. 1979. Parent involvement in the process of special education: Establishing the new partnership. *Focus on Exceptional Children* 11 (2):1–15.

Marion, R. L. 1981. *Educators, parents, and exceptional children.* Rockville, Md.: Aspen Systems Corporation.

Moersch, M. S. 1978. History and rationale for parent involvement. In *Parents on the Team,* ed. S. L. Brown and M. S. Moersch. Ann Arbor, Mich.: University of Michigan Press.

Murphy, A. T. 1981. *Special children, special parents: Personal issues with handicapped children.* Englewood Cliffs, N. J.: Prentice-Hall.

Murray, M. A. 1959. Needs of parents of mentally retarded children. *American Journal of Mental Deficiency* 63:1078–88.

O'Connell, C. Y. 1975. The challenges of parent education. *Exceptional Children* 41 (8):554–56.

Odle, S. J., J. G. Greer, and R. M. Anderson. 1976. The family of the severely retarded individual. In *Educating the severely and profoundly retarded,* ed. R. M. Anderson and J. G. Greer, 251–61. Baltimore: University Park Press.

Pasanella, A. L., and C. B. Volkmor. 1977. *To parents of children with special needs. A manual on parent involvement in educational programming.* Los Angeles: California Regional Resource Center, University of Southern California.

Patterson, G. R., and M. E. Gullion. 1969. *A guide for the professional for use with living with children.* Rev. ed. Champaign, Ill.: Research Press.

Rockwell, R. E., and K. J. Grafford. 1977. *TIPS (Teachers Involve Parent Services).* Edwardsville, Ill.: School of Education, Southern Illinois University.

Ross, A. O. 1964. *The exceptional child in the family: Helping parents of exceptional children.* New York: Grune and Stratton.

Rowell, J. C. 1981. The five rights of parents. *Phi Delta Kappan* 62 (6):441–43.

Rutherford, R. B., and E. Edgar. 1979. *Teachers and parents: A guide to interaction and cooperation.* (Abr. ed.) Boston: Allyn and Bacon.

Sayler, M. L. 1971. *Parents: Active partners in education.* Washington, D.C.: American Association of Elementary-Kindergarten-Nursery Education.

Schleifer, M. J., S. D. Klein, and J. Q. Griffin, eds. 1978. Parent-professional communication: Practical suggestions. *The Exceptional Parent* 8 (2):F15–F18.

Schopler, E. R., R. J. Reichler, and M. Lansing. 1980. *Individualized assessment and treatment for autistic and developmentally disabled children.* Baltimore: University Park Press.

Seligman, M., and P. A. Seligman. 1980. The professional's dilemma: Learning to work with parents. *The Exceptional Parent* 10 (5):S11–S13.

Shea, T. M. 1978. *Teaching children and youth with behavior disorders.* St. Louis, Mo.: C. V. Mosby.

Shearer, M. S. 1974. A home based parent training model. In *Training parents to teach: Four models, first chance for children,* Vol. 3, ed. J. Grim. Chapel Hill, N.C.: Technical Assistance Development System, North Carolina University.

Shigley, R. H. 1980. Parent and professional: Personal views from both perspectives. *The Pointer* 25 (1):8–11.

Simpson, R. L. 1982. Future training issues. *Exceptional Education Quarterly* 3 (2):81–88.

Stewart, J. C. 1978. *Counseling parents of exceptional children.* Columbus, Ohio: Charles E. Merrill.

Stigen, G. 1976. *Heartaches and handicaps: An irreverent survival manual.* Palo Alto, Calif.: Parents' Science and Behavior Books.

Susser, P. 1974. Parents are partners. *The Exceptional Parent* 4 (3):41–47.

Taccarino, J. R., and M. A. Leonard. 1976. Coping strategies for parents of the mentally retarded. In *Tomorrow's flower,* ed. A. M. Burke. Chicago: Illinois Association for Retarded Citizens.

Turnbull, H. R., A. P. Turnbull, and M. J. Wheat. 1982. Assumptions about parental participation: A legislative history. *Exceptional Education Quarterly* 3 (2):1–8.

Warfield, G. J. 1975. Mothers of retarded children view a parent education program. *Exceptional Children* 41 (8):559–62.

Wolfensberger, W. A. 1978. *A multicomponent advocacy protection scheme.* Toronto: Canadian Association for the Mentally Retarded.

Wood, M. M. 1975. *Developmental therapy: A textbook for teachers as therapists for emotionally disturbed young children.* Baltimore: University Park Press.

Yoshida, R. K., K. S. Fenton, M. J. Kaufman, and J. P. Maxwell. 1978. Parental involvement in the special education pupil planning process: The school perspective. *Exceptional Children* 44 (7):531–33.

CHAPTER FOUR

A MODEL FOR PARENT-TEACHER INVOLVEMENT

■ This chapter introduces a model to help education, special education, mental health, and social service professionals work effectively with parents in raising exceptional children. This tool, essentially a procedural framework, parallels processes mandated by Public Law 94-142 for individualized education programs (see Chapter Three). It, or similar service delivery models, will be an essential component of quality special education programs in the 1980s and beyond.

The model aims to respond to parents' and exceptional children's varied informational, educational, and social-emotional needs, keeping in mind the importance of individualizing the activities designed to do so. It recognizes the importance of teachers and other human service professionals in child raising but assumes that parents are primarily and ultimately responsible for educating and training their children.

The model is essentially a prescriptive teaching methodology. Activities emphasize exclusively positive, humane child-raising practices and behavior management techniques that recognize each parent and child as an individual with unique abilities, needs, and environmental influences. Aversive interventions are inappropriate in this framework.

The model involves parents, and in some circumstances the exceptional child, with the teacher and other professionals in all decision making. It emphasizes cooperation and collaboration—sharing rather than one-way dispensing of information and skills. All channels of communication among parents, children, and teacher are essential and of equal worth in furthering exceptional children's development.

The primary goal of the model presented here is to further, through parent-teacher activities, the optimal development of the exceptional child, as a person, a son or daughter, and a learner. It views parents and teachers as the primary agents of change in the child's life.

Teachers design individualized programs based on assessment data gathered through formal and informal information-gathering techniques such as those described later in this chapter. Once they have a thorough understanding of parents' and children's needs, teachers can develop appropriate activities. These activities will aim to develop the child's cognitive, affective, and psychomotor abilities, each essential to the exceptional child's overall growth and development.

The model is applicable to nonexceptional as well as exceptional populations. However, it is especially sensitive to the needs of parents and children confronting problems which lie outside normally anticipated child growth and development processes. It is not designed for treating parents with social-emotional conflicts, psychopathologies, or marital difficulties, however. It is not a form of psychotherapy, as important as such treatment may be for some parents. Teachers and other professionals using the model will find that some parents cannot benefit their child through this or similar programs. In such cases, they must refer to qualified and certified therapists, counselors, or social service professionals. Clearly, too, the effectiveness of the model, as of any model, depends on the interest, willingness, and ability of the parents and teachers participating in the program.

THE MODEL

The parent-teacher involvement model (Figure 4-1) includes five phases: (1) intake and assessment, (2) selection of goals and objectives, (3) planning and implementation of activities, (4) evaluation of activities, and (5) termination review. The flowchart in Figure 4-1 illustrates various decision points in the involvement process, and the following sections describe each phase in more detail.

Phase 1: Intake and Assessment

Ideally, parent-teacher involvement begins before the exceptional child's placement in a special education service program. However, in the real world of special education, this early contact is not always feasible.

Consequently, parent–teacher contact should occur at the first possible opportunity during referral, diagnosis, and placement.

Intake and assessment consist of a series of conferences between parents and teachers. These conferences have the following goals:

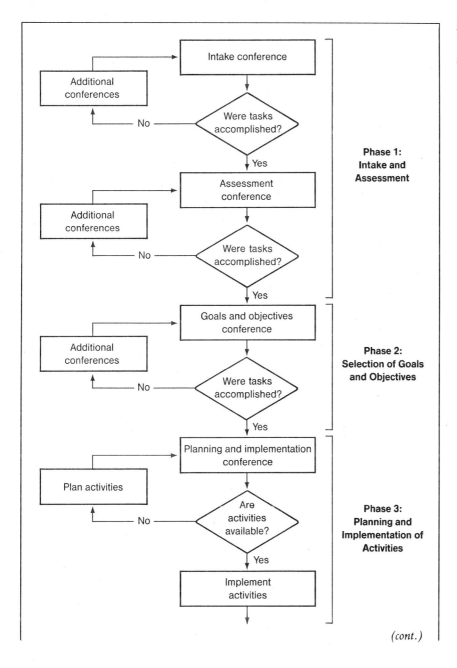

FIGURE 4-1
The Parent-Teacher
Involvement Model

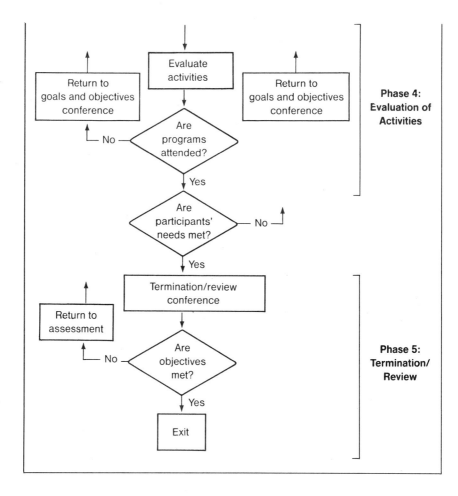

FIGURE 4-1
(cont.)

1. To establish a positive interpersonal relationship between parents and teachers

2. To ease parents' introduction to and acceptance of the parent-teacher involvement program

3. To share with parents their child's assessment information and describe his or her special and regular educational programs

4. To ascertain parents' perceptions of their children and their exceptionality, as well as their special needs, prognosis, and educational programs

5. To determine parents' needs, desires, interests, and competencies in parenting their children and responding to their special needs.

During the intake conference, the first meeting between parents and teacher, the teacher seeks to establish a positive interpersonal relationship, review and discuss the child's assessment information, and review and discuss the child's regular and/or special educational placement and program. He or she reviews with the parents the parameters of the child's exceptionality, attempting to ascertain the parents' perception of the child's problems in the process. The intake conference is complete only when parents and teacher agree that they have accomplished the tasks cited above.

Assessment conferences focus primarily on parents' perception of their children and their exceptionality. These conferences help the teacher determine the parents' capacity to attend to their child's problem and to verify their understanding of the information presented to them during the intake conference. Although the conferences rely primarily on interview techniques for assessment, teachers can use various formal and informal checklists and inventories to supplement the interview (see Appendix A: Assessment and Information-Gathering Techniques). During assessment, parents and teacher attend to the following tasks:

■ Parents provide their perspective on their child and their assessment of his or her exceptionalities.

■ The teacher and parents assess the parents' readiness, interest, willingness, capacity, and need for a parent-teacher involvement program.

The assessment is complete when parents and teacher agree that they have sufficient information and understanding to proceed to phase 2 of the model. If they do not have adequate information or if they have not reached consensus, they continue to seek an agreed-upon assessment of the child's status.

Phase 2: Selection of Goals and Objectives

In phase 2, parents and teacher synthesize the assessment data they accumulated during phase 1 to develop goals for the child's program. Phase 2 tasks generally require one or more conferences to clarify the unmet needs of parents and teachers in working with the exceptional child.

The unmet needs identified by parents and teacher translate into program goals and objectives. Goals are global (or general) targets of the involvement program; they state the desired outcomes of the collaborative activities yet to be determined. Objectives are precise, specific, and limited statements of the desired results of collaborative activity. They state the behavior, knowledge, or skill the parent, child, or teacher will exhibit upon completing an activity; the conditions under which the new behavior will be exhibited; and the criteria for acceptable performance of the new behavior.

Program objectives are essential precursors to planning and implementing activities in phase 3. Parents and teacher should select objectives independent of their knowledge of whether a suitable activity is available. If one is not available, they will later design an appropriate activity to respond to their objective.

Frequently, parents and teachers select more objectives than they can reasonably attain during the time available. Thus, they must organize objectives by priority. It is prudent to include at least one of the parents' and one of the teacher's high priority objectives among those selected for immediate implementation. The collaboration will break down if either party insists on placing his or her objectives first. When parents and professionals have completed phase 2, they can proceed to the next phase.

Phase 3: Selection and Implementation of Activities

Phase 3 includes two steps: selecting activities in one or more conferences, and carrying out the agreed-upon activities. During the activities planning conferences, parents and teacher translate the objectives of phase 2 into involvement activities. In many cases, they will find needed activities in the school and community. However, if appropriate programs are not available, parents and teacher will plan a suitable activity or select a viable alternative from those available.

Parents and teacher will generally select activities such as written and telephone communications, individual parent-teacher conferences, parent-teacher groups, and classroom, school, and community activities (see Chapters Five through Nine). These activities represent a continuum from minimum to maximum involvement (see Figure 4-2), and parents and teacher will establish in their conferences the most appropriate level of involvement. Thus, the activities selected will reflect the intensity of personal involvement required for success, the openness of communication between the parents and the teacher, the degree of personal content in the activity, and the duration and frequency of participation required.

During planning, parents and teacher agree on when, where, and how they will complete each activity. Phase 3 is complete when they

FIGURE 4-2
Continuum of
Involvement

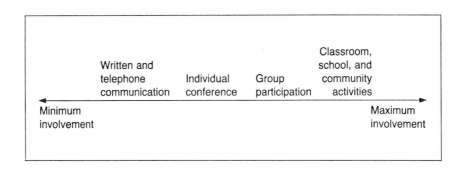

have carried out all agreed-upon involvement activities. As parents and teacher proceed through activities, they evaluate their effectiveness.

Phase 4: Evaluation of Activities

In phase 4, parents and teacher evaluate the effectiveness and efficiency of the activities under way. This stage includes both process and content evaluations that ask two basic questions: Is the prescribed activity available to the right people, and do they participate in it? Is the activity effectively changing the participants' behavior—that is, improving performance, knowledge, or skill?

Parents and teacher evaluate process using accountability procedures to answer such questions as the following:

■   Is the activity available?

■   Is the activity offered as scheduled?

■   Are all parties attending the activities?

■   Are all parties participating in the activities at the agreed-upon level?

The answers to these questions help both the teacher and parents determine if they are maintaining their part of the agreement. For example, if an activity does not take place as scheduled and both parties had agreed that the teacher was to organize and conduct the activity, the person responsible for the failure is clear. Alternatively, if an activity takes place as scheduled and parents do not attend or do not participate as prescribed, the parents are clearly responsible for the breakdown in the program. By conferring periodically to review the process evaluations, the parents and teacher have a mechanism for remedying problems.

The second type of evaluation is content evaluation, which responds to the question, Are the participants learning the knowledge and skills promoted by the activity? For example, teachers can examine parents participating in a study group on the content of the accompanying text or lectures. Or the teacher can assess competency using a newly learned teaching or behavior management skill by observing changes in the parents' or exceptional child's behavior.

Phase 5: Termination/Review

The final phase of the parent-teacher involvement model is the termination/review conference. Generally, the involvement process ends only when the parent or teacher leave the school or community or when the student graduates from school or moves to another program, classroom, or teacher. However, parents and teacher should meet at least annually to review the program plan and modify it if necessary. This step assures that the program remains responsive to the ever-changing needs of the child, parents, and teacher. The child's annual individualized educational program conference (IEP conference) may be an appropriate and convenient time to conduct the review.

A program development form, such as the one in Figure 4-3, can be an invaluable tool for the teacher as he or she moves through the five phases of the parent-teacher involvement model. By noting each step of the process as it occurs, teacher and parents have a complete record of their interactions and mutual decisions. Notes in each column of the form provide data for use in the following phase. Teachers can also use the form as a focal point for discussions. (Chapter Ten provides completed examples of the form.)

COMMUNICATION SKILLS AND INFORMATION-GATHERING TECHNIQUES

Mutually respectful communication lies at the heart of the parent-teacher involvement model. Thus, professionals need special interpersonal skills to work effectively with parents in launching an involvement program. Some of these skills and techniques are basic to any communication process; others are specific to components of the model. This section outlines those communication skills and special techniques that are the building blocks for effective parent-teacher interactions throughout the five-phase process making up the involvement model. Always, the goal is to help teachers understand parents' and children's needs so that they can support them in developing important coping skills and a positive self-image.

Interpersonal Communication

Communication is a basic human need essential to human existence (Chinn, Winn, and Walters 1978). People communicate to affect others, the environment, and themselves; they send messages in order to obtain a response and thus influence others' behavior. Communication also provides catharsis, relieving tension, frustration, and anxiety, which in turn can lead to self-discovery and self-insight.

Goolsby (1976) suggested that the critical determinant of the success or failure of a service program requiring interpersonal cooperation is the quality of communication. Effective communication is a complex dynamic process requiring people to extend themselves and to take personal risks. Frequently, however, parents and teachers lack the interpersonal skills to communicate effectively (Duff and Swick 1978).

Humans communicate at several levels simultaneously: through verbal expressions, or what they say; through body language or non-verbal expressions, or how they behave; and through emotional re-

Parents' Names _____ Teacher _____ Date _____

I	II	III	IV
Assessment	Goals and Objectives	Activities	Evaluation
A. List the assessment techniques used to obtain the data synthesized in IB.	A. List the goals, by priority, derived from the assessment process and mutually agreed on by parents and teacher.	List the activities designed by parents and teacher to meet the objectives in IIB.	A. Process: List the procedures parents and teacher will use to evaluate the processes for carrying out the activities in III.
B. List the needs mutually agreed upon using the assessment techniques in IA.	B. List the objectives derived from the goals in IIA.		B. Content: List the procedures parents and teachers will use to evaluate the content of the activities in III.

FIGURE 4-3
Program Development
Form

sponses, or how they show what they feel. The more congruent these levels of expression, the more meaningful or understandable the messages become to others. To fully interpret others' messages, one must both listen to the words and interpret the accompanying nonverbal components of body language and emotional content.

In an interview, communication is circular and forward moving. An act of communication is not repeatable; it is impossible to "uncommunicate" a message. Through continuing communication, however, people can amend their messages (Webster 1977). By understanding and monitoring three important forms of language—descriptive, inferential, and evaluative—people can reduce the need to amend original messages.

Descriptive language relates information about things the communicator has observed using his or her senses of sight, hearing, taste, touch, and smell. Inferential language describes patterns a person has become aware of through multiple observations. Such language is tentative, qualifying observations with such words as "appears," "seems," and "maybe."

Evaluative language communicates judgments and conclusions. It "tells about what is going on inside the head of the person making the evaluation. Evaluations can be positive or negative statements because they refer to the speaker's values; such statements will reveal what the speaker considers right or wrong, worthy or unworthy, beautiful or ugly, and so forth" (Webster 1977, 18). Evaluations use forms of the verb "to be" and words like "always," "never," and "must."

The teacher should be skillful in differentiating between the three forms of language in both the messages sent to and received from parents. He or she should be able to relate objective information to parents about their child (descriptive language), communicate patterns which seem to emerge from observations (inferential language), and formulate conclusions (evaluative language). By the same token, with an awareness of the different levels used by parents, the teacher can be more sure of the accuracy of their perceptions of the parents' message.

Numerous barriers exist to effective communication, however. Webster suggested that human projections can interfere with communication, especially people's perceptions of the messages they receive from others. In an admitted oversimplification, Webster stated that "one projects what one expects to perceive and then proceeds to perceive that which will support his conception; one imagines what one will find in the outer world, sets out to find it, and sometimes does find it" (1977, 6). No stronger statement can be made about the importance of self-insight and self-awareness for teachers wishing to communicate positively and productively with parents. People's perception is selective, reflecting their experiences, associations, and needs.

Humans are also expert communicators. They develop self-protective devices, ways or habits of reacting to each other that do not simplify or ease communication. Such habits protect or defend people against making undesirable revelations about themselves, or presenting themselves to others unfavorably. Most people understandably want to appear intelligent, thoughtful, and virtuous to others.

People also want to avoid being influenced by others against their will. As experienced communicators, they may anticipate what others are going to say and respond to what they expect to hear rather than to what the other person actually says. In addition, most people constantly evaluate, sort, accept, and reject messages as they hear them, consequently changing them in an attempt to assimilate them.

Memory failure is another potential barrier. People's selective memory and forgetfulness can unwittingly distort communication. No matter how cooperative they may want to be, people are often unable to recall information and occurrences in an understandable way.

Words are essentially symbols for concepts and as such, they both help and hinder communication (Sheridan 1972). Language is relatively static and inflexible next to the reality it attempts to reflect, limiting people's ability to express what they see, hear, feel, touch, taste, and believe.

People's place of birth, residence, culture, education, occupation, age, and experience all determine the language they use. Thus, two people may use very different words to describe the same experience. It is easy to see how a teacher's choice of words may ease or inhibit communication with parents.

Indeed, teachers' professional jargon and technical terminology may be an enigma to parents, inhibiting communication. Schuck (1979) noted that educators are often unable or unwilling to use jargon-free language. Special educators appear to have a particularly large arsenal of technical terms; the following offers only a few examples of terms likely to be incomprehensible to many parents:

■ IQ, Intelligence Quotient

■ Visual perception, auditory perception, gross and fine motor skills

■ Multidisciplinary, interdisciplinary

■ PIAT, ITPA, PPVT, WISC-R, WRAT, Binet

■ BD, ED, EMH, TMH, LD, severe-profound

■ Mainstreaming, least restrictive alternatives.

In communicating with parents, teachers should use clear language, avoiding or defining specialized terms while treating parents as equals. Teachers who find themselves in a conference with a parent and another professional who is using jargon can subtly assist the parent by asking the professional to define each acronym or unfamiliar term. This approach saves parents the embarrassment or anxiety of asking and provides them with clearer explanations and information. The use of clear language helps parents, specifically minority parents, by reducing their fear and anxiety during the conference (Marion 1981).

The prudent teacher also avoids words and phrases that may give parents false or undesirable impressions of their children or their exceptionality. Many words in the vernacular can anger and alienate others if used inappropriately. Table 4-1 offers examples of inappropriate expressions and possible alternatives.

Goolsby (1976) suggested several guidelines for teachers wishing to improve their communication skills:

1. Assume that parents are acting in good faith and sincerely wish to cooperate on behalf of their child.

2. Allow parents to express their individuality. Accept them as they are and do not expect or demand perfection.

3. Solicit parent involvement in planning communication and cooperative activities and assure their agreement with proposed objectives.

4. Give parents feedback to assure their communication and cooperation.

5. Continually practice effective communication skills.

TABLE 4-1 Sample Word Choices

Avoid:	Use instead:
Must	Should
Is lazy	Can do more with effort
Culturally deprived	Culturally different, diverse
Is a troublemaker	Disturbs class
Is uncooperative	Should learn to work with others
Cheats	Lets others do his or her work
Is below average	Works at his (her) own level
Truant	Absent without permission
Impertinent	Discourteous
Steals	Takes things without permission
Is dirty	Has poor grooming habits
Disinterested	Complacent, not challenged
Is stubborn	Insists on having his (her) own way
Insolent	Outspoken
Wastes time	Could make better use of time
Is sloppy	Could be neater
Is mean	Has difficulty getting along with others
Time and time again	Usually, repeatedly
Dubious	Uncertain
Poor grade or work	Work below his (her) usual standard
Will flunk	Has a chance of passing if . . .

According to Lichter (1976), parent-teacher communication begins with listening—active listening. Teachers who are skilled active listeners state their understanding of what the parents said (and the feelings accompanying the words) and provide feedback for the parents' verification and clarification.

Active listening is not a mechanical process of hearing and repeating words; the listener's attitudes are as important as his or her verbal and nonverbal communication (Gordon 1970). The active listener wants to hear and takes the time to hear what the parents are saying and wants to help them with the problems they face. Teachers who are active listeners accept parents' feelings whether they concur with those feelings or not. Finally, they show faith in parents' capacity to solve their problems with assistance.

Teachers wishing to increase their active listening skills should listen for the basic message in parent's communication and restate to the parents a brief, precise summary of the verbal, nonverbal, and feeling tone of the message as they perceived it. They should be sensitive to parents' verbal or nonverbal cues to their restatement of the initial message and encourage parents to correct inaccurate perceptions.

The Interview

The parent-teacher involvement model uses an interview as the primary assessment technique. This interview is an information-gathering process and is distinct from a therapeutic interview designed to explore with parents their personal, marital, or social problems.

The parent-teacher involvement interview should help parents develop an undistorted perception of the realities of their child's exceptionality so that they can make rational decisions about the child's education and treatment. Thus, the inverview focuses on the child, the child's exceptionality, and the parents' responses to both.

Though a highly useful process, an interview is not an end in itself; it is a means to an end—providing needed assistance to the parents and, ultimately, to the child. An interview is also an art, a specialized form of communication:

> An interview is not a conversation. A conversation is a two-way exchange of information in which all parties involved may contribute equally or alternately to the flow of the communication. The implicit rules of a social conversation state that all parties have a responsibility for keeping the exchange from coming to a standstill, periods of silence are avoided, "personal" topics are generally taboo, and the content of the conversation may range widely as the participants introduce new topics in association to something another may have said. (Ross 1964, 76).

Kahn and Cannell offered this definition:

[An interview is] a specialized pattern of verbal interaction—initiated for a specific purpose, and focused on some specific content area, with consequent elimination of extraneous material. Moreover, the interview is a pattern of interaction in which the role relationship of interviewer and respondent is highly specialized, its specific characteristics depending somewhat on the purpose and character of the interview. (1957, 16)

According to Kroth and Simpson (1977), one of the most profound realizations an interviewer can have is the interview's tendency to encompass all the complicated aspects of human behavior. Human interactions prove far too varied to submit to a formula approach to interviewing. Teachers can learn to perform the role of interviewer and can learn techniques for getting parents to talk and for obtaining certain types of information; nonetheless, much of the interviewing process remains an art.

According to Morgan, the essential prerequisite for a successful interview is the teacher's genuine concern for and desire to help the parents and the exceptional child. Parents quickly perceive a teacher who does not truly care about them and their child and who will not make an all-out effort to assist them and their child.

Teachers must understand and appreciate both conscious and unconscious human motivation, remaining sensitive to what parents feel as well as what they say. As interviewers, teachers must also recognize that parents do listen and act on their suggestions. Consequently, effective interviewers are aware of the actual and potential impact of their personal experiences, prejudices, attitudes, and training on their communication with the parents and the parents' future action. Conversely, they recognize and appreciate the potential impact the parents' behavior will have on them.

Kroth (1975) pointed out several deterrents to effective communication during an interview:

1. *Fatigue.* Interviewing is difficult work, requiring considerable energy. Both parent and teacher can tire and become distracted during an interview, particularly if the conference takes place after a day's work.

2. *Strong feelings.* Strong emotions can prohibit people from perceiving reality clearly, thereby inhibiting communication. Interview participants must recognize and control their feelings to maintain productive communication.

3. *Words.* The use of emotionally loaded words and phrases can stop or retard communication. A word or phrase used inappropriately may anger or embarrass parents. In addition, the skillful and concerned interviewer knows what topics are inadmissible.

4. *Teacher talk.* A teacher who talks continuously is not listening to the parents. Parents can only communicate if allowed to do so. Teachers should monitor the amount of time they talk and allow plenty of time for listening. An interview is not the time for lengthy conversation, lectures, and sermons.

5. *The environment.* A distracting or uncomfortable meeting place limits the possibilities for a productive interview. Parents who are physically and emotionally uncomfortable will end an interview as quickly as possible. Interview locations should be private and comfortable.

The effective parent-teacher involvement interview requires careful preparation and planning by the teacher, preferably several days before the session. Part of this process is mental preparation—reviewing knowledge about human behavior and remembering the importance of positive communication. The other aspect of planning is to review and analyze all available information of the parents, the child, and the family. Teachers can form judgments of the reliability and validity of the information that will help them direct the interview. Gaps or inconsistencies in the information will guide the teacher in developing questions or topics for the interview agenda. At a practical level, teachers must also determine the parents' primary language, arrange for an interpreter if necessary, and establish an agreed-upon location, hour, and date for the session.

A relaxed, confident parent can more readily share knowledge and feelings with an interviewer. Thus, teachers should make every effort to put the parents at ease at the beginning of an interview. A friendly greeting and handshake, indicating a comfortable chair, or offering refreshments all help break the ice. A few minutes chatting about current events will help the parents relax and gain confidence in their communication skills.

During the interview, teachers have several responsibilities: to listen actively to what parents are saying, to be alert to the parents' central message or messages and seek clarification when necessary, to discern topics the parents do not or cannot discuss, and to observe and interpret the parents' nonverbal messages and feelings. With culturally different parents, teachers must communicate acceptance of the parents' values (Marion 1981).

An active listener avoids interrupting parents when they are making a genuine effort to respond to a question; minority parents in particular are not always afforded the courtesy of being heard. If teachers find it difficult to follow what the parent is saying, they can concentrate on getting the tone and essence of the parents' comments (Marion 1981). On the other hand, teachers may have to redirect the discussion gently when parents depart from the purpose of the interview. Effective interviewers tolerate and encourage appropriate silences for thought and meditation and try to remedy those caused by embarrassment and discomfort.

Questions are an important part of the communication process during the parent-teacher interview. Teachers will generally ask questions for two purposes:

■ To obtain specific, necessary information or to clarify available information

■ To redirect the interview when parents stray from pertinent information.

These questions may be *closed,* requesting a specific item of information, or *open-ended,* soliciting a detailed response (Webster 1977). The following are examples of closed questions:

■ What is your full name and address?

■ How old are your children?

■ When was your child last evaluated?

According to Webster (1977), open-ended questions are also of two types, soliciting conversation information or requesting ideas on a particular topic. The following are examples of open-ended general questions:

■ How did the week go?

■ What's your opinion?

■ Where shall we begin?

The open-ended question on a particular topic is far more specific:

■ How is your work going today?

■ How do you feel about John's exceptionality?

■ How do you think we should explore the problems of residential care for Mary?

Open-ended general questions are often useful at the beginning of the interview. As the interview progresses, open-ended questions on a particular topic can probe parents' perceptions, opinions, and evaluation of a specific issue. Marion (1981) encourages the use of open-ended questions, especially with minority parents, to encourage discussion.

Before ending the interview, teachers should review and summarize the discussion with the parents, allowing both parents and teacher to clarify the topics discussed during the session and agree on what has transpired. If additional sessions are desirable, this time is a good one to establish location, date, and hour.

When the parents leave, the teacher should record the information gathered during the interview. This is a good time to begin developing an agenda and writing questions for the next session since the information is still fresh in the teacher's mind.

The Intake Conference. Parents and teachers usually first meet at the individualized education program (IEP) meeting, at which time the child is placed in the teacher's program. This meeting is attended by several school district representatives and parents and generates an educational plan for the child. The intake conference is the first substantive step in a parent-teacher involvement program and probably the first interview the teacher will conduct with parents. Intake activities frequently require more than a single session, for they must accomplish several purposes:

1. To establish a positive working relationship between parents and teacher

2. To review and discuss diagnostic findings, the child's exceptionality, its parameters, and education prognosis

3. To review and discuss the child's individualized education program (IEP) for the special and regular educational settings

4. To review and discuss the roles and functions of the special education teacher and other educational personnel, such as the regular teacher, school psychologist, nurse, and aide, in the child's program

5. To review and discuss the role and functions of the parents in the child's education program

6. To introduce the parents to the parent-teacher involvement program and invite their participation.

In some cases, parents and teacher may have accomplished the first two goals before the intake conference—if the teacher has been involved in the diagnosis and placement decision, for example.

Raech (1966), the parent of a mentally handicapped child, believes that the first contacts between parents and professional have an enduring impact on the parents' perceptions of themselves and the child. At this time, "miscounseling" in the intake interview can cause permanent shock and trauma for the parents.

> It is my firm belief that the vast majority of parents of retarded
> tend to develop something less than a balanced outlook on life.
> I do not mean to imply from this mental imbalance. I do imply

that they tend to be unable to enjoy life to the optimum degree because of their preoccupation with their problem. (1966, 25)

Thus, Raech saw the initial interview as an opportunity for the teacher to offer empathy and wisdom. Communications between parents and teachers must be truthful, sensitive, and in language understood by the parents.

Sawyer and Sawyer (1981) suggested that during the first contact parents often confront teachers with difficult questions and responses. They described several aspects of the interview that may be particularly difficult as a result:

1. Opening the interview

2. Responding to the parents' overprotective behavior toward the child and helping them consider alternative behaviors

3. Dealing with parents' feelings of denial and anger

4. Using open-ended questions to gain more information about parents' and child's behavior

5. Responding to parents' recognition of new responsibilities as the parents of an exceptional child

6. Responding to questions about the child's future

7. Dealing with silences.

If teachers anticipate these problems and develop strategies to deal with them, they can avoid some uncomfortable periods during the intake interview.

Rockowitz and Davidson (1979) viewed the presentation and discussion of diagnostic findings as the first step in developing a cooperative parent-professional relationship. This part of the intake conference is a two-way flow of information between parents and professional, not a lecture by the teacher. It has four equally important components: the entry pattern, presentation of diagnostic findings, discussion of educational suggestions, and summary. The teacher will have carefully prepared for the presentation by establishing when and where the interview will take place, who will attend, who will act as discussion facilitator, what professional expertise is necessary to explain the findings, and what information will be shared.

The purpose of the first part of the interview, the entry pattern, is to increase parents' comfort in the conference setting and establish rapport. The entry pattern includes an introduction of all people present, a review of the techniques used to obtain the diagnostic findings, a discussion of the parents' perceptions of the child's current functioning, and a statement of the parents' expressed worries and concerns.

The second phase, the presentation of diagnostic findings, includes an overview of the findings, a discussion of parents' reactions to the overview, and a detailed presentation of the findings specifying the child's strengths and deficits. The presentation of findings should be honest and precise, avoiding unnecessary technical terms and professional jargon and allowing time to discuss parents' reactions to the findings. In this discussion, the teacher should describe the probable effects of the child's exceptionality on performance and explore the overall educational prognosis. In turn, the teacher should encourage parents to discuss possible issues at home that may affect the exceptionality. Teachers should not offer false hope that the child will eventually function fully if in fact this probability is limited. Alternatively, they must be sensitive to parents' feelings, avoiding being cruel, blunt, and inconsiderate.

Test results are frequently an issue of concern for parents of culturally diverse children, and minority parents may react strongly to results indicating their child is not functioning at the same level as other children. Marion (1981) suggested that the teacher ask minority parents to state their understanding of the information shared to make sure parents understand the results as fully as possible. Marion also suggested that the teacher make a sincere attempt to alleviate any anxiety parents express over possible misuse of test results.

Once the diagnosis is on the table, the teacher presents educational suggestions and options. These suggestions should be practical and within reach. Most likely a discussion of the child's individual education program (IEP), developed earlier by parents and teacher, will be appropriate at this point in the interview. Again teachers should encourage parents to react to their comments.

If the interview takes place in the child's instructional setting, teachers can use "show and tell" methods to present IEP content to parents. They can demonstrate the instructional materials and equipment the child will be using. When they can actually see and use the material, parents gain great understanding of their child's program.

Parents also want to know who is responsible for their child. Thus, during the conference, teacher and parents review the professional and paraprofessional personnel who will work with the child and how each will participate in the child's overall program. The teacher may want to prepare a written outline of the functions of each professional to help clarify roles for the parents.

The parents should also know the teacher's perceptions of their proper roles as parents in their child's educational program. The conference can then provide a format for ironing out differences in perceptions and negotiating necessary modifications. This discussion of the parents' role is a natural opening for a closing discussion of the parent-teacher involvement program. Teachers should describe the program and communicate the importance of parents' participation in their child's education. However, they should not imply that parents who cannot or choose not to participate are neglectful of their child.

Parents, preferably both mother and father, and the teacher are the major participants in the intake conference, but special education teachers, regular teachers, school social workers, and psychologist may contribute important information as well. However, the presence of too many professionals during the intake conference may threaten parents who are already anxious about their child and the conference. In some cases, an older sibling, aunt, uncle, grandparent, or other person attends the conference with the parents. The parents may wish to include a friend, interpreter, or advocate. Occasionally, the exceptional children participate as well; many can contribute significantly to decision making about their future education and training.

As for any interview, the teacher must prepare for and plan the intake conference, reviewing the child's cumulative record, individualized education program, recent tests, work samples, and health records. If possible, the teacher should meet or observe the child.

An interview agenda in the form of an informal checklist or series of questions can be useful. Teachers can share the agenda with parents at the beginning of the interview and use it as a focusing device to keep the interview on track and assure that it covers all key points.

Some teachers prefer to organize the intake conference agenda around a detailed information-gathering guide that structures the conference and assures that all needed information is obtained. However, the guide may inhibit communication if either parents or teacher become overly concerned with the information-gathering process itself.

Kroth (1975) suggested that teachers use interview guides much as those used by medical and social workers, to get a "picture" of the child from the parents. His guide, reproduced in Figure 4-4, is designed to guarantee that the interviewer cover all pertinent topics. It solicits information on aspects of the child's growth and development with implications for his or her education. Beginning interviewers may wish to adhere closely to the guide. However, as teachers gain confidence and experience in interviewing, they need not rely on it as heavily.

The teacher brings to the intake conference all materials needed to attain the interview objectives, including the child's assessment data, recent tests, progress reports, work samples, individualized education program, pertinent texts, workbooks, and worksheets. Providing copies of these materials to parents is useful for family records and also solidifies parents' understanding of their child's exceptionality and the remedial options available.

At the end of the intake conference, the teacher should repeat the diagnostic findings, restate the parents' comments, and review the plan for future action. This summary assures the teacher that the parents understand the information. The intake conference ends only after parents and teacher agree that they have satisfied the objectives of the interview to their satisfaction.

Assessment Conferences. The assessment conferences are the second substantive step in the parent-teacher involvement model. Generally en-

A. Present Status

   1. Age
   2. Sex
   3. Grade/Class/Last year's teacher's name

B. Physical Appearance and History

   1. General impression made by child
   2. Obvious physical strengths and limitations
   3. General mannerisms, appearance, etc.

C. Educational Status

   1. Present school achievement/Kind of work/Samples of work
   2. Promotions, accelerations, retardations/Causes
   3. Relations with individual teachers, present and past
   4. Books, etc., used in last educational setting
   5. Tests, individual or group/Types of measures used

D. Personal Traits

   1. Personality, general statement
   2. Attitudes towards home, friends, self, family, other students, school
   3. Hobbies, play life, leisure time activities
   4. Educational and vocational goals
   5. Marked likes and dislikes—foods, toys, TV programs, etc.

E. Home and Family

   1. Individuals in the home
   2. Socioeconomic level
   3. Relations with home—favorite brothers/sisters, parent/other relative
   4. Regular chores, pets, etc.
   5. Home cooperation
   6. Record at social agencies

F. Work Experience

   1. Part-time jobs (summer, after school)
   2. Attitude toward work, etc.

G. Additional Information Needed

   1. Sending school
   2. Outside agencies
   3. Private sources, doctor, mental health center, etc. (need release forms)
   4. Health information

FIGURE 4-4
Interview Guide

(Kroth 1975, 20)

compassing one or two sessions, the assessment process seeks to accomplish two purposes:

■ To assess parents' perceptions of their child, the exceptionality, and its implications

■ To assess parents' readiness, interest, capacity, willingness, and need for parent education and training.

The assessment conference helps the teacher evaluate the parents' understanding of the information they received during the intake conference and provides an opportunity to clarify misperceptions or alleviate unrealistic or unfounded fear and guilt. This conference is also the time for teachers to identify those parents who cannot benefit from parent-teacher involvement activities or who are averse to participating.

The assessment helps parents and teacher determine the following:

1. The parents' needs for information, social-emotional support, services, and training

2. The parents' major concerns about their child's present and future functioning

3. The areas of their child's functioning that parents would like to modify.

Thus, it asks whether the parents have the background and experience to perform certain activities to benefit themselves, their child, or the teacher. For example, parents who want to change their child's social behavior may be ineffective without training in behavior management techniques. Similarly, parents cannot teach their children language, reading, or motor coordination skills if they lack the training needed to teach these skills.

If parents have only recently learned of their child's exceptionality, they may not be ready to participate in a structured educational program, in which case the teacher may refer them to a counselor or other parents of exceptional children to help them sort out and clarify their feelings. Some parents, though very willing to help their child, may not have the energy or time to participate in an organized program of parent-teacher activities, in which case the teacher should respect the legitimate duties and responsibilities that prohibit their consistent long-term participation.

The parents and teacher are the primary participants in the assessment conferences, with additional participants as appropriate (the exceptional child, a parent advocate, or an interpreter, for example). All parties review the significant information exchanged during the intake conferences before attending the assessment session. In addition, the teacher should prepare materials specific to the assessment interview.

The teacher should understand the purpose, administration, and interpretation of the assessment materials to be used, especially commercially available scales, inventories, and questionnaires that may require special explanation or use unfamiliar procedures.

After determining which assessment aids will supplement the conference interview, the teacher should establish an agenda to guide the conference. Sloman and Webster (1978) suggested a procedure for interviewing parents of learning-disabled children, for example, that allows teachers to rate parents on five dimensions of parental functioning that affect the child significantly: evaluation, permissiveness of autonomy, mutual affection, hostility, and pressuring. The evaluation scale determines how the parent defines and reacts to the child as a person. Permissiveness of autonomy measures the extent to which parents encourage their child's independence. Mutual affection gauges the warmth of parent-child interactions. Hostility measures the parents' hostility toward the child. And pressuring looks at the emphasis parents place on their child's academic performance.

Sloman and Webster designed their interview technique for use in a study at a summer camp for learning-disabled children. However, teachers will find it useful in a nonresearch environment as well.

The questions are open-ended questions and keyed to the five dimensions noted above (see Figure 4-5). This semistructured approach organizes the information-gathering process and allows interviewers to

---

(Evaluation)

1. Are there any activities that you particularly enjoy doing with your child?

2. What do you feel are some of your child's greatest problems?

3. Are there any ways in which you have been able to help him with this?

4. Do you feel that this approach has helped?

5. How did you come to try this?

6. Inquire specifically about areas that have not been covered (physical, social, language, academic).

(Permissiveness of Autonomy)

7. Do you feel that it is important for a child to learn to do things and to manage on his own? Give examples of things your child does on his own. Give examples of things your child does on his own at home. How often during the day do you find yourself helping your child with something?

8. When you think about your child, do you ever feel that he grew up too fast or not fast enough?

9. Does your child give up easily with things he finds difficult to do? Give an example of things he might give up on.

(cont.)

FIGURE 4-5
Interview Questions

10. Do you feel that your child needs a lot of praise and encouragement? Give examples of situations where you would give him this.

(Affection)

11. Is your child very affectionate with you?

12. In what way does your child express his affection? Physically? Verbally? How often?

13. Are there any ways in which your child gives you more pleasure than your other children? Or are there any little things about your child that you especially enjoy? Give examples.

14. Are there any ways in which your child is more difficult to enjoy than your other children? Give examples.

(Hostility)

15. When during the day does your child place demands on you?

16. Does your child ever become annoyed when you try to help him with something? Give examples.

17. When do you become most annoyed with your child? How frequently do you end up feeling irritated and angry with your child?

18. When is your child the easiest to manage? When is your child the most difficult to manage?

(Pressuring)

19. Give an example of a recent situation in which your child really wanted to do something that you didn't want him to do. What happened?

20. When during the day do you feel that you place the most demands on your child?

21. Do you have any special rules for your child in your home? Do these apply to your other children as well?

(Hostility)

22. Are there ever situations that are likely to end up with both you and your child feeling angry or frustrated with each other? Give an example.

23. Can you give me a recent example of a situation when you lost your temper with your child? What did your child do? What did you do?

(Affection)

24. How do you usually express your affection for your child? Verbally? Physically? Special privileges or presents?

25. Do you feel you more often show your affection to your child when he has achieved something?

26. Are there ever times when you show your affection for no special reason?

27. Are there any particular situations when you are more apt to show your affection for your child? Give examples.

*FIGURE 4-5
(cont.)*

(Sloman and Webster 1978, 74–79)

gauge the accuracy of their intuitive judgments about parents, children, and families.

Needs Assessment Techniques

This section reviews formal and informal needs assessment and information-gathering techniques that can supplement parent-teacher interviews. The teacher uses the techniques to clarify parents' perceptions of their children and their exceptionality. The instruments also ascertain parents' interest, readiness, capacity, willingness, and need to participate in parent-teacher programs and specific parent-teacher activities.

Teachers must judge which, if any, aids are appropriate for a given situation, using expressed needs, wishes, and interests as cues. For example, if parents express concern about their child's behavior and the teacher requires additional information to respond, an aid designed to assess parents' perceptions of the child's social behavior would help in developing a solution. Other procedures are available to respond to parents' concerns about their child's self-help skills, motor skills, or vocational readiness. The techniques reviewed here can be administered anytime during the assessment process that the teacher or parents require additional information for decision making.

Formal Techniques. Scales, inventories, checklists, and questionnaires are formal assessment techniques that are clinically useful in obtaining information for discussion and clarification. However, because the statistical reliability and validity of these aids are questionable, they are appropriate only as components of a total assessment program.

Commercial aids include the Vineland Social Maturity Scale (Doll 1965), Burks' Behavior Rating Scale (Burks 1977), the Denver Developmental Screening Test (Frankenburg, Dodds, and Fandal 1970), and Behavior Scales (Nihira, Foster, Shellhaas, and Leland 1975). (See Appendix A for descriptions of several formal instruments.)

Several criteria, similar to those suggested by Lambert and Bower (1961) for identifying special needs children, should guide a teacher's selection of formal assessment tools:

1. The parents and teacher working together should be able to complete the procedure without assistance.

2. Extensive training or explanation should be unnecessary to complete the procedure.

3. The results obtained should be sufficiently clear to ease discussion between parents and teacher.

4. The information requested should be within the confines of good taste and standards of privacy.

5. The procedure should not pose a threat or cause unnecessary discomfort to either parents or teacher.

6. The procedure should not be excessively time-consuming.

7. The procedure should be economical.

Informal Techniques. The teacher may find it desirable to use informal needs and interest assessment techniques to respond to the individual needs and interests of specific parents or to look at the characteristics of a particular type of exceptionality. Informal techniques may also be an answer when personnel or working conditions impose practical limitations on information-gathering efforts.

Bauer (1981) designed two techniques for use with parents. The "Parents' Needs Form" helps the teacher to determine parents' needs and allows parents to indicate their preferences of methods to meet their needs for information, training, counseling, and so on (Figure 4-6). The "Parents' Activities Form" is a checklist of over thirty items of concern to the parents of exceptional children (Figure 4-7). Teachers can add items as necessary. Parents check items of personal interests and then rank them in priority. Both forms are open-ended to encourage parents to elaborate or include additional concerns.

*FIGURE 4-6
Parents' Needs Form*

Confidential   Date: _____

Parent's Name _____

Child's Name _____

Introduction:
    Listed below are several statements describing concerns common to the parents of exceptional children. The items may or may not concern you at this time. Please complete only those items that currently concern you.
    The information on this form is used *only* to help plan and implement a parent-teacher involvement program. All information is held in strict confidence.

Directions:
  1. Read each statement carefully.
  2. Circle the number on the 1–5 scale that most closely approximates your current need in each area. Circle *1* to indicate a low priority need and *5* to indicate a high priority need.
  3. Below the 1–5 scale are several statements suggesting ways you may prefer to meet your stated needs. Please check only *two* of the four statements listed below each item.
  4. You may write additional comments in the space provided.

(cont.)

I. I need the opportunity to discuss my feelings about my exceptional child and myself with someone who understands the problem.

(Circle the appropriate number.)

1	2	3	4	5
Low Priority				High Priority

(Check *only* two statements.)

_____ I prefer to talk to a professional.
_____ I prefer to talk to the parent of an exceptional child.
_____ I prefer to be referred to another agency for counseling.
_____ I prefer to read articles and books discussing the reactions of parents of exceptional children.
_____ I prefer _____

_____.

II. I would like to talk with other parents and families who have exceptional children.

(Circle the appropriate number.)

1	2	3	4	5
Low Priority				High Priority

(Check *only* two statements.)

_____ I prefer to be in a discussion group.
_____ I prefer to participate in social gatherings (picnics, parties, potluck dinners).
_____ I prefer to meet informally.
_____ I prefer to participate in general meetings, workshops, lectures, demonstrations, and other informational gatherings.
_____ I prefer _____

_____.

III. I would like to learn more about my child's exceptionality.

(Circle the appropriate number.)

1	2	3	4	5
Low Priority				High Priority

(Check *only* two statements.)

_____ I prefer to obtain information through reading.
_____ I prefer to observe teachers and other professionals working with my child and then discuss my observations.
_____ I prefer individual parent-teacher conferences.
_____ I prefer a parent-teacher discussion group.
_____ I prefer _____

_____.

(cont.)

IV. I would like to learn more about how children develop and learn, especially exceptional children.

(Circle the appropriate number.)

1	2	3	4	5
Low Priority				High Priority

(Check *only* two statements.)

_____ I prefer to obtain information through reading.

_____ I prefer to participate in a formal behavior management training course.

_____ I prefer a parent-teacher discussion group.

_____ I prefer individual training in my home by a teacher or other professional.

_____ I prefer to attend meetings at which specialists present information on behavior management.

_____ I prefer _____

VI. I would like to work with a teacher or other professional so that I can use the same instructional methods at home that the school uses.

(Circle the appropriate number.)

1	2	3	4	5
Low Priority				High Priority

(Check *only* two statements.)

_____ I prefer to observe my child in school.

_____ I prefer to attend a training program in observation.

_____ I prefer to attend a course in instructional methods.

_____ I prefer to work with the teacher in my child's classroom.

_____ I prefer in-home training by a teacher or other professional.

_____ I prefer to learn through readings, newsletters, telephone communication, and similar resources.

_____ I prefer _____

VII. I would like _____

(Circle the appropriate number.)

1	2	3	4	5
Low Priority				High Priority

(Write the appropriate statements.)

_____ I prefer _____

_____ I prefer _____

FIGURE 4-6
(cont.)

(cont.)

Comments:

Thank you.

*FIGURE 4-7
Parents' Activities Form*

Confidential   Date: _____

Parent's Name _____

Child's Name _____

Introduction:

Listed below are thirty-five topics and activities generally believed of interest to the parents of exceptional children. Not all parents are interested in any single item, nor is any parent interested in all the items.

Your response to this questionnaire is used *only* to assist in planning and implementing a parent-teacher involvement program for you. All information is held in strict confidence.

Directions:
1. Read the entire form carefully.
2. In Column A check 15 items of interest to you.
3. In Column B rank 5 of the 15 items you checked in Column A. Number the item of highest priority to you 5, the next highest 4, and so on.
4. You may write additional comments in the space provided.

A	B	
_____	_____	1. Help my child learn.
_____	_____	2. Build my child's self-confidence.
_____	_____	3. Select activities to help my child learn (books, games, toys, projects, experiences).
_____	_____	4. Teach my child to follow directions.
_____	_____	5. Help my child enjoy learning.
_____	_____	6. Assist my child in language development.
_____	_____	7. Teach my child problem-solving skills.
_____	_____	8. Fulfill my role as (father) (mother) to my child.
_____	_____	9. Avoid emotional involvement in my child's emotional outbursts.

(cont.)

_____ _____   10. Protect my child from getting hurt.

_____ _____   11. Care for my child when he or she is sick or injured.

_____ _____   12. Discipline my child.

_____ _____   13. Deal with my child's misbehavior.

_____ _____   14. Teach my child respect for people and property.

_____ _____   15. Teach my child to express feelings in a socially acceptable manner.

_____ _____   16. Teach my child to show love, affection, and consideration for other family members.

_____ _____   17. Teach my child to live in harmony with the family (television, bedtime, meals, sharing, responsibilities).

_____ _____   18. Develop a positive and productive relationship with my child.

_____ _____   19. Develop my problem-solving skills.

How can I obtain information on the following topics affecting my child:

_____ _____   20. Art activities

_____ _____   21. Creative dramatics

_____ _____   22. Educational games and activities

_____ _____   23. Exercise

_____ _____   24. Health and hygiene

_____ _____   25. Music

_____ _____   26. Nutrition and diet

_____ _____   27. Puppetry

_____ _____   28. Recreation

_____ _____   29. Sleep

_____ _____   30. Toys

Other topics and activities of interest to me are:

_____ _____   31. _____

_____ _____   32. _____

_____ _____   33. _____

_____ _____   34. _____

_____ _____   35. _____

*FIGURE 4-7
(cont.)*

(cont.)

Comments:

Thank you!

ADDITIONAL RESOURCES

As Clements and Alexander (1975) maintained, the special education teacher is the front-line practitioner, the person primarily responsible for parent services in the school. Experience bears out that teachers initiate most requests to talk with parents and most actively organize services for parents. Nonetheless, special teachers can make excellent use of a wide range of parent, professional, and paraprofessional resources in conducting a parent-teacher program. Prudent use of these resources allows special teachers more time and energy to manage or coordinate an involvement program and to concentrate their efforts on those areas in which they have the greatest expertise.

Parents and professionals can provide information and expertise during all phases outlined in the involvement model.

Professionals and paraprofessionals, acting essentially as consultants, provide direct and indirect services. They may offer direct service in specialized areas, and they can serve as mediators between parents and teachers (Heron and Harris 1982).

It is essential to program success that the teacher conduct an inventory of the skills and potential contributions of those parents, professionals, and paraprofessionals in the school and community willing to assist in the involvement program. The available resource consultants can then be used to the extent feasible.

Teachers should view parents as experts on their children, for they are the people most intimately involved with the child's birth, growth and development, health, behavior, exceptionality, family, home, neighborhood, and other influences on the child. As such, parents are an invaluable resource that cannot be ignored or neglected. Many parents also have personal and professional knowledge and skills that can help the teacher, other parents, and exceptional children. The teacher should recognize that some parents of exceptional children are professionals and skilled workers in their own right who can contribute significantly to the program. They may have counseling, interviewing, leadership, administrative, organizational, instructional, or other skills; they may also have the time and energy to conduct activities for which the special teacher has no training or time.

School district and community professionals are available to both the teacher and parents. Frequently, they work in the exceptional child's school, though their availability will vary. School and community administrators, psychologists, social workers, nurses and physicians, regular class teachers, subject matter specialists, communication specialists, guidance counselors, diagnosticians, supervisors, and paraprofessionals all can provide invaluable services and practical or social-emotional support.

Many of the parent involvement activities described in the remainder of this book require help from resource consultants. Below are examples of the contributions these consultants can make to the parent-teacher involvement program.

1. *Administrators.* School administrators and special education directors and supervisors can provide considerable logistical support by granting official permission to start a parent program, setting aside time for the program, supplying facilities, materials, equipment, and so on. They may help draw in parents, as well as school and community consultants, to the program and offer social-emotional support through public recognition of their efforts. Administrators can also provide information on special education programs, school organization, administration, placement, available services, and legal issues.

2. *Psychologists, counselors, and diagnosticians.* These professionals offer a broad understanding of personality development and functioning, individual and group counseling skills, and assessment, diagnostic, and observation skills. They can conduct individual or small group training sessions, offer therapeutic services, and provide information to support assessment, diagnosis, and placement. They can observe and evaluate parent-teacher activities, such as conferences and group meetings, and supply the knowledge and skills that make certain parent-teacher activities possible.

3. *Social workers.* Social workers are trained in interviewing, assessment, and counseling skills and can contribute directly to a parent involvement program by referring parents to the teacher, encouraging participation, conducting intake and assessment interviews, counseling individuals and small groups, and connecting parents and children with community and school services. Social workers' knowledge of and relationship with community and school social services is one of their greatest contributions.

4. *Medical professionals.* Nurses and physicians can contribute their expertise on medical diagnostic and treatment services. They are

valuable sources of information on medical examinations, diagnostic labels, treatments, medications, diets, and related aspects of caring for exceptional children.

5. *Regular teachers and subject matter specialists.* These professionals are highly trained in general and special areas of instruction, teaching methods, and child growth and development. They can contribute significantly to programs for parents of exceptional children who are integrated into regular and specialized instructional programs through diagnosis and treatment of disabilities in reading, mathematics, spelling, writing, and other academic subjects. They can also support art, music, physical education, and other areas of instruction. The communication specialist can advise on the development and remediation of language.

6. *Paraprofessionals.* Paraprofessionals are among teachers' most important allies. They can help with many parent-teacher activities, as well as research, prepare, organize, and evaluate them. Many times the paraprofessional is a professional person and skilled worker in another area and can bring special skills to the classroom. Frequently, too, the paraprofessional is a member of the community, is familiar with the culture and language, knows the parents and children of the community, and understands their living situation.

To work effectively in parent-teacher involvement programs, teachers should consider themselves leaders of a team. As such, they are responsible for involving all appropriate people in program planning and activities, whether they be parent, professional, or paraprofessional resource consultants.

SUMMARY

This chapter introduces a five-phase model for parent-teacher involvement that guides teachers through a process of intake and assessment, goal selection, planning and implementation of activities, evaluation, and termination/review.

Succeeding sections highlight special skills and techniques essential to effective use of the model.

The chapter discusses criteria for effective interpersonal communication and emphasizes its importance in the parent-teacher involvement program. It highlights the interview as the primary intake and assessment technique used in a parent-teacher program and discusses the use of formal and informal needs and interest assessment techniques to supplement the central interview process. The concluding sections of the chapter describe the use of parents and professionals as resource consultants, specifying the contributions that administrators, psychologists and diagnosticians, social workers, medical professionals, regular teachers and subject matter specialists, and paraprofessionals can make to parent involvement programs.

EXERCISES AND DISCUSSION TOPICS

1.   Read another book or several articles that present a model for parent-teacher collaboration. Write a paper comparing the model in this text with the one you studied, considering each model's definition, purposes, limitations, participants and their contributions, organization, phases or steps, and comprehensiveness.

2.   Research an assessment instrument either from Appendix A or elsewhere. Present a critical evaluation of it to your class. Demonstrate its administration and the integration of its results.

3.   Using a case with which you are familiar or a case study from Appendix B, complete a sample "Program Development Form."

4.   Discuss with your class the following statement: "People communicate to affect others, the environment, and themselves; they send messages in order to obtain a response and thus influence others' behavior. Communication also provides catharsis, relieving tension, frustration, and anxiety, which in turn can lead to self-discovery and self-insight."

5.   Carefully observe a presentation by an individual you consider a "great communicator," such as an instructor, employer, television personality, or politician. (You may want to record the presentation if you can obtain permission.) Analyze and evaluate the presentation considering verbal communication, body language or nonverbal expression, affective tone, and the use of descriptive, inferential, and evaluative language.

6.   Discuss in class the following quotation: "One projects what one expects to perceive and then proceeds to perceive that which will support his conception; one imagines what one will find in the outer world, sets out to find it, and sometimes does find it" (Webster 1977, 6).

7.   Study the section of this chapter entitled "The Interview." Develop a checklist of interviewing tasks to be accomplished before, during, and after a parent-teacher information-gathering interview.

8.   Study the section on the intake conference; then conduct a conference with the parent of an exceptional child. Have a colleague observe

the conference with the parent's permission; later critique the session together. If a parent is not available for this task, role play a conference with your study group doing a case from Appendix B.

9. Study the section on the assessment conference; then conduct a conference with the parent of an exceptional child. Have a colleague observe the conference with the parent's permission; later critique the session together. If a parent is not available for this task, role play a conference with your study group using a case from Appendix B.

REFERENCES

Bauer, A. M. 1981. Program for parents of severely handicapped students—A plan. Edwardsville, Ill.: Southern Ilinois University.

Burks, H. F. 1977. Burks' behavior rating scales: Manual. Los Angeles: Western Psychological Services.

Chinn, P. C., J. Winn, and R. H. Walters. 1978. *Two-way talking with parents of special children: A process of positive communication.* St. Louis: C. V. Mosby.

Clements, J. E., and R. N. Alexander. 1975. Parent training: Bringing it all back home. *Focus on Exceptional Children* (5):1–12.

Doll, E. A. 1965. The Vineland Social Maturity Scale. Circle Pines, Minn.: American Guidance Service.

Duff, R. E., and K. J. Swick. 1978. Parent-teacher interaction: A developmental process. *The Clearing House* 51 (6):265–68.

Frankenburg, W. K., J. B. Dodds, and A. W. Fandal. 1970. *Denver developmental screening test manual.* Rev. ed. Denver: University of Colorado Medical Center.

Goolsby, E. L. 1976. Facilitation of family-professional interaction. *Rehabilitation Literarure* 37 (11, 12):332–34.

Gordon, T. 1970. *Parent effectiveness training.* New York: Peter H. Wyden.

Heron, T. E., and K. C. Harris. 1982. *The educational consultant: Helping professionals, parents, and mainstreamed students.* Boston: Allyn and Bacon.

Kahn, R. L., and C. F. Cannell. 1957. *The dynamics of interviewing: Theory, technique, and cases.* New York: John Wiley and Sons.

Kroth, R. L. 1975. *Communicating with parents of exceptional children: Improving parent-teacher relationships.* Denver: Love Publishing.

Kroth, R. L., and R. L. Simpson. 1977. *Parent conferences as a teaching strategy.* Denver: Love Publishing.

Lambert, N. M., and E. M. Bower. 1961. *A process for in-school screening of children with emotional handicaps: Manual for school administrators and teachers.* Sacramento: California State Department of Education.

Lichter, P. 1976. Communicating with parents: It begins with listening. *Teaching Exceptional Children* 8 (2):66–71.

Marion, R. L. 1981. *Educators, parents, and exceptional children.* Rockville, Md.: Aspen Systems.

Morgan, W. G. (No date.) Skills in working with parents. Champaign-Urbana: Institute for Research on Exceptional Children, University of Illinois.

Nihira, K., R. Foster, M. Shellhaas, and H. Leland. 1975. American Association on Mental Deficiency Adaptive Behavior Scales. Rev. ed. Washington, D.C.: American Association on Mental Deficiency.

Raech, H. 1966. A parent discusses initial counseling. *Mental Retardation* 4 (2):25–26.

Rockowitz, R. J., and P. W. Davidson. 1979. Discussing diagnostic findings with parents. *Journal of Learning Disabilities* 12 (1):11–16.

Ross, A. O. 1964. *The exceptional child in the family: Helping parents of exceptional children.* New York: Grune and Stratton.

Sawyer, H. W., and S. H. Sawyer. 1981. A teacher-parent communication training approach. *Exceptional Children* 47 (4):305–6.

Schuck, J. 1979. The parent-professional partnership—Myth or reality? *Education Unlimited* 1:26–28.

Sheridan, M. D. 1972. The child's acquisition of code for personal and interpersonal communication. In *The child with delayed speech,* eds. M. Rutter and J. A. M. Martin. London: Heinemann.

Sloman, L., and C. D. Webster. 1978. Assessing the parents of the learning disabled child: A semistructured interview procedure. *Journal of Learning Disabilities* 11 (2):73–79.

Webster, E. J. 1977. *Counseling with parents of handicapped children: Guidelines for improving communications.* New York: Grune and Stratton.

PARENT-TEACHER INVOLVEMENT ACTIVITIES

■ Chapters Five through Ten offer examples of collaborative parent-teacher activities appropriate to the involvement model introduced in Chapter Four. Depending on program needs, parents and teachers will be able to use many of these activities directly, may want to modify others, and in some cases, will design alternative activities to fit specific needs.

Chapter Five suggests ways to modify and extend several traditional parent-teacher communications activities—such as daily and periodic report cards, notes, notices, newsletters, and telephone communications—for a program for exceptional children. It also introduces two innovative activities, passports to positive communication and learning charts.

Chapter Six discusses ways to approach individual parent-teacher conferences, including problem-solving conferences, behavior management training conferences, and conferences for progress reports. It reviews the individualized education program meeting and home visit as well.

Chapters Seven and Eight look at parent-teacher groups. Chapter Seven reviews those factors essential to organizing small and large parent-teacher groups, such as establishing group objectives, purpose, size, planning, structure, limitations, and leadership. Chapter Eight discusses ways to run specific types of groups—informational, communication, problem-solving, discussion, and training groups.

Chapter Nine introduces important parent-teacher home, school, and community activities that encourage parent involvement as paraprofessionals, instructors, volunteers, and home-based teachers. It discusses parents' roles in classroom, school, and community environments and looks at their responsibility as child advocates.

Chapter Ten integrates much of the material in this book by illustrating an extensive application of the parent-teacher involvement model and supporting activities. It also provides an overview of the school year, showing how teachers can establish program priorities and plan ahead for parent-teacher cooperation.

Teachers' ability to carry out the activities described in this section depend on several factors, including the following:

1. The thoroughness and reliability of the assessment procedures that determine the child's and parents' needs

2. The time available to parents and teachers to participate in the activities

3. The teacher's level of expertise and skills to conduct the activities

4. The resources available.

Clearly, the assessment process is important because it determines whether parents and teachers have a clear enough understanding of the child's strengths and weaknesses to design appropriate activities. It also determines whether parents and teachers agree on the activities and can work in concert to the child's benefit.

Both parties must also be realistic about their workloads and available time when selecting activities so that they neither shortchange the child nor design overly ambitious activities doomed to failure. Parents cannot devote large amounts of time to the exceptional child at the expense of their spouses, other children, family, employers, church, and community. Similarly, teachers must spread their time among many children and also act as a husband or wife, parent, housekeeper, employee, and so on. Both parents and teachers must be sensitive to the other's practical limitations.

Teachers must also match the skill level needed for specific activities with the people available. Some activities require few specialized skills; others call for highly specific and specialized competencies. If teachers are not sufficiently expert in the skills needed, they should seek out training, enlist the help of an appropriately trained resource person, or develop alternative activities.

Finally, teachers and parents should verify they have the resources they need to do it right. They must assure the availability of the needed personnel, materials, equipment, facilities, and funds.

WRITTEN AND TELEPHONE COMMUNICATION

■ Written and telephone communication can be a quick, efficient way for parents and teacher to keep in touch about the exceptional child's progress. Most written communications and phone contacts require minimal time and energy of parents and teachers, and do not require much, if any, instruction (Lordeman and Winett 1980). They are generally indirect forms of communication, requiring little personal contact. Thus, they are most appropriate for communicating on relatively impersonal topics.

Though the activities discussed in this chapter—daily and periodic report cards; learning charts; a passport to positive communication; notes, letters, and notices; newsletters; and telephone communication— require considerably less effort than those presented in later chapters, parents and teacher must devote some time and energy to planning them and carrying them out effectively. If properly conducted, written and phone feedback techniques can transfer important information and support the exceptional child's educational progress (Lordeman and Winett 1980).

Teachers must use their professional judgment to gauge when and for whom written and telephone techniques are most appropriate. Parents' needs for information, ability to understand the message, personalities, time restrictions, and environments will all determine their responsiveness to a specific technique.

It is important to ascertain the willingness and competence of parents to participate in activities requiring reading, writing, and verbal skills. Teachers should determine the primary language of the home and use that language in all written and telephone communication. Many adults lack the academic and verbal skills needed to meaningfully participate in many activities discussed in this chapter. These parents will need more detailed instruction and support in written and telephone activities.

REPORT CARDS

Daily Reports

The report cards and grades issued periodically by elementary and secondary schools and universities probably influence students' performance positively. This effect is probably also short-lived. Observations of school and university students suggest that they study more and behave better in the few weeks immediately before and after report cards or grades are due. Unfortunately, this high level of performance does not persist during those times when report cards are not imminent (Kroth 1975).

Thus, it appears that more frequent feedback on students' academic and behavioral performance is more likely to inspire continued positive performance—a proposition that has led several investigators to explore the use of daily report cards with normal and exceptional children at several grade levels (Edlund 1969; Dickerson, Spellman, Larsen, and Tyler 1973; Kroth, Whelan, and Stables 1970; Kroth 1975; Powell 1980). The daily report card has several advantages: It is an efficient method of coordinating and monitoring training and assuming the teacher obtains the parents' commitment to a daily system, it is a forum for two-way communication.

In 1969, Edlund designed and implemented a daily reporting system that did in fact improve children's academic performance and behavior. In Edlund's system, individual and small group sessions introduce parents to the daily report card concept, presenting the behavior modification principles and procedures used in the reporting system. Parents learn about daily checklists, principles of reinforcement, reward selection, and application of the Premack Principle (reinforcing a nonpreferred activity with a preferred one) in these sessions, which are followed up by weekly parent-teacher meetings or telephone conferences.

Before daily reporting begins, the teacher gathers baseline data on each student's academic performance and social and personal behaviors in order to individualize the daily reporting.

A child earns points at school for completing academic assignments and for acceptable school behavior and also receives rewards at home. Edlund designed three checklists for recording points: one for academic performance, one for personal-social behavior, and one that serves as a composite report. (Figure 5-1 is an example of a composite report.)

The teacher awards points in the form of check marks at the end of predetermined periods or activities throughout the school day. At the end of the day, the teacher reviews the child's checklist and initials it. The child takes the checklist home, the parents review it and initial it, and the child returns it to school the following day. A child cannot receive rewards without the checklist. Thus, children who fail to take the checklist home return to school for it or a duplicate.

Parents give rewards to the child at home during the afternoon and evening hours. These rewards are tailored to the child so that they will be meaningful. Parents try to ensure that their child only receives rewards when he or she earns them. Children who do not earn rewards are assigned tasks at home, such as housekeeping chores, yardwork, homework, and so on. They receive special rewards for a "perfect day" or several "perfect days."

When children show acceptable academic performance and behavior over several weeks, parents and teacher phase out the reward system over days or weeks. The children will most likely continue to respond to parents' and teachers' praise and social recognition for high-level performance. Professionals have used the Edlund daily report card system successfully with children from kindergarten to high school and with exceptional children classified as emotionally disturbed, mentally retarded, disruptive, school phobic, truant, economically deprived, or culturally different.

Another daily system reported effective is the teacher-parent communication program (TPCP) (Dickerson, Spellman, Larsen, and Tyler 1973). The TPCP calls for teachers to issue report cards throughout the school day. Children then take the cards home at the end of the school day, and parents reward them or not depending on the day's performance. TPCP cards allow the teacher to check evaluations of the child's academic performance and social behavior, with allowance for elaboration on the back of the card if necessary (Figures 5-2 and 5-3). The example card in Figure 5-2 is generally used with children in grades K–3, while the example card in Figure 5-3 is used with older elementary school age children. Dickerson and his associates recommended that the teacher's comments be noncommittal and positive. (Note: Teachers developing their own versions of TPCP cards may want to provide space for parents' signatures and notations.)

122

FIGURE 5-1
Composite Daily Report

Name _____

| | Reading | | Spelling | | Arithmetic | | Health | | Social Studies | | Physical Education | | Total | Initials | |
	Academic	Behavior	Academic	Behavior	Academic	Behavior	Academic	Behavior	Academic	Behavior	Academic	Behavior		Parent	Teacher
Monday															
Tuesday															
Wednesday															
Thursday															
Friday															
Total															

Consider card satisfactory *only* when 1 and 3 boxes are checked.

1. ☺ ☐ Social behavior good

2. ☹ ☐ Social behavior bad

3. ☺ ☐ School work done

4. ☹ ☐ School work not done

_____/_____/_____   _____
      Date   Teacher's Signature

FIGURE 5-2
Daily Report Card for Grades K–3

(Dickerson, Spellman, Larsen, and Tyler 1973, 171)

Consider card satisfactory *only* when boxes 1 and 3 are checked.

1. ☐ Social behavior satisfactory

2. ☐ Social behavior unsatisfactory

3. ☐ Academic work satisfactory

4. ☐ Academic work unsatisfactory

_____/_____/_____   _____
      Date   Teacher's Signature

FIGURE 5-3
Daily Report Card for Grades 4–6

(Dickerson et al. 1973, 171)

The teacher begins the TPCP by soliciting parents' cooperation and participation and explaining the program's purpose and benefits to parents in a first conference. The teacher outlines the duties and responsibilities of all participants using the checklist in Figure 5-4 to ensure thorough coverage.

Whether teachers adopt one of the systems described here or devise their own systems, the reporting method they choose should be specific and easy to complete. It should also accentuate the child's positive be-

1. Ten cards will be sent home each day whether academic work is done or not.

2. One bad check makes a card unacceptable.

3. Cards must be signed by the teacher and free of erasures and extra marks.

4. The minimum number of good cards necessary to earn privileges should be explained.

5. The number of acceptable cards will be increased sometime in the future.

6. The program will at first emphasize the quantity of work and later the quality of work.

7. The backs of the cards should always be examined for notations.

8. Weekend bonuses may be earned for each week the specified number of good cards has been earned.

9. After-school and evening activities should be a direct result of performance in school.

10. Cards not received at home should be counted as unacceptable.

11. Cards should be reviewed with the child as soon as he arrives home.

12. The cards should be counted each day.

13. Praise and encourage the child for earning the acceptable number of good cards.

14. LET THE CARDS DO THE TALKING.

FIGURE 5-4
Checklist for TPCP
Parent-Teacher
Conference

(Dickerson et al. 1973, 175)

havior or performance. Such a system is a shared responsibility; it will succeed only if both teacher and parents meet their obligations.

Periodic Reports

The traditional report card has limited value to parents of exceptional children, whether it uses letter, number, satisfactory-unsatisfactory, or pass–fail grading (Shea 1978). Current dissatisfaction has several roots:

> [The] modern school's concerns have broadened. The 3R's are still important but there are many other R's: Reliability, Responsibility, Reasoning, Rhythm. . . . And, in addition, there are A's for Appreciation, Adjustment, and Attitudes; B's for Balance and Bladder Control and Bravery and Buoyancy; C's for Cooperation, and so on through the whole alphabet. (Hymes 1974, 84)

These broader objectives, reflecting parents' interest in their children as people as well as academic achievers, makes the traditional report card an inadequate vehicle for reporting a child's overall development and special strengths. According to Hymes, an effective report card is a communication technique that leads parents and teachers to action. Thus, it goes beyond simple transmittal of information.

To Granowsky and associates, the traditional report card is "like letting the team in on only one play out of every thirty" (1977, 56). They maintain that parents cannot intelligently and constructively follow their child's progress if they receive only three or four report cards annually.

> The report card is supposed to provide the parent (and at times the child) with a standard measure for evaluating performance. It should inform parents what skills their children are working on, how well they are doing, what the specific areas of concern are, and how they are behaving in class. (Rutherford and Edgar 1979, 6)

Rutherford and Edgar suggested that teachers explain the report card to parents at a conference at the beginning of the school year. At this time, teachers can also spell out for the parents in writing their child's instructional or performance objectives in each area of study and the grading system for each.

In a study of the evaluation and reporting methods preferred by parents of educable mentally handicapped children, Ryan and Ryan (1973) found that the parents preferred written progress reports, especially those offering specific behavioral data. Although parents wanted schools to administer achievement tests, these test results were of secondary interest. A majority of the parents were dissatisfied with traditional reporting systems, such as letter grading. Overall, they wanted a combination of written reports and parent-teacher conferences.

A report card such as the one in Figure 5-5 can provide valuable information to parents on their child's progress during the preceding

---

PUPIL PROGRESS REPORT

_____

Student's Name _____

Placement _____

Teacher _____

Principal _____

School _____

(cont.)

FIGURE 5-5
*Overall Evaluation,
Pupil Progress Report*

Message to Parents

This report will be sent to you at the end of each nine weeks of school unless it is felt that a conference can better inform you of your child's progress in school.

Please study each area carefully and feel free to discuss this report with your child's teacher. Your interest in and cooperation with the school program are essential parts of your child's education.

The grading system used in this pupil progress report is based upon your child's individual progress at his level of capability.

Grading System

A = Excellent
B = Very Good
C = Average
D = Poor
F = Unsatisfactory

	Grading Periods			
	1	2	3	4

WORK HABITS

	1	2	3	4
Follows directions				
Completes work on time				
Takes care of materials and equipment				
Thinks and works independently				
Asks for help when necessary				
Allows others to work				
Stays in seat				
Talks only with permission				

SOCIAL ADJUSTMENTS

	1	2	3	4
Shows self-control				
Is courteous				
Carries out responsibilities				
Accepts constructive criticism				
Shows respect for authority				
Respects rights of others				
Cooperates in group activities				
Shows good sportsmanship				

FIGURE 5-5
(cont.)

(cont.)

HEALTH AND SAFETY HABITS

Practices good health habits				
Hair is washed and combed				
Is neat and clean				
Obeys safety rules				
Behaves on bus				
Behaves on playground				
Behaves in lunchroom				

ATTENDANCE RECORD	1	2	3	4	Year-End Total
DAYS PRESENT					
DAYS ABSENT					
TIMES TARDY					

PARENT COMMENTS:

1st Quarter

2nd Quarter

3rd Quarter

4th Quarter

PARENT'S SIGNATURE

1st Quarter _____

2nd Quarter _____

3rd Quarter _____

4th Quarter _____

(Courtesy of the administration and staff of the Cahokia Area Joint Agreement, Cahokia, Ill.)

marking period. Because of the detailed reporting format, parents can review their child's competence in specific skills, which helps them supplement the child's educational program at home. This evidence of their child's strengths and weaknesses may also encourage parents to seek the teacher's assistance in improving their child's performance of specific tasks.

This progress report format is applicable in many special education programs. The final page is particularly useful, for it allows the teacher to rate achievement and effort in the subject areas while commenting in a more detailed manner as well (see Figure 5-6).

Teachers whose special education programs do not use task analysis report cards can strongly encourage their adoption and if these efforts fail, prepare informal task analysis forms for enclosure with the child's traditional report card. The progress report selected should reflect the special needs and curriculum of the students. For example, a progress report for emotionally and behaviorally disordered children would emphasize overall appropriate behavior, social adjustments, and personal interaction skills, whereas a progress report for the moderately or severely handicapped would pay little attention to academic subjects and focus on self-help skills, independent living and community living skills, leisure skills, and home-living skills.

LEARNING CHARTS

Thorman (1979) introduced the idea of *learning charts* as supplements to pupil progress reports. He maintained that these charts are useful evaluation devices that offer clear images of a student's progress over time that is readily understandable to parents and students.

A completed chart provides students, parents, and teachers with four types of information:

1. The student's level of information and/or skill before formal instruction

2. The level of mastery the student must achieve during formal instruction

3. The student's level of information and/or skill upon completing formal instruction

4. The effectiveness of the teacher's instructional methods.

The teacher determines the student's level of information or skill before formal instruction by administering a pretest and then plots the results on the learning chart. Next, the teacher establishes a realistic goal for the student and plots this mastery level on the chart. A posttest determines the student's mastery of the course or unit content, and these results are plotted on the chart.

_____ Winter _____ Quarter

NAME _John S._____

SUBJECT _Reading_____

The ACHIEVEMENT grade reflects your child's progress at his level of learning in each subject area.

The EFFORT grade reflects how hard your child is working within the given subject area.

ACHIEVEMENT *C*

EFFORT *A*

Though John's reading skills are currently at the functional level, he has increased his comprehension skills. He is now able to read directions and complete a job application with little help. His use of the newspaper has improved so that he can now locate all parts of the paper and find specific information, such as movie times and prices of items.

John is still reluctant to pursue reading as a leisure activity and needs encouragement to pick up a book during free time. High-interest, low vocabulary books available at the school library may be of help.

Susie Smith
_____
Teacher

FIGURE 5-6
Sample Subject Area
Evaluation, Pupil
Progress Report

Comparing pretest and posttest results shows parents how far their child has progressed and comparing post-test results with the target level of mastery shows them how far the child has to go to achieve acceptable performance. Figure 5-7 shows examples of a learning chart

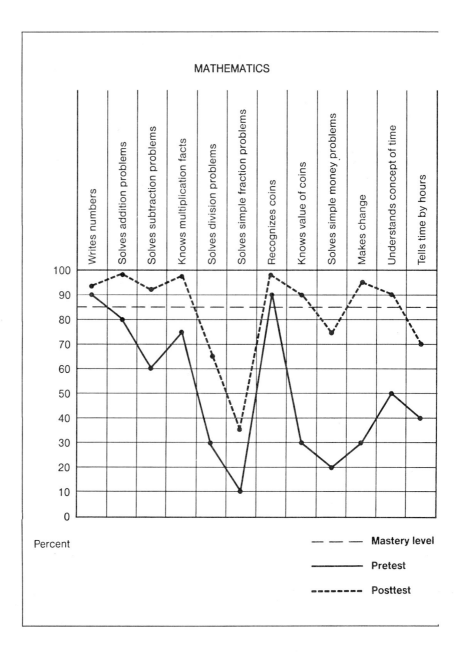

*FIGURE 5-7
Sample Learning Charts
for Performance in
Mathematics (left) and
Social Skills (right)*

for a student's progress in mathematics and in social behavior. The charts use a graphing system to measure students' performance against a desired level of 85 percent competence.

THE PASSPORT

The *passport* to positive parent–teacher communication (Runge, Walker, and Shea 1975) is an effective technique for starting, increasing, or

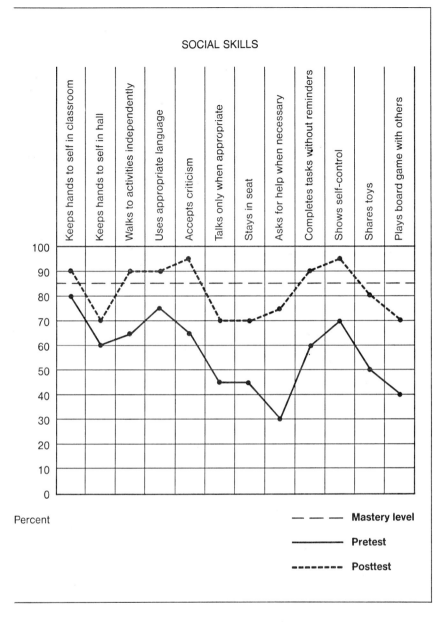

SOCIAL SKILLS

maintaining systematic parent-professional cooperation. It is an ordinary spiral notebook that the child carries daily—to and from home, to and from classrooms, to the gym, cafeteria, music room, and so on. Parents, special teachers, regular teachers, teacher aides, physical education instructors, playground monitors, bus drivers, and other people influencing the child's academic and behavioral performance all may write notations in the passport.

The teacher's first step is to introduce the passport to the child, emphasizing its positive aspects and explaining that he or she will receive rewards for carrying the passport, presenting it to the teacher and other adults during the day, and showing acceptable academic and behavioral performance. Teachers award points at school for carrying the passport, for appropriate behavior, for academic effort, and for academic accomplishment. Parents award points at home for acceptable behavior, completion of assigned tasks, and completion of home-study assignments. Children who forget or refuse to carry the passport cannot accumulate points. Some parents and teachers incorporate *response-cost* procedures into the passport program whereby the child loses points, and thus rewards, for unacceptable behavior and performance.

At appropriate intervals, children can exchange points for rewards that they have helped select. Parents and teachers agree on the time, place, frequency, amount, level, and kind of reinforcers the child will receive at home and at school.

Most elementary school students are enthusiastic about carrying the passport, receiving points and rewards, and reading the comments in their passports. They respond to the passport program as a form of systematic positive attention from the adults they care about.

Teachers introduce parents to the passport concept and procedures at an orientation session, at which time they respond to parents' questions, concerns, and suggestions and provide instructions for writing in the notebook. Parents also learn how to give points and rewards to their child, and parents and teachers agree on the specific behaviors they wish to help the child change.

Parents and teachers follow certain guidelines in writing notes in the passport:

1. Be brief. (Parents and teachers are busy.)

2. Be positive. (Parents know their child has problems and need not receive constant negative reminders.)

3. Be honest. (Don't say a child is doing fine if he or she is not. However, write noncommittal comments or request a face-to-face or telephone conference in place of negative notes.)

4. Be responsive. (If the parent or teacher asks for help, respond immediately.)

5. Be informal. (All participants are equals.)

6. Be consistent. (If the passport is the communication system of choice, use it consistently and expect the same from other participants.)

7. Avoid jargon. (Parents may not understand educational jargon, and even professionals may use jargon at cross-purposes.)

8. Be careful. (No one should project personal feelings or the frustrations of a bad day onto the child, parent, or teacher.)

Figure 5-8 offers examples of notes following these guidelines.

9:00 AM

TO: Ms. Dolores

   Good day on the bus. Tom sat in his assigned seat and waited his turn to leave the bus. I praised his behavior and gave him two points.

Mr. Parker, Bus Driver

10:30 AM

TO: Ms. Dolores

   During PE today the group played kickball. Tom was well-behaved but had difficulty participating effectively. I awarded him six points and praised his behavior. Can we meet to discuss some means of increasing his participation?

Ms. Minton, Physical Education

2:30 PM

TO: Mr. and Mrs. Hogerty

   As you can see from the notes above, Tom had a good day at school.
   He received 89 percent on his reading test this morning. That's real progress. Please praise him for this accomplishment.
   This evening, Tom is to read pp. 1–5 in his new reading book.
   Even better news! Tom remembered to walk in the hallways today. He is very proud of himself.
   I shall talk to Ms. Minton today about increasing Tom's participation in PE. I'll let you know what we decide at tomorrow night's parent meeting.

Ms. Dolores

9:00 PM

TO: Ms. Dolores

   We praised and rewarded Tom for his hard work on the reading test, the bus, and the hallways. You're right; he feels good about himself today.
   Tom read pp. 1–5 in the new book with his father. The words he had trouble with are underlined.
   We will see you at parent meeting tomorrow night.

Mary Hogerty

FIGURE 5-8
Sample Passport Notes

NOTES, LETTERS, AND NOTICES

Notes, letters, and notices are good ways to notify parents of administrative and record-keeping problems and concerns, schedule changes, special events, holidays, workshops, field trips, attendance, fees, and so on. However, unless used systematically, these techniques have limited value in reinforcing the child's academic performance or social-emotional behavior and are best used as one component of overall parent-teacher communication.

Notes, letters, and notices can provide continuous positive contact if teachers use them appropriately (Magnusson and McCarney 1980).

Most authorities agree that the vast majority of teachers' notes and letters bear bad news. Rutherford and Edgar (1979) suggested that this process can create a negative relationship between parents and teachers. Poorly composed, negative communication can also lead to unwarranted punishment for a child and unnecessary anxiety for the parents. Consequently, Rutherford and Edgar proposed that teachers aim for a ratio of four good news notes for every bad news note.

Effective notes are clear, concise, and positive and speak to the parents in their primary language. Rutherford and Edgar suggested that these notes and letters serve four purposes: to praise the child's general academic performance and behavior; to informally (handwritten) and positively address specific academic and behavior problems; to informally evaluate the child's performance; and to provide a structured performance evaluation, such as the periodic report cards discussed earlier.

Marion (1979), urging caution in writing to minority parents, offered the following guidelines, which in fact apply to all parents:

1. Determine the parents' educational level before sending written communications. By adjusting the language of the message accordingly, teachers increase the likelihood that parents will understand it and perceive it positively.

2. Affix Mr. and/or Mrs. to all communications. Minority parents do not widely accept Ms. as a form of address.

3. Be positive. Highlight the child's positive attributes before discussing the problem at hand.

4. Guard against a condescending or superior tone. Reread the message before sending it to exorcise educational jargon.

5. Be brief, but clear and precise. Parents often complain that they do not hear about certain problems or hear only part of the story. Messages must clearly convey the teacher's meaning, leaving little room for supposition.

6. Offer a clear reason for requesting visits to the school. Parents resent losing time from work or home tasks for unclear reasons.

7. If appropriate, include a sign-off portion for the parents. This practice provides a feedback mechanism to assure teachers that parents have received their messages.

Fedderson (1972) described his use of notices and brief letters in the kindergarten he instructed. His goals were to communicate with parents throughout the school year about classroom program, specific class occurrences, children's instructional goals and objectives, and children's progress; he also sought additional information about the child. Further, Fedderson wished to communicate *with* parents as well as *to* them. He used brief conversations before and after school and formal parent-teacher conferences to communicate with parents and found notices and letters most helpful in communicating information to them. However, he stated, "Teachers need not delude themselves into believing that all parents read and use *all* the ideas and information in *all* the letters sent home" (1972, 76).

Croft (1979) pointed out that persistence pays even when communication appears to be one-way. Though parents may not respond to notes the way the teacher would like, they do gain greater awareness with each note of their child's school program.

Many teachers use notes to schedule parent-teacher conferences. When Clements and Simpson (1974) investigated methods of encouraging parents' attendance at conferences, they found that parents responded most positively to personal handwritten notes sent through the mail. This method was nearly twice as effective as sending mimeographed notices home with the child. The positive consequences of mailed, handwritten notes were, in fact, reversed when mimeographed notices were sent home instead. Personal appointment notes also allow the teachers to be specific about the reasons for meeting, and thus avoiding unnecessary parent anxiety (Magnusson and McCarney 1980).

Personal letters are one way for teachers to let parents know they perceive them as important to the child's success at school and vital members of the child's educational team (Granowsky et al. 1977). A letter of introduction mailed to parents at the beginning of each school year is an opportunity for teachers to initiate positive contact and to demonstrate an interest in the child's home life (Magnusson and McCarney 1980). Many investigators recommend sending such a welcome letter to each child's parents (Olson et al. 1976; England 1977; Magnusson and McCarney 1980). The letter should be positive, friendly, and full of hope, emphasizing the parents' importance to the child's educational program and the teacher's desire to help the child (see Figure 5-9). Olson and colleagues (1976) suggested that the welcome letter contain the following:

■ A welcome to the child

■ A list of the year's scheduled subjects, activities, and events

■ An invitation to the parents to visit the school and class

■ An invitation to the parents to contribute to the class as an aide, volunteer, or instructor

August 20, 198_

Dear _____,

I am happy to welcome you and your child _____ to Airport School for the 198_–8_ school year. Your child is a member of the Special Education School District resource program. _____ will be in regular class for most academic and special subjects and will receive support services and remedial instruction in the resource program.

Let me tell you a little bit about myself. I have taught in this school district for nine years. In my first five years, I taught exceptional children in a special classroom. Four years ago I transferred to the resource program. This transfer was in large part a result of new guidelines contained in The Education of All Handicapped Children Act (Public Law 94-142). According to this law, all children are educated in the least restrictive environment possible to meet their individual needs. Your child is most effectively served in the resource program.

In the near future, I will meet with parents to discuss their children's individualized educational program and to review the goals and objectives established for each child at the end of the last school year. During the conference, we will discuss expectations for your child this year, and I will suggest ways you can help your child at home and in school. I will try to respond to your questions and concerns about your child's educational program at this conference. I will telephone you for an appointment in early September.

This year, we are implementing a new program in which parents can volunteer in the resource program. This will be an excellent means for us to get to know each other and collaborate in activities to help the children. Also, it will help familiarize you with the child's educational program. We can discuss this exciting project during our conference.

I look forward to a very rewarding and productive school year with _____. With your support and assistance, I am sure we will make significant progress. Please feel free to contact me at Airport School (555-5534).

Sincerely yours,

*FIGURE 5-9
Welcome Letter*

- The teacher's school and home telephone numbers

- A list of materials the child needs for school

- Suggestions for parents wishing to help the child at home.

England (1977) suggested the following purposes for an introductory letter to the parents of secondary school students:

- To introduce the teacher

- To state course goals and expectations

- To describe classroom procedures

- To list readings and projects

- To describe the evaluation process

- To inform the parent about other parent-teacher activities, such as conferences and visits

- To provide the teacher's telephone number and appointment schedule.

England also recommended brief, positive notes and letters to communicate with parents the remainder of the year, as did Hymes (1974) and Kroth (1975).

Thank you letters are also effective communications devices. Using this format, teachers can express their appreciation for parents' contributions to the special education program during the school year (Figure 5-10). They can also offer continued assistance and consultation during the summer months. Kaplan, Kohfeldt, and Sturla (1974) and Kaplan and Hoffman (1981) developed formats for awards, glad notes, and certificates for teachers to duplicate and send home, either as part of a systematic communication program or as periodic rewards (Figures 5-11 and 5-12). Imber, Imber, and Rothstein (1979) developed another positive device, a praise note (Figure 5-13), and studied its effects on the academic performance of three exceptional children. The research design consisted of three phases: (a) baseline, (b) intervention 1 (a teacher-child conference to praise the child and distribute earned praise

May 10, 198_

Dear _____,

Thank you for the fine job you've done in supporting our educational team this year. You have been vital to the success of _____'s program. It is a real pleasure to have worked with you. We look forward to future years with you and

_____.

It is my sincerest hope that your summer will be a relaxing and enjoyable one. I hope you will have time to enjoy your children.

During the summer, if you have any concerns, please feel free to call me (555-0839). I will provide whatever assistance I can. Enclosed are copies of some "Summer Ideas" you may want to try with your child.

Have a nice summer. See you in the fall.

Sincerely,

FIGURE 5-10
Thank You Letter

FIGURE 5-11
Behavior and
Achievement Award

noted), and (c) intervention 2 (parent-teacher telephone contact and praise notes). The three children's performance improved significantly during both interventions using praise notes.

It is important that teachers let the children know the content of any notes, letters, or notices that go home. This practice can allay the children's anxiety about possible "bad news" and counteract the traditional negativity that has surrounded parent-teacher written communication.

FIGURE 5-12
Behavior and
Achievement Awards

TELEPHONE CONTACTS

A telephone call demonstrates the teacher's personal interest in the parents, and positive, periodic, and consistent telephone contacts can significantly affect the child's school performance. (Alternatively, of course, negative telephone contacts can have a negative effect on parents' and exceptional children's attitudes toward teacher and school.)

Teachers must exercise care in using the telephone to communicate with parents about their child. Telephone contacts are good ways to encourage parents to attend meetings, conferences, and other school events. However, teachers should refrain from burdening an already

Success — (☺) — Gram

This is an announcement and remembrance of a great deed or accomplishment.

_____ has _____

_____

_____

Congratulations are in order!

Keep up the good work!

Date _____   Signed _____

busy parent with calls about the child's classroom or school behavior problems. It is impossible, in most circumstances, for a parent to control the child's school performance and behavior from home.

Olson (1976) encouraged teachers to telephone each parent in the first days of the school year to introduce themselves and demonstrate to parents their genuine concern with the child's welfare. Periodic telephone contacts with parents increase the probability of positive interactions (England 1977). Cory (1974) recommended the systematic use of "glad phone calls"—brief, polite, and positive telephone calls to tell parents about their child's positive and productive activities at school. Such calls supplement the periodic report card and other parent-teacher communication techniques.

Some teachers have used recorded telephone messages citing the day's spelling words, for example, and other school activities as an effective, nonthreatening way to increase parent contacts (Chapman and Heward 1982). Answering machines also allow parents to leave messages for the teacher to respond to later in the day.

According to Granowsky and associates, "Many parents are afraid to come to school, and they feel uncomfortable when they do" (1977, 54). These authors encourage teachers to reach out to parents and communicate their wish to know the parents as well as their child. The telephone can be an effective means for beginning this process.

If teachers cannot make home visits, they can conduct telephone miniconferences with the parents. Using this technique, teachers should communicate with parents consistently—for example, biweekly or monthly—to report on student progress, behaviors, and achievements to be reinforced at home. Teachers should plan these telephone miniconferences in advance.

A telephone call from school is extremely threatening to many minority parents, for they have come to expect bad news (Marion 1979). Indeed, many nonminority parents probably share this negative perception of telephone calls from school.

Marion proposed guidelines for minimizing parent-teacher misunderstanding and misperceptions in telephone communications with minority parents; they are in fact applicable with nonminority parents as well:

1. Address parents as Mr. or Mrs. for two reasons: Minority parents do not always receive the same courtesy and respect as other people. They may also resent or mistrust a professional who seems to want to become too friendly too soon. Common courtesy can make the difference between a good or poor beginning in the parent-teacher relationship.

2. Use a tone of voice that expresses respect and courtesy. Because a phone call from the school usually raises anxiety in many parents, a respectful, polite, calm tone of voice can be reassuring.

3. Discuss some of the child's good points before launching into a report of the problems. This approach will reduce the parent's anxiety, set the tone for conversation, and enhance the parent's perception of the teacher. Parents respond to a helpful person who treats them with kindness and respect and who makes positive comments about their children.

4. Use language the parent understands. Teachers must tune into parents' articulation, response, and level of understanding and adjust their language accordingly as the phone conversation progresses. Teachers should talk at parents' level without condescending. Most people have built-in "antennae" that pick up the difference between a patronizing and a respectful attitude.

5. Ask parents to repeat essential parts of the conversation. Teachers should listen and respond appropriately at the parent's level of understanding and communicate empathy if parents have difficulty understanding unfamiliar educational concepts.

Croft (1979) suggested making telephone calls to parents during the evening hours or at times when parents are less likely to be busy. As a rule, calls to parents at work are inadvisable except in an emergency for many employers frown on employees' accepting personal telephone calls during working hours.

NEWSLETTERS

The newsletter is a valuable component of a comprehensive parent-teacher involvement program that can serve several needs. Newsletters can provide information on long- and short-range program plans, explain instructional methods, and report on activities and events (Granowsky et al. 1977). Newsletters are a good way to maintain regular contact with parents, especially those unable to participate in group meetings (Liddle, Rockwell, and Sacadat 1967) and may be an integral part of a program designed to communicate both with and to parents (Fedderson 1972).

England (1977), Cooke and Cooke (1974), and Cory (1974) viewed the newsletter primarily as a technique for communicating information to parents. Hymes (1974) suggested that newsletters explain the "why" of class activities and events.

A newsletter may be weekly, biweekly, or monthly depending on classroom needs, personnel, time, and materials. However, it should be distributed regularly. Cory (1974) urged teachers not to wait for an all-school newsletter or newspaper to communicate with their group of parents because a classroom newsletter can better transmit information when it is timely. In all probability, classroom newsletters are as well-received at home as all-school newspapers.

Parents usually read newsletters "on the run" or during a spare minute between activities. Thus, newsletters should not exceed four to six typewritten pages, should be written in common language, and should be positive and personal.

Teachers can supplement their contributions to the newsletter by soliciting contributions from other professionals, parents, and children. Children's and parents' contributions increase the newsletter's readership because parents enjoy this type of personal material. Every child in a class should contribute an article or drawing to the newsletter sometime during the year.

Parents may be willing to help prepare and distribute newsletters—often writing articles, typing manuscripts, or duplicating. Teachers can send newsletters home with the children, distribute them at parent meetings, or mail them.

Diversity makes for interesting and inviting newsletters. By developing an annual plan for newsletter content, teachers can assure that they include relevant items at key points during the year. They might include any or all of the following items, for example.

1. An explanation or description of the what and why of class activities

2. General news from classroom and school

3. Announcements (future activities, materials and equipment needed, resource people needed, holidays, birthdays, celebrations, workshops)

4. Suggestions for reading and viewing (new and significant books, current articles, motivational and inspirational literature, news articles, movies, lectures, and television and radio presentations)

5. Abstracts and summaries of articles and books

6. Learning activities for parents and children to do at home

7. Recreational activities and games for parents and children

8. Recognition of volunteers and other classroom contributors

9. Introduction of community resource people and groups serving parents and exceptional children

10. Program descriptions, including personnel working with the children, functions of resource personnel, class schedules, school calendars, materials and equipment, class organization, and behavior management techniques

11. Children's drawings, poems, and stories

12. A question-and-answer column

13. Want ads for volunteers, equipment, materials, and suggestions.

The Carbondale Special Education Cooperative in Carbondale, Illinois, produces "The Co-op Connection" for parents, friends, and supporters of a program serving children and youth who are severely and profoundly mentally handicapped and multiply handicapped (Figure 5-14). The young people live in a residential environment and seldom see their parents, siblings, and relatives. Consequently, the newsletter is an important vehicle for highlighting the residents, their activities, and their progress. It also introduces the co-op faculty and staff to parents and others interested in the program in an informal, visually attractive, and cheerful format.

CARBONDALE SPECIAL EDUCATION COOPERATIVE   Carbondale, Illinois   April, 1980

What happened to spring? Temperatures have been in the 90s this week and
everyone is talking about splash parties, picnics, and other summer activities.
The Co-op's wading pool has been unpacked and cleaned up, One afternoon a
number of our children dunked their feet in and splashed up a storm!

We welcome two new students to C.S.E.C.:

    Joan is in Sue's class and

    Mike is in Louise's class.

Mrs. Smith also has two new teacher aides, Elizabeth Riley and Dan Train. We
are all glad to have them with us.

                    DID YOU KNOW. . . .

. . .that Jill, our secretary, was the guest of honor at a "Spring Sing"

    during National Secretary's Week?

. . .that Dr. Johnson of the SIU Department of Music has volunteered

    to provide music therapy for our students twice weekly since 1976?

    She is really APPRECIATED. Thank you.

                   ARTS AND CRAFTS

The change of season always brings
a change of artwork displays. A
trip down the hall features trees in
full blossom, (blossoms of pop-corn,
that is), fluffy white clouds made of
soapsuds with brightly colored tissue
paper kites. Another wall has kites
flying every which way with shiny
cellophone tails. Spring cannot be
complete without lovely "pudding
painted" flowers! Gardens are
popping up all over.

FIGURE 5-14
Sample Newsletter:
"The Co-op
Connection"

"Kiddie Kapers" is a monthly newsletter for parents of exceptional children attending a public preschool program (Figure 5-15). This newsletter highlights classroom learning activities, as well as introducing activities parent and child can do at home. The newsletter is informational: "We want to tell you . . . ," "We are learning . . . ," "We need . . . ," and so on. Newsletter sections aim for brevity and clarity in an attractive format.

NEWS FLASHES!

Vincent plays the drum in music class all by himself!

Joe puts his shirt on and takes it off with very little help!

Betty is learning to use her new communications board! (Her pet mouse, Felix, (or is it Felicia) is enjoyed by all her friends.)

Andrew side-steps along the handrail independently and walks holding an adult's hand on one side and the handrail on the other side!

Dwayne drinks from a cup independently!

Jenny matches identical objects!

Sarah holds her own cup and needs just a little help to scoop her food at lunch time!

Mona's toileting program has been very successful. She has had 12 accident free days!

Mickey is putting circles into a shape box independently!

Timothy really gets around taking small steps in his walker and goes just about any place he wants in his classroom!

John is the V.I.P. of the month in the Intermediate I room. He has become a very outgoing young man. Frequently, John may be seen heading for the candy jar in the secretary's office. He is also learning to climb the stairs.

Mary Ann is making great strides in self-feeding.

Eileen enjoys sitting in a teacher aide's lap. It is nice to see her relaxed and enjoying herself.

Kathleen looks forward to strumming the autoharp and playing the tambourine during music.

SPEAKING OF KITES. . . .

The first annual kite flying contest was held on April 23rd. Each room made a kite and eagerly anticipated its launching. Tension was high! Would it fly! How long would it stay up! Which one would go the highest!

It was a beautiful day with a slight breeze. Everyone gathered in the field behind the Co-op. The time has finally come to see everyone's kite in the air - or so we thought!

FIGURE 5-14
(cont.)

SUMMARY

This chapter describes several techniques for parent-teacher involvement that depend on written and telephone communication: daily and periodic report cards; learning charts; a passport to positive parent-teacher communication; notes, letters, and notices; telephone communication; and newsletters. These techniques require the least amount of

The pre-schoolers had a very pretty little kite and won the award for longest flying kite. It stayed up for 23 seconds.

The primary room's kite was a big red and white striped bird. It was the highest flying reaching an altitude of about 12 feet (if you stretch it a bit).

Every kite flying contest has a dragon and our dragon was judged the funniest kite of the day! It tried to fly but its power source fell down.

The prettiest kite was made by the people in the Intermediate I classroom. It looked like a stained glass windmill.

A double kite which was awarded the prize for most original kite was entered by the Intermediate II class. It also made every effort to fly but couldn't quite make it.

Despite the fallen kites, everyone had a high flying good time!

THANK-YOU!

Many visitors have been to the Co-op since the threat of bad weather has passed. As always we are pleased to see our students' families and friends.

FIGURE 5-14
(cont.)

parent–teacher involvement and are most appropriate for transmitting information. Thus, they communicate primarily *to* parents, providing only limited opportunities to communicate *with* them.

The techniques are most effective as components of a comprehensive parent–teacher involvement program. They are valuable for initiating interaction, bridging the gap between parents and teachers, and

Mr. and Mrs. William Smith
Mrs. William Jones
Mr. & Mrs. William Davis
Mr. and Mrs. Kurt Swoboda
Mrs. Janice Lang

Phone calls are always welcome. Recently we have heard from Mrs. Marcus and Mrs. Mines.

Some of our children have recently gone home for a visit.

Mickey
Elizabeth
Barbara
JoAnn

JUST FOR FUN

Our children have participated in a number of special activities in addition to the kite flying contest!

Two of our talented aides organized a super afternoon at the Co-op. Our very own clown entertained with stunts and acrobatics. She is none other than Paula (Her mother was a "real circus clown"!) Gwen assisted her by leading a sing-a-long, an event considered to be a favorite by students and staff.

Paula and Gwen also planned a spring dance for everyone. A great time was had by all! The activity therapists cooperated by providing refreshments. Thank you!

Some of the teachers and one of the nurses have had four-legged visitors at school. Most of the children enjoy feeling the soft fur of kittens, puppies, and dogs. It's fun to watch them, too!

FIGURE 5-14
(cont.)

supporting ongoing activities. The chapter suggests the best use of each communication method, provides guidelines for productive use of the techniques, and offers samples of each.

The next four chapters present techniques suited for communicating *with* parents. Chapter Six discusses the most frequently used of these techniques, the parent–teacher conference.

A trip to the stables is planned for this Spring. We also hope
to have some baby farm animals visit the schoolyard.

Our traditional picnic will take place during the last week of school.

It will be a super special picnic this year at "Touch of Nature,"
the Southern Illinois University's outdoor laboratory and camp for
the handicapped located on Little Grassy Lake. Some of the exciting
activities which are planned are a pontoon boat ride, sand play, a
nature hike, and cook-out. We might even fly a kite!

                              SPLASH!

We have a new swimming program every Friday at the YMCA. Our group
started out with five children from various rooms and has expanded to
include three more.

The eight children have been responding to the water very well. Mary
seems to have acquired the name "fish" after displaying her ability
to kick and move her arms with very little support. Naomi finally
found the bottom of the pool and is now standing while holding on to
the side. Enos has been working with one of our new volunteers and
has finally <u>lost</u> the bottom. He is floating very nicely with support.
Joshua is "warming up" more easily each session and has kicked one of
the nerf balls several times in the water. Drew is our rowdy in
the bunch! Besides managing to drench himself he also likes to splash
everyone that comes near. Dora is kicking and moving her arms in a
very progressive manner. Pamela made her debut in the water a couple
of weeks ago and holds great potential in moving her arms with more
control. Laura is scheduled to come this week and we eagerly anticipate
her participation.

FIGURE 5-14
(cont.)

EXERCISES AND
DISCUSSION TOPICS

1. Design and carry out a daily report card system for one or more
children in your class (or for a child described in Appendix B). Train
parents and children in the system.

2. Design a task analysis report card for your class (or for a child
described in Appendix B). Individualize the card to respond to each

A special thanks goes out to all the joint efforts put forth in helping to make the swimming program the success that it is:

The staff from Styrest, staff from the school, our volunteers, and especially Mr. Miller who originally said, "yes" to the whole idea!

SPECIAL PROJECT

The entire staff of the Co-op salutes Joel for an ENORMOUS project filled with love, devotion, creativity, and time. A dream has come true due to Joel's talent and interest in the seed of an idea. He nurtured that seed and helped it develop. What is it? It is a stimulus controlled learning center large enough for two people to comfortably work inside. All sights, sounds, and smells are under complete control. More information will be included in next year's first issue of the Co-op Connection. Until then, thanks, Joel.

SCHOOL'S OUT

Another school year is about to end. It seems as though it just started. We have seen progress in our students and growth in our staff. It has been out pleasure to have had a small part in developing each child's potential and providing love and security so vital for growth.

FIGURE 5-14
(cont.)

child's academic or preacademic and behavioral objectives. Train parents (and children, if appropriate) in using the report card.

3. Design one or more learning charts for each child in your class (or for the children described in Appendix B). These charts may record preacademic, academic, or behavioral performance. Train parents to use the learning chart and implement the reporting system.

4. Design and carry out a *passport* system of communication with one or more children in your class (or for those described in Appendix B).

We want to tell you:

that January is an especially busy month here at school. By this time in
the school year, parents are usually noticing many signs of maturation
and growth in their children. Please remember to talk with your child
about what he is doing here at school. It is not uncommon for children
to refuse to talk immediately when they get home. However, most children
will share later when they have had a chance to unwind or relax. If
your child refuses or is not able to tell you about his school experiences,
let me know so that we can make up some type of notebook.

We are learning:

these new words:

Fall	Spring
New Year	Summer
Seasons	Winter
Snow	

We need:

you. Please plan on coming to visit school if you have not done so already.

We want to thank:

our room mothers, Mrs. Dale and Mrs. Hill for coordinating another fantastic
party. They said that they couldn't have done it without the help of all
of you.

We want you to remember:

January 19th - No School. Teacher Institute.
January 29th - No. P.M. Session. Teacher Conferences.

FIGURE 5-15
Sample Newsletter:
"Kiddie Kapers"

Train the children, parents, and other professionals and paraprofessionals to use the passport, implement the system, and evaluate it.

5.   Using the material in this chapter, develop a checklist for the content of an introductory letter to parents. Write one or more examples of an introductory letter for the parents of the children in your class (or for parents of those in Appendix B). Ask several colleagues or parents to critique the letter, and rewrite it based on their critiques.

6.   Write several notes to parents to accomplish the following objectives:

a.   To praise the child for appropriate behavior

b.   To praise the child for superior academic performance

c. To alert parents to potential academic difficulties

d. To tell parents about a behavior problem

e. To invite the parents to a conference.

Ask several colleagues or parents to critique the notes, and rewrite them to reflect their comments.

7. Call several parents of children in your class on the telephone (or role play telephone calls using the cases in Appendix B) to convey the messages listed in 6 above.

8. Plan a monthly newsletter for your class (or a hypothetical class) for distribution ten times a year (September to June). After establishing the content for each of the ten newsletters, develop a format and prepare at least two samples.

REFERENCES

Chapman, J. E., and W. L. Heward. 1982. Improving parent-teacher communication through recorded telephone messages. *Exceptional Children* 49 (1):79–82.

Clements, J. E., and R. L. Simpson. 1974. Establishing parental support. *The Pointer* 19 (1):70–71.

Cooke, S., and T. Cooke. 1974. Parent training for early education of the handicapped. *Reading Improvement* 11 (3):62–64.

Cory, C. T. 1974. Two generations of volunteers: Parents. *Learning* 3 (2):76–79.

Croft, D. J. 1979. *Parents and teachers: A resource book for home, school, and community relations.* Belmont, Calif.: Wadsworth.

Dickerson, D., C. R. Spellman, S. Larsen, and L. Tyler. 1973. Let the cards do the talking—A teacher-parent communication program. *Teaching Exceptional Children* 4 (4):170–78.

Edlund, C. V. 1969. Rewards at home to promote desirable school behavior. *Teaching Exceptional Children* 1 (4):121–27.

England, D. W. 1977. Hearing from the teacher when nothing is wrong. *English Journal* 66 (6):42–45.

Feddersen, J., Jr. 1972. Establishing an effective parent-teacher communication system. *Childhood Education* 49 (2):75–80.

Granowsky, A., A. Hackett, J. Hoffman, A. Keller, J. Lamkin, F. Morrison, J. Rabbit, M. Schumate, S. Schurr, E. Stranix, and J.

Woods. 1977. How to put parents on your classroom team. *Instructor,* Nov., 54–62.

Hymes, J. L., Jr. 1974. *Effective home-school relations.* Sierra Madre, Calif.: Southern California Association for the Education of Young Children.

Imber, S., R. Imber, and C. Rothstein. 1979. Modifying independent work habits: An effective teacher-parent communication program. *Exceptional Children* 46 (3):218–21.

Kaplan, P. G., and A. G. Hoffman. 1981. *It's absolutely groovy.* Denver: Love Publishing.

Kaplan, P. G., J. Kohfeldt, and K. Sturla. 1974. *It's positively fun: Techniques for managing learning environments.* Denver: Love Publishing.

Kroth, R. L. 1975. *Communicating with parents of exceptional children: Improving parent-teacher relationships.* Denver: Love Publishing.

Kroth, R. L., R. J. Whelan, and J. M. Stables. 1970. Teacher application of behavior principles in home and classroom environments. *Focus on Exceptional Children* 1 (3):1–9.

Liddle, G. P., R. E. Rockwell, and E. Sacadat. 1967. Education improvement for the disadvantaged in an elementary setting. Springfield, Ill.: Charles C. Thomas.

Lordeman, A. M., and R. A. Winett. 1980. The effects of written feedback to parents and a call-in service on student homework submission. *Education and Treatment of Children* 3 (1):33–44.

Magnusson, C. J., and S. B. McCarney. 1980. School-home communication. *The Pointer* 25 (1):23–27.

Marion, R. 1979. Minority parent involvement in the IEP process: A systematic model approach. *Focus on Exceptional Children* 10 (8):1–15.

Olson, S. A., E. Gaines, J. H. Wilson, N. Voldstad, and P. A. Smith. 1976. Reinforce that home-school link. *Instructor,* Oct., 112–114, 116, 119.

Powell, T. H. 1980. Improving home-school communication: Sharing daily reports. *The Exceptional Parent* 10 (5):S24–S26.

Runge, A., J. Walker, and T. M. Shea. 1975. A passport to positive parent-teacher communications. *Teaching Exceptional Children* 7 (3):91–92.

Rutherford, R. B., Jr., and E. Edgar. 1979. *Teachers and parents: A guide to interaction and cooperation.* Abr. ed. Boston: Allyn and Bacon.

Ryan, S. B., and R. E. Ryan. 1973. Report cards? Why not ask the parents? *Teaching Exceptional Children* 6 (1):34–36.

Shea, T. M. 1978. *Teaching children and youth with behavior disorders*. St. Louis: C. V. Mosby.

Thorman, J. H. 1979. A supplement to the report card. *Education and Treatment of Children* 2 (1):65–70.

CHAPTER SIX

PARENT-TEACHER CONFERENCES

◻

■ The parent-teacher conference is "an individualized, personalized meeting between two or three significant persons in the child's life with the purpose of accelerating his or her growth" (Kroth and Simpson 1977, 2). The approach to a given conference depends on its purpose and content (Barsch 1969). This chapter discusses the types of conferences most likely to be useful to teachers of exceptional children: progress report, problem-solving, and behavior management training conferences. In addition, it discusses the individualized education program meeting mandated by Public Law 94-142 as a special type of conference. Sections on home visits, the three-way conference, and coping with negative reactions are discussed.

The quality of the communication between parents and teacher in a conference is key (Kroth and Simpson 1977). Just as positive communication can help improve the child's performance, so can negative interactions cause performance to deteriorate (Truax and Wargo 1966).

Consequently, it is important to structure every conference to encourage a positive exchange.

Individual conferences are one part of a comprehensive parent-teacher involvement program. They require more planning, preparation, and personal involvement than do written and telephone communication. However, because communication is face to face, the probability of miscommunication decreases. The content of the parent-teacher conference is more personal than that of traditional written and telephone communications. Both parents and teacher must devote time and energy to planning, scheduling, attending, and evaluating each conference.

PROGRESS REPORT CONFERENCES

The progress report conference supplements traditional reporting procedures, such as the report card, providing an opportunity for personal interactions that decrease misunderstandings (Rutherford and Edgar 1979).

The conference is an opportunity for parents and teachers to exchange information about the child's school and home activities, and it is an occasion to involve parents in planning and carrying out their child's program. Based on systematic evaluation of the child and information from the parents, the conference can guide the teacher in modifying the child's educational program. Ultimately, the progress report conference is a forum for sharing wisdom, knowledge, and skills to benefit the child ("The parent-teacher conference" 1973; Farr 1977).

When teachers contact parents to schedule progress report conferences, they should explain the purpose of the conference and possibly give the parents a written agenda. These steps help reduce parents' anxiety about the coming session.

As a verbal report card, the progress report conference centers on the child and the program, not on the parents' or teacher's personal, social, emotional, or marital problems (as important as they may be to the parent and teacher). Its proper focus is the child's progress in various areas of school and home functioning.

In many cases, the conference is a "show and tell" session. The teacher presents and discusses the child's work and the instructional materials used in the educational program. Many parents welcome an invitation to try out instructional materials and equipment.

Conference planning and preparation is as important as, if not more important than, the actual conduct of the conference. Teachers should write a jargon-free report before the session evaluating the child's educational program and progress (Figure 6-1). They give parents a copy

A. Social behavior (in the classroom, during recess, on field trips, on the bus)

   1. Self-control (in large and small groups, during activities)

   2. Affective behavior (enthusiasm, leadership, followership, obedience, responsibility, reactions to rewards and discipline)

   3. Group participation (in the classroom, during recess, on field trips, during activities)

   4. Social amenities (manners, courtesies, respect for others and their property)

B. Communications

   1. Modes of communication (speaking, conversing, eye contact, reading, writing, spelling, music, gestures)

   2. Listening (responsiveness, direction following, stories, music)

   3. Language activities (awareness, receptive language, expressive language, language development, verbal communication of experiences)

   4. Language skills (speech, spontaneous language, words, sentences)

C. Basic knowledge

   1. Information (name, age, address, siblings, parents, friends, places, things, colors, shapes, letters, numbers)

   2. Reading (or readiness)

   3. Spelling

   4. Arithmetic

   5. Social studies (current events)

   6. Art (second and third dimensional)

   7. Music

   8. Sensory-motor skills (recreation, physical education)

   9. Perception (auditory, visual, tactile)

D. Self-care, practical and work skills

   1. Work tools (paste, paper, pencil, blocks, puzzles, knife, spoon, fork, scissors, saw, hammer, cutting torch, level)

   2. School chores and duties (hanging up clothes, serving table, setting table, cleaning, washing)

   3. Bathroom and grooming (toilet training, cleaning hands and face)

   4. Body use (awareness, climbing, walking, running, moving self and objects)

FIGURE 6-1
Outline for Preconference
Report

(Shea 1978, 244)

at the beginning of the conference for their home records, for future reference, or to inform an absent parent if necessary.

The teacher guides the actual conference, systematically reviewing the report and encouraging and responding to the parents' questions and comments. Because parents' questions and comments reflect their most pressing concerns, teachers should take care to respond fully and reassuringly. They should also see that they obtain the information they need from parents.

After making parents comfortable at the beginning of a session, teachers clarify the time available for conferring. The conference tone is positive: The teacher accentuates the positive and encourages the parents to do likewise. Thus, rather than saying "Tommy does not recognize fourteen letters of the alphabet," the teacher says "Tommy recognizes twelve letters of the alphabet; this is three new letters since we last conferred." Instead of "Jean is out of her seat without permission sixteen times a day," the teacher says "We are seeing some progress in Jean's in-seat behavior. Last month when we conferred, I reported that she left her seat twenty times per day. Now she's out of her seat about fifteen times per day. That's an improvement." Teachers should also review and accent the areas of functioning in which the child demonstrates skill, competency, and progress. This approach provides a balanced view of the child as a learner rather than as an exceptional child only.

Except for the initial conference, the teacher focuses on the child's progress since the last scheduled session. However, once each year, parents and teachers may find it valuable to review the child's progress since the beginning of the year or since the implementation of a specific educational program.

If the teacher sees that parents wish to and can increase their involvement in their child's educational program, he or she can encourage them to do so at this time although it is not an immediate objective of the progress report conference. However, the teacher has the duty to ensure that such parent involvement is helpful to the child, which it generally is.

Freeman (1975) proposed that teachers end progress report conferences with a specific plan of action for helping the child. Parents, teacher, and child write a "Student-Parent-Teacher Commitment" or contingency contract. Subsequent conferences review and modify this contract and develop new contracts.

Parents and the teacher may all want to take notes during the conference, but the teacher should make sure that all participants are comfortable with note taking and drop it if necessary. Immediately after the conference the teacher writes a conference summary to attach to the report and file in the child's folder. This summary includes questions the teacher wishes to raise with the parents at the next conference.

Investigators disagree on the proper number of conferences annually. Kean (1975), speaking as a parent, recommended four or five conferences a year. Shea (1978) recommended a conference every nine to twelve weeks. The editor of *The Exceptional Parent* (1979) recommended developing a one-year conference plan for four sessions in August or September, Thanksgiving season, early spring, and at the end of the school year.

Rutherford and Edgar (1979) published a guide for teachers planning a progress report conference (Figure 6-2) as well as a sample agenda (Figure 6-3), which offers an alternative to a conference outline presented previously. Several authors have suggested "dos and don'ts" for teachers conducting the progress report conference (Long 1976; Gaines 1976; Instructional Materials Center, Illinois; Bailard and Strang 1964):

■ Don't make parents defensive by criticizing them, their children, their employment, their neighborhood, or other personal matters.

■ Don't argue. Teachers are not always right, nor do they always have the answer.

Purpose	To inform parents of their children's progress in school
Needs of Teacher	To ensure parents understand how their children are doing
Preplanning of Teacher	• Inform parents of purpose of meeting • Agree on meeting time • Collect samples of the children's work • Prepare materials explaining teaching goals and strategies • Schedule enough time for parents to ask questions and express concerns
Materials	• Daily schedule of classroom activities • Checklist of skills areas and notes on how children are doing • Samples of the children's work • Test scores and reports from others on the children
Needs of Parents	To find out how their children are performing, what they are learning, what activities they are engaged in, and what their teacher is like.

FIGURE 6-2
Guide for Basic
Information Conference

(Rutherford and Edgar 1979, 10)

General Impression of Johnny:
Alert, talkative, happy, well-liked. A good reader but needs work in spelling.

ACADEMIC AREAS

Reading: Lippincott Book D, mid-second level. Advanced reading group. Good sounding-out skills. Great comprehension.

Arithmetic: Counts, writes numerals to 100, and understands addition and subtraction facts.

Writing: Manuscript—all upper and lower case letters. Nice creative stories.

Spelling: Needs some help in phonetic spelling; suggest place in special help group.

Art: Good creative work.

Music: A leader with gusto.

Science: Likes to tell about his "collections": Does he have bugs, spiders, and rocks?

Test Scores: (IQ, Lorge-Thorndike, and group test): Follows directions well.

Metropolitan Achievement Test: 2.8 on word attack skills, 2.9 on word meaning, and 2.1 on arithmetic.

GOALS		How
Reading:	To progress through beginning third-grade level; should be able to read on own books like *Little House on the Prairie.*	Reading group Language Master Fifth-grade tutor
Arithmetic:	To add and subtract two place numbers with renaming (46 + 75; 74 − 28). Time, money ($1.00, $5.00, $10.00, $25.00, $50.00, $100.00). Fractions (1/2, 1/4, 1/3).	Total group Seat work
Writing:	To write all cursive letters.	Total group
Spelling:	To spell all words on grade 3 test correctly.	Special help group
Art:	To become familiar with pottery techniques.	Art teacher
Music:	To become familiar with all the instruments of an orchestra.	Music teacher
Science:	To become familiar with domestic and wild animals.	Experiments Group discussion
Social Activities:	To know the rules of group games.	Playground Free time

(Rutherford and Edgar 1979, 11)

FIGURE 6-3
Sample Agenda

■ Do let the parent who is speaking or thinking do so without interruption. Don't persist in making your point to such an extent that the parents are angered or bored.

■ Do listen. Parents have some important things to say.

■ Don't belittle students, the school, the administration, or the school system.

■ Don't talk about or compare other children or parents.

■ Don't gossip. Maintain confidentiality.

■ Don't become too personal. Avoid embarrassing the parents.

■ Don't assume the parents of an exceptional child are problem parents. Don't assume they need, want, or will accept teachers' help or advice.

■ Don't dwell on negatives. Seek the positive and remain positive throughout the conference.

■ Don't promise things that are not deliverable.

■ Don't assume full responsibility for the child. Share responsibility with the parents.

■ Don't take yourself too seriously. Teachers are human. They make mistakes.

■ Don't avoid conferring with parents because of your anxiety. Everyone is nervous but gets over it with success and experience.

■ Do listen to parents. Be friendly, relaxed, and empathetic.

Teachers can help parents participate fully in several ways. Providing parents with a handout offering tips is one way (Figure 6-4). Kroth (1972) suggested preconference, conference, and postconference activities for parents who wish to actively participate in progress report conferences. He advised parents to discuss the coming conference with their spouses and children and to write a list of questions, any information they wish to give the teacher, and suggestions for dealing with the child. Kroth also encouraged parents to invite a spouse, friend, or advocate if they feel uneasy about the conference.

During the conference, Kroth recommended that parents ask the teacher how much time is allotted for the conference so that they can pace their discussion. He advised parents to take notes during the meeting, ask for clarification of items they do not understand, and ask to see any records with which they are unfamiliar and have them explained. Parents should sign only those papers they understand clearly.

If the teacher does not summarize at the end of the conference, the parent should do so, according to Kroth. Moreover, if they feel they

Before the conference:

1. Make arrangements for your other children, if necessary. The conference is for you and your child's teacher; small children can be distracting and take time away from the discussion.

2. Jot down any questions you may have for the teacher, such as:
   • Is my child working to the best of his (her) ability?
   • How is he (she) progressing in reading, math, handwriting, and other subjects?
   • Does he (she) get along well with teachers, children?
   • Does he (she) follow classroom rules?
   • What is his (her) attitude in class?
   • How do you handle (specific behaviors)?
   • What do the tests say about his (her) ability?

3. Talk to your child about the conference. Ask if he or she wants you to ask any questions or voice any concerns.

4. Collect any records or information that may help the teacher. Try to anticipate questions and prepare answers.

At the conference:

1. Please be on time and stay only for your scheduled time. You may schedule another conference if you do not cover all the necessary information in the allotted time.

2. Discuss only the child at issue. Try not to stray off the subject. Do not bring up your other children's problems.

3. Ask any questions about your child's education. Advocate for your child. Know your child's and your rights.

4. Volunteer information that may help the teacher plan programming for your child.

5. Feel free to take notes to review later.

After the conference: Feel free to contact your child's teacher for further clarification.

FIGURE 6-4
Parent Handout for
Conference Preparation

do not have closure, they should request another conference. After the conference, Kroth urged parents to review their notes and write down questions and concerns for the next conference.

PROBLEM-SOLVING CONFERENCES

Conferences to plan and carry out solutions to academic or behavior problems are often useful to both parents and teachers. According to Kroth (1972, 1975), the successful problem-solving conference considers in detail the environment in which the problem is taking place, the nature of the problem, conference preplanning, conference timing, required data and information, needs of parents' and teachers' for reinforcement, and provisions for training parents to help solve the problem.

Parents and teacher must recognize that a child may have a problem in one environment but not in another. Thus, they must determine if the problem is primarily at school, at home, in the neighborhood, or in several places. Similarly, they should avoid projecting their personal and social problems or behaviors onto the child and should determine if the problem rests with the child or with the parent or teacher.

Stewart (1973) suggested that early conferences look at one specific problem in order to avoid diluting parents' and teachers' effectiveness. Generally, the teacher is responsible for specifying the problem with the parents; Kroth (1972a) recommended the following procedure:

1. Select the behaviors of concern by listing observable behaviors or asking the child to select his or her own targets.

2. Define the behaviors in enough detail to allow accurate measurement.

3. Rank the behaviors. Because success in remedying academic deficits often alleviates excessive social behaviors as well, academic behaviors may often rank above social behaviors.

4. Label each behavior on the ranked list *P* (parent) or *T* (teacher) to designate parent involvement or teacher-only work on a solution.

5. Keep an accurate record of the frequency, duration, and rate of occurrence of the selected behavior(s) for a week.

6. Graph the data as a visual record for presentation to the parents.

7. Prepare a plan for intervention, specifying what the teacher will do and what the parents will do. (This plan, of course, depends on the parents' ability or willingness to carry out their part of the plan.)

Clearly, the problem-solving process is a cooperative activity among parents, teacher, and child, who may participate during planning as well as in carrying out solutions. Regularly scheduled conferences are the best way to develop this relationship. Crisis conferences, when feelings run high, are less likely to be productive; an ill-timed conference can create tension between parents and teacher that interferes with effective problem solving.

In a study of parent-counselor conferences before students enter junior high school, Duncan and Fitzgerald (1969) found that contacting parents before the child's entrance into school, before the beginning of the school year, or before the onset of a crisis seems to encourage parent involvement in the child's education. The study indicated that an individualized first contact may be more effective in ensuring continued involvement than a traditional large group orientation session.

Parents and teacher need all pertinent information to solve problems effectively. Thus, parents need background information on the child's overall performance at school, and the teacher needs information on the child's performance at home and in the neighborhood. Both need specific information about the problem at hand, including answers to who, what, where, when, how, and how often. Before the conference, both parents and teacher should observe and record the frequency, intensity, and duration of the behavior.

Parents and teacher can structure their cooperation through the problem-solving process by following these steps:

1. Set goals.

2. Select potential interventions.

3. Carry out interventions.

4. Provide feedback.

5. Evaluate results.

In the first step, parents and teacher agree on the problem they want to solve together. At this time, they also determine the desired outcome of their efforts or the performance standard that will indicate success, and they develop a plan for evaluating the effectiveness of the intervention. Next, the parents and teacher suggest potential interventions to solve the problem until they can agree on an action.

During the third step, they put their plan in action for a specific period of time under specific conditions. Parents and teacher collect information on the frequency, intensity, and duration of the behavior and report their experiences at home or at school. Because parents do not have educational expertise, they may require additional training to participate fully in problem-solving activities. The teacher can provide opportunities for the parents to learn about, observe, and practice various instructional methods and behavior management interventions.

Parents and teacher confer periodically to evaluate the effectiveness of the intervention, offering each other the systematic feedback and positive reinforcement so important to the process. During these prescheduled conferences, they evaluate the effectiveness of the intervention, the standards of performance, the intervention procedures, and the reinforcers.

Rutherford and Edgar (1979) have proposed a general problem-solving process applicable to several theoretical problem-solving models. They have discussed parent-teacher problem-solving conferences using applied behavior analysis, interpersonal communication, and assertiveness strategies. Their model and the prerequisite skills for its effective implementation can guide teachers and parents in their problem-solving activities (Table 6-1).

Applied behavior analysis systematically approaches observing and analyzing behaviors where they occur. Specific behavior change strategies are used to increase or decrease selected behaviors. Interpersonal communication stresses effective communication skills as an intervention procedure. Assertiveness strategies stress helping people better control their destinies while learning to feel better about themselves.

TRAINING CONFERENCES

Training conferences teach parents how to design, carry out, and evaluate home and home-school behavior management interventions. Blackard and Barsch (1982) suggested that professionals underestimate

TABLE 6-1   *A Problem-Solving Model*

Problem-Solving Model	*Skills*
Defining the problem.	Applied behavior analysis: Pinpointing observable, measurable behaviors; recording; charting. Communication: Expressing ownership and "I" messages; listening actively. Assertiveness: Recognizing irritation; defining territorial issues.
Developing the solution.	Applied behavior analysis: Analyzing the antecedents and consequences of the behavior. Communication: Employing bilateral decision making to determine solutions and develop a written contract. Assertiveness: Stating needs; defending against weapons; drawing up written contract.
Implementing the solution.	Applied behavior analysis: Aiming for consistent application of procedures. Communication: Allowing ample time for understanding the problem. Assertiveness: Testing the contract.
Evaluating the results.	Applied behavior analysis: Conducting an ongoing assessment; charting; maintaining; generalizing. Communication: Using "I" messages to discuss whether the problem is resolved. Assertiveness: Renegotiating agreements if there is displeasure.

Source: Rutherford and Edgar 1979, 198.

parents' teaching abilities and lack confidence in parents as teachers of their own children. However, the literature amply documents that training in the principles and practices of behavior management helps parents change their children's behavior (Patterson 1969; Bandura 1969; Schopler and Reichler 1971; Ross 1972; Nardine 1974; O'Dell 1974). After reviewing thirty-four research studies, Berkowitz and Graziano (1972) concluded that parents can be trained to apply behavior modification techniques effectively. Kelly (1974), suggesting that parental "ignorance," not "malignance," causes many child-raising problems, recommended involving and training parents in behavior modification.

This section discusses the parent-teacher conference as the appropriate instructional setting for this training. Preferably, both parents should attend the training sessions to ensure that they use the same management interventions at home with consistency. With the teacher using the same techniques at school, the child has the security of consistent expectations throughout the day.

The teacher, as a conference leader and parent educator, should aim for a positive tone that communicates personal interest, enthusiasm, knowledge, and faith that the training will pay off in a happier, more competent child. The training program must be specific, starting with problems significant to the parents. The more the teacher enlivens the conferences with real life examples speaking to the parents' needs, the more useful it will be.

Adhering to structured conference procedures in the early stages of parent training also helps both teachers and parents feel secure and develop faith in the potential effectiveness of their cooperative efforts. As parent and teacher become more comfortable, the teacher can relax the structure somewhat. Several behavior management training techniques are available for teachers to match with their instructional purposes and the parents' level of knowledge and skill. Beginning teachers will find them useful in establishing a framework for their work with parents; as they gain more experience, they can adapt them to fit specific circumstances.

Walker and Shea (1984) suggested a psychosituational assessment interview designed by Bersoff and Grieger (1971) as an effective behavior modification interviewing technique. Teachers can use the interview to analyze unacceptable behaviors, uncover their antecedents, and examine the consequences that elicit, reinforce, and sustain them. This information guides parents and teachers in their decisions to use specific behavior management interventions.

Bersoff's and Grieger's interview departs from the predominant assumption that personality needs and traits predispose people to respond in certain ways; operating on this assumption, professionals try to fix the individual rather than the setting in which the behavior occurs. Alternatively, Bersoff and Grieger proposed that behavior results from the individual's inability to respond in certain ways in certain situations rather than from inherent needs and traits. Thus, their model views behavior as a consequence of prior learning and the situation or environment.

A psychosituational assessment interview is designed to help teachers determine to what extent the environment reinforces the exceptional child's behavior and to what extent changes in the environment may alter the behavior. Thus, it focuses on three major aspects of any behavior problem: the child's behavior, including its antecedents and consequences (for example, the responses of parents, siblings, and others); the environmental variables surrounding the behavior, including the presence of significant others; and the parents' attitudes and expectations. Thus, the interview should accomplish four tasks: defining the target behavior(s), explicating specific situations in which the behavior occurs, uncovering the contingencies that seemingly sustain the behavior, and detecting any irrational ideas that stand in the way of understanding, accepting, and modifying the behavior.

To define the target behavior, the interviewer gathers information on its frequency, its intensity, and its duration. Looking at the problem within this framework not only helps narrow it down to manageable proportions but also helps parents check their perceptions of the behavior and focus on its most important aspects. Next, obtaining information about the specific situations in which the behavior occurs is important to clarify links that may lead to a solution.

Third, by exploring the antecedents and consequences of the behavior, parents and teacher can become aware of the role they play in the problem.

Finally, by looking at parents' possibly irrational and unrealistic ideas about their child, teachers may learn of unwarranted short- or long-term expectations burdening the child or causing inappropriate responses to specific behaviors. The following are irrational ideas that commonly emerge during the interview:

1. The notion that the child is infallible and has wide-ranging competence. When parents expect their child to be competent in all respects, they may view inefficient functioning in one or two areas as general failure.

2. The idea that the child should meet certain absolute, unsupportable, or unreasonable standards. Parents often express this belief in "ought" and "should" statements: "He should be able to sit longer," or "He ought to know better."

3. A belief that anger is the most helpful response to the child's misbehavior. This feeling may cause parents to feel guilty and anxious, thereby interfering with positive parent-child interactions.

4. The belief that the exceptional child is blameworthy and should be punished for misdeeds.

The psychosituational assessment interview may be a single session or a series of sessions. One or two sessions may be sufficient to design an intervention for a single behavior. However, the interview technique is most effective in an ongoing series of behavior management training conferences.

During the assessment interview, the teacher has several objectives:

1. Establish rapport with the parents. Sample questions: How was your day? How is your child today?

2. Obtain the parents' description of the behaviors concerning them, including their frequency, intensity, and duration. Sample questions: What exactly does the child do that you find unacceptable or annoying? What exactly does he do that makes you say he is hyperactive, nonresponsive, or disobedient? In the course of an hour, how often is he hyperactive, nonresponsive, or disobedient?

3. Obtain the parents' description of the situations and environments in which the behavior occurs and the people present when the behavior occurs. Sample questions: Where does this behavior occur? In the house? In the yard? On the playground? In a store? Does it occur when the child is working on a particular project? With a particular group? While watching TV? When getting ready to go to bed? When getting up in the morning? Who is present when the behavior occurs? Mother? Father? Brothers? Sisters? Playmates? Visitors?

4. Explore the contingencies that may stimulate and sustain the behavior. Sample questions: What happens just before the behavior occurs? What happens just after the behavior occurs? What do you usually do when the child behaves in this way? How do other people indicate to the child that the behavior is unacceptable?

5. Attempt to determine the ratio of positive-to-negative interactions between the child and the parents. Sample questions: Is your relationship with the child usually pleasant or unpleasant? Do you usually praise his accomplishments? Do you think you praise his successes as much as you reprimand his failures, or do you think you do one more than the other?

6. Explore the parents' methods of behavior control. Sample questions: Do you punish the behavior? How do you punish inappropriate behavior? Who administers the punishment? Do you always use this method of punishment? What other methods do you use?

7. Determine how aware parents are of the way they communicate praise or punishment and its effect on the child's behavior. Sample questions: Can the child tell when you are angry? How? Can he tell when you want him to stop doing something?

8. Explore how parents communicate their expectations to their child. Sample questions: How clearly do you spell out the rules you expect the child to follow? Does he know what you expect him to do?

9. Detect irrational and unrealistic ideas that make it difficult for the parents to understand, accept, or modify the child's behavior. Restate these irrational ideas but avoid reinforcing them. Sample questions: What do you feel is the reason for the behavior? Do you think the behavior can be changed?

10. Conclude the interview by restating the unacceptable behavior and clarifying the desirable behavior.

At the end of the interview, the teacher may suggest that the parents keep a log of their child's unacceptable behavior (Figure 6-5). The teacher should complete the top portion of the form, describing the target behavior in behavioral terminology. The parents write the day or date of the target behavior's first occurrence each day in the far left column. They then note the time the behavior begins and ends each time it occurs. If the behavior ends quickly, they note the time only in the "Begins" column. Each time the target behavior occurs, parents also note its antecedents (what happened immediately before the behavior) and the consequences (what happened immediately after the behavior) in the designated columns. In the "Applied Interventions" column, they note what they or someone else did to change the child's behavior. In the "Comments" column, parents note any additional observations. See supplementary materials, pp. 187–192.

Parents return the completed log at the next conference, usually scheduled at the end of the psychosituational interview, at which point the teacher analyzes and discusses the information with them. Graphing the data can be helpful in such discussions. The next step is to plan and put into effect a behavior management intervention.

Kelly (1974) suggested that teachers can help parents with their children's behavioral problems in two ways: By training parents in behavior management principles and techniques and applying them to specific problems; by generalizing from parents' successes modifying specific problem behaviors to teach behavior management principles and techniques. The approach selected is dependent on the parents' needs, interests in learning, and the specific problems under consideration. Perhaps a combination of the two approaches is most effective. The psychosituational assessment interview represents Kelly's second approach in that the teacher starts with the parents' experience, reinforcing positive uses of behavior management techniques and guiding parents to alter less positive approaches. (Note: Walker and Shea (1984) developed a parent behavior management training program that incorporates both approaches and is described in Chapter Eight.)

Target behavior _____

Observer's name _____ Child observed _____

Day or Date	Time		Antecedents	Consequences	Applied Interventions	Comments
	Begins	Ends				

FIGURE 6-5
Behavior Log Form

169

INDIVIDUALIZED EDUCATION
PROGRAM MEETINGS

The *individualized education program* (IEP) mandated by Public Law 94-142 is central to providing effective education and related services to exceptional children. Public Law 94-142 reaffirmed the legitimate and essential role of parents in the education of their exceptional children, requiring that parents be active participants in the development, approval, and evaluation of their children's individualized education program. Specifically, parents participate with professionals in the assessment, planning, approval, placement, and evaluation processes. They may also participate actively in implementing their children's education program and related services.

The IEP meeting is the vehicle that brings parents and professionals together in a formal setting to plan the exceptional child's program. Crawford (1978) indicated that the following people attend the meeting:

1. An administrator of the local school district or special education district who can assure the availability of necessary resources (staff, programs, funds)

2. The teacher primarily responsible for the exceptional child's education, who is qualified to assess the skills, educational programs, and related services the child needs

3. The child, if parents and professionals consider it appropriate

4. The parents, who are ultimately responsible for the child's welfare and who possess a wealth of information and experience pertinent to the meeting

5. Others with important information and expertise, subject to parents' and professionals' approval.

Losen and Diament (1978), on the other hand, suggested limiting the number of professional staff to avoid overwhelming parents. Scanlon, Arick, and Phelps (1980) found that in practice, only the special education teacher and mother attended 75 percent of the meetings they analyzed. When other people did attend, their roles were perceived as more important and they may be more influential in decision making than the parents and special teachers.

Gilliam and Coleman (1981) found that parents were perceived as low in actual contribution and influence in IEP meetings. Psychologists were most influential in the diagnostic portion of the meetings, the special educator in planning and implementation of the program, the special education director in placement decisions, and the special education supervisor in assuring due process. Parents tended to be passive, serving as listeners and "consenters."

The IEP written at the meeting is "a documented agreement between all parties. It sets forth in clear terms the provisions of certain services" (Crawford 1978, 2). McAfee and Vergason (1979) suggested that current legislation is weaker than it could be because the IEP is not a contractual agreement between parents and professionals. Currently, the professional alone is responsible for initiating and fulfilling the terms of the IEP. McAfee and Vergason suggested that if the IEP became a contract outlining professionals' and parents' responsibilities, parent-teacher cooperation would be more effective and thus improve the child's education and related services program.

Both the IEP concept and the IEP meeting are unfamiliar to the vast majority of parents, especially parents who have just learned about their children's exceptionality. Thus, to avoid inefficient use of time at the meeting, the teacher should prepare the parents. Several authors have suggested that parents receive the following preparation for the IEP meeting: (Lusthaus and Lusthaus 1979; Winslow 1977; Bauer 1981):

1. Adequate notice of the meeting

2. An opportunity to review the child's educational records with a competent professional familiar with the information

3. A meeting agenda stating the session objectives, discussion topics, and questions to be addressed to the parents

4. A list of the people to attend the meeting and descriptions of their positions and functions

5. Information on obtaining an independent or supplemental assessment of their child if they so desire

6. Information on who may accompany them to the meeting (the child, an attorney, an interpreter)

7. A list of the materials they may wish to bring.

Winslow suggested that parents maintain a notebook recording informal notes on the child's behavior, formal observations, significant changes and differences in the child, and treatments attempted. In addition, parents can file in the notebook copies of all records, test results, and reports, as well as the child's interests, hobbies, likes and dislikes, skills, weaknesses, family, and friends.

Before the IEP meeting, parents should talk to their children about their feelings about school, the teacher, and peers. They may also wish to ask their child whether they want to attend the meeting. Gillespie and Turnbull (1983) suggested that parents and teacher consider three factors before inviting a child to participate in the meeting: Will the child understand the language used in the conference, and will he or she be able to communicate preferences and interests? How comfortable will the child feel, and how will he or she react to possible disagreements during the conference? Will the child understand the purpose of the conference and the possible benefit of his or her attendance?

Uninitiated parents may benefit from talking with other parents of exceptional children who have participated in IEP meetings. They may also wish to observe their children in the classroom and discuss the child and his or her educational performance with the teacher. If a change in placement is under consideration, parents should visit the potential classroom and confer with the teacher.

Parents should prepare a list of the questions they wish to ask at the meeting. They should also clarify their personal short-term and long-term expectations for their child. This type of preparation is time-consuming and, on occasion, frustrating for parents inexperienced in exceptionality and special education. However, the more thorough their preparation, the greater the chance that the meeting will result in a responsive program.

Goldstein and Turnbull (1982) found that two actions are especially effective in encouraging parents to participate. The first is sending questions home to the parent, followed by a phone call for clarification. The second is including the school counselor in the conference as a parent advocate. These two strategies increased fathers' attendance at the conference and increased the parents' participation during the meeting.

During the meeting, parents should feel free to make comments, ask questions, and offer recommendations. Thus, teachers should be approachable, listen to parents' ideas, and communicate a sense of unity in working for the child. Teachers should also be flexible, adaptable, responsive to parents' needs, and sensitive to each parent's uniqueness (Swick, Flake-Hobson, and Raymond 1980). Professionals are responsible for seeing that the education and related service program responds directly to the child's assessed needs and that the child is to be placed in the least restrictive environment in which he or she can be effectively educated. Parents must be sure they have a complete understanding of their child's educational program and related services, including who is to provide the agreed-upon services.

Shevin (1983) stated that too often professionals focus more on obtaining parents' signatures on the appropriate line by the correct date than on encouraging them to participate fully in decision making for their children. He described four typical levels of parent participation at IEP meetings. The first level is that of uninformed consent, in which parents agree to the IEP without sufficient information on the risks, implications, and alternatives. In this situation, the teacher may outline IEP goals, ask parents if they have any questions, request that they sign the IEP, and take the signature as consent. Professionals typically present only positive possible outcomes in such cases, omitting programming alternatives.

Shevin's second level is uninformed participation, whereby parents are requested to identify goals for the teacher to implement but the parents are provided with no information on which to base their decisions. The third level is informed consent. Here parents fully understand the rationale behind the program, its potential benefits and risks, and available programming alternatives, but are not really full participants because the professionals view them as "informed laypersons" who can either consent or not.

Shevin's final level of participation is informed participation, which involves parents in identifying educational priorities, developing instructional strategies, and reviewing and modifying goals. This level of interaction develops continuity between home and school in the child's program, provides parents with information about resources and alternatives, and yields more appropriate and feasible goals than lesser degrees of participation. It also guarantees the child strong advocates, the parents, on his or her educational team.

Shevin suggested a procedure for assuring parent involvement in goal setting.

1. The teacher identifies and clarifies the parents' personal values.

2. Parents and teacher brainstorm alternative approaches.

3. Parents and teacher set priorities for the ideas generated during the brainstorming session.

4. Participants explore available and potential resources.

5. Participants specify the period in which goals are to be achieved or reassessed.

The IEP meeting can be a valuable learning experience for parents. They learn a great deal about their child, special education and related services, placements, professionals, and themselves. In addition, they learn the answers to these questions (Lusthaus and Lusthaus 1979):

■ What are the professionals' views of the child's special needs?

■ How do they define the child's strengths and weaknesses?

■ What do they consider the child's current level of performance?

■ What are the possible placements for the child?

■ What potential problems exist in each placement? What solutions exist to these problems?

■ What potential benefits does each placement offer?

■ What do meeting participants think is the best placement for the child?

■ If the placement is new, when will it begin and how long will it last? How will the transition take place?

■ What are the goals for the child in this placement?

■ Who will determine if the goals are attained? How and when?

■ What related services (speech therapy, for example) will the child receive in this placement? When will each service begin and how long will it last? How will meeting participants evaluate the usefulness of these services?

■ What percentage of time will the child spend in special education and what percentage in regular education?

■ Who in the school is responsible for the child's progress?

■ How and when will the effectiveness of the placement and the program be evaluated?

■ How do the professionals think the parents can help in the child's educational program?

■ Who in the school system is responsible for communicating the child's progress to parents? How and when will progress reports take place?

■ To whom should the parent convey concerns about the child's education?

At the end of the meeting, parents should either receive or arrange to receive a copy of the child's individualized education program.

Morgan (1982) provided the following guidelines for parental involvement in the IEP process:

1. Parents should participate in the process as much as they want to and are able to.

2. Schools should deal with parents on a program level rather than a legal level.

3. Professionals should not view parent participation as an intrusion but as a help in controlling arbitrary evaluation, placement, and instruction.

Parents should remain calm, cool, and collected during the IEP meeting to preserve the spirit of cooperation. However, they should not allow professionals to intimidate them and dominate the meeting, or to do all the planning and assume responsibility for all services. Nor should parents settle for inadequate or inappropriate services for their child. Clearly, parents' responsibilities do not end with the meeting, for they should monitor implementation of the child's educational program as well, continuing to meet with and otherwise communicate with those responsible for service to the child.

HOME VISITS

Home visits by teachers are increasingly common. Indeed, many elementary and secondary school teachers are discovering that annual home visits are an expected part of their jobs. The practice is standard in many special education and preschool programs.

Boards of education and school administrative personnel are demonstrating greater willingness to adjust school schedules to accommodate home visits. A few schools provide time for teachers to prepare, conduct, and evaluate home visits, sometimes employing substitute teachers or dismissing classes to permit visits during school time. Some school districts provide transportation, pay mileage, or offer escorts to teachers making home visits.

A home visit helps the teacher get to know the child's family, environment, and culture better in order to serve both child and parents more effectively. A conference at home is an occasion for the teacher to meet the other members of the child's educational team—mother, father, siblings, grandparents, relatives, and other people living with the family (Hymes 1974). Teachers can use home visits for several purposes: information gathering, reporting the child's school performance, problem solving, preliminary discussions for the formal IEP meeting, and parent training.

Because the home conference takes place in the child's natural environment, the teacher's careful observation can often answer questions about the child's behavior and academic achievement, particularly the quality of the interactions between the child and other people in the household. In the home setting, the teacher can express concerns about the child directly in a face-to-face discussion; because the parents are in a familiar and secure environment during the home conference, they are more willing to express concerns about the child, teacher, and school (Rutherford and Edgar 1979).

Children usually enjoy teacher visits. Young children in particular see a visit by the teacher as a very special and exciting occasion. Children are eager to have the teacher meet their parents and brothers and sisters, see their bedrooms, and share the delight of personal treasures. They like to tell their friends and classmates about the visit, for it makes them feel important (Croft 1979). Before the conference itself begins, parent and teacher must decide whether the child should participate.

Parents' reactions vary. Some parents are very pleased by the visit and welcome the teacher into their homes. Others are reluctant to permit a visit. A few become annoyed and angry at this attempt to invade their privacy. Those families who do not accept a visit may cite illness or death in the family, a previous appointment, an emergency, the demands of work, or other reasons. Some parents will never feel free to tell the teacher their reason. However, the teacher should accept the parents' stated reason. Time and patience may eventually make the parents more receptive to the idea.

If parents are reluctant to participate in a home conference, Croft (1979) suggested several things a teacher could do:

1. Become acquainted with the parents on neutral territory, such as a park, a coffee shop, a community center, or a church

2. Establish a positive relationship before requesting a home visit

3. Discuss the purposes and advantages of a home visit

4. Enlist the assistance of a third party respected by the parents, such as a friend, neighbor, or minister

5. Focus the proposed visit on a subject of special interest to the parents.

Hymes (1974) suggested that a teacher guided by common sense, politeness, and friendliness—in other words, who acts normally—will have little difficulty arranging and conducting a home visit. He advised treating the home conference as one part of the child's total educational program, not to be emphasized disproportionately.

A teacher should never make an unannounced visit to a child's home. An advance telephone call or note can establish a time convenient for parents (preferably both parents) and teacher.

When teachers schedule a visit, they should tell parents the purpose of the conference and let them know if they must prepare or have specific information or questions ready for the discussion. Teachers should let parents know approximately how long the visit will last and be careful not to overstay their welcome. They should recognize when it is time to end the conference and then do so promptly and politely.

At the beginning of a visit, teachers should talk informally with parents and child for a few minutes to establish a friendly tone and reduce parents' anxiety. At all times, teachers must remember that they are guests and avoid judging affairs and conditions in the home. A home conference is not an inspection tour. Parents will have greater confidence in the teacher if they know the content of the discussion will be confidential as well. Marion (1979) urged teachers to dress properly and conduct themselves with dignity in the child's home. Many minority group families view teachers as extremely important people in the community, deserving of honor and respect, unless they prove otherwise.

Home visits do have disadvantages. They are time-consuming and often inconvenient for both parents and teachers. Both parties must prepare for the visit. However, the many advantages of meeting on the child's home ground generally outweigh the disadvantages.

SPECIAL ISSUES

The Exceptional Child's Participation

Interest in three-way conferences—including parents, teacher, and child—has grown in recent years. This trend reflects parents' renewed participation in their child's formal education, the growing recognition of the child as an active participant in the educational planning process, and recent legislation mandating parent involvement in decision making for their exceptional children's individualized education programs.

Hogan suggested that children should attend and participate in conferences because "it is the child who has the greatest investment and the most important involvement in the conference" (1975, 311). Hogan's statement reflects two years' feedback from teachers of first through fifth grades in an 800-student elementary school. McAleer (1978) and Carberry (1975) confirmed this belief, though Carberry suggested that children below third-grade level would probably not benefit significantly from conference participation.

Children benefit in several ways from three-way conferences:

1. They become aware that their parents and teacher are interested in their welfare and see them work cooperatively.

2. They hear firsthand the teacher's and parents' evaluation of their performance.

3. They feel involved in efforts toward personal achievements.

4. They sharpen their perceptions of parents' and teachers' problems and concerns.

5. They develop a task-oriented view of improving performance.

Children excluded from the parent-teacher conference are less likely to learn responsibility for personal behavior and achievement; parents and teacher tend to assume total responsibility for the child's learning. Excluded children also become curious about what the parents and teacher are saying about them in the conference and become anxious unnecessarily. Children receive information about the conference either secondhand from their parents or teacher or not at all. When they do receive information, it may mispresent or distort the discussion, or they may misinterpret it. Such miscommunication can cause conflict among the three parties.

Occasionally, parents resist including their child in the conference. Their reluctance may stem from various reasons:

1. They expect the child's presence to inhibit their behavior.

2. They fear their child will expose private family information during the conference.

3. They are unsure they can express themselves positively with their child present.

4. They fear their child's anxiety will be too high if he or she has to participate in a personal evaluation.

Teachers can discuss such concerns with parents before including the child in the conference. They should never include the child over parents' objections, however.

According to Hogan (1975), children generally want to participate in conferences because they can show their work to their parents, hear their teacher's evaluation of them, and receive positive reinforcement from the teacher with their parents present. Those children who do not want to participate in a conference usually fear their parents' reactions to the teacher's report or fear their parents will focus entirely on negative issues.

Freeman (1975) encouraged teachers to carefully prepare children for three-way conferences by taking the following steps:

1. Meeting with the children early in the school year to encourage them to select one or two personal goals and to inform them that they will discuss these goals in a three-way conference with their parents

2. Role playing a conference with the children

3. Conducting a preliminary teacher–child conference to tell the children what the parents will hear and to reach a consensus on the material the teacher will and will not present to parents.

After the three-way conference, the teacher should talk with the children and telephone the parents to determine their evaluation.

Parents, too, benefit from their children's presence in a three-way conference:

1. They sharpen their understanding of the problems concerning their children and the teacher.

2. They become aware of their children and the teacher as individuals and see how they relate to each other.

3. They develop greater understanding of their role in their children's development.

Three-way conferences help teachers in their work in several ways:

1. They gain greater understanding of the parents' and children's problems and concerns.

2. They get a feel for how parents and children interact.

3. They have everyone together at one time to simplify planning and communication.

Three-way conferences are especially appropriate for progress reports (Glasser 1969; Carberry 1975; Hogan 1975) and education and behavior management program planning sessions (Freeman 1975; McAleer 1978). Like all conferences, the three-way conference requires careful planning, preparation, and organization. The teacher must select a manageable conference goal, and collect the information needed to discuss it. As always, the teacher's observations and recommendations should be positive. Moreover, the teacher should involve both the parents and the child in the discussion, actively listening to their messages and responding appropriately. According to Carberry (1975), the teacher's empathy, nonpossessive warmth, and genuineness are essential ingredients of a successful three-way conference. Freeman (1975) suggested that three-way conferences incorporate formal contracting procedures as a means of recording agreed-upon academic and behavior goals and providing impetus for all parties to fulfill their obligations.

Negative Reactions to Conferencing

Parents' reactions to conference requests depend on their personalities and life conditions, the child's exceptionality, their awareness of and experience with the exceptionality, their past experiences in conferences with school personnel, and the quality and circumstances of the request. According to Losen and Diament (1978), some parents become angry when invited to a parent-teacher conference, often for one of the following reasons:

1. They received little warning from the teacher of their child's academic or behavioral difficulty.

2. Previous information led them to believe their child's problem was either resolved or caused by another child or the teacher.

3. Past experiences with the school, either in their own childhoods or their attempts in seeking help for their child, have been negative.

4. They have a negative attitude toward the school or education in general.

5. They cannot attend fully to their child's problem because of personal or family circumstances.

Teachers must respond appropriately to parents' anger, avoiding meeting anger with anger, if they are to encourage positive and productive communication. Prudent teachers acknowledge the parents' anger and express concern, perhaps suggesting a meeting in the immediate future to discuss the parents' feelings. In addition, teachers can assure parents they will personally investigate their concerns before meeting with them.

The key to working effectively with angry parents is to focus on the present. It is avoiding unproductive discussions of past errors and attempting to focus parents' attention on what can be done *now* and in the *future* to help the child (Wallbrown and Meadows 1979; Carberry 1975). "Active listening" skills are particularly important (Gordon 1970); teachers should encourage parents to "talk out" their anger by using open-ended questions, neutral responses, and brief pauses (Table 6-2).

TABLE 6-2 *Conferring with Angry Parents*

Do	*Don't*
Listen	Argue
Write down what they say	Defend or become defensive
When they slow down, ask them what else is bothering them	Promise things you can't produce
Exhaust their list of complaints	Own problems that belong to others
Ask them to clarify complaints that are too general	Raise your voice
Show them the list of complaints and ask if it is complete	Belittle or minimize the problem
Ask for suggestions for solving the problem	
Write down suggestions	
As much as possible, mirror their body posture	
As they speak louder, speak softer	

Source: University of New Mexico 1979.

In addition to angry parents, the professional must confer with other difficult parents, such as self-centered parents, passive-resistive parents, overwhelmed parents, and denying parents (Carberry 1975; Losen and Diament 1978). Self-centered parents perceive the world only as it affects them and their well-being and comfort. Teachers must help these parents see their children as separate from them. When conferencing with self-centered parents, professionals can emphasize their children's individuality, highlighting strengths and weaknesses, for example.

Passive-resistive parents can be difficult in conferences for they reject any and all recommendations. They might state that a neighbor or friend already tried the recommended technique without success. The best approach with such parents is to involve them in all planning, using their recommendations whenever possible.

Some parents are overwhelmed by personal, marital, and family problems and are unable to attend to the child's problem. In such cases, the teacher can listen to the parents' difficulties, reschedule the conference if possible, and refer the parents to a trained professional.

Teachers must also learn to communicate with parents who are unable to keep a confidence by discouraging gossip about other children and parents, guarding information and impressions the parents could use against others. In conferences, teachers should politely but firmly keep the parents' attention on their child and their role as parents.

Some parents deny that their child has a problem, adopting a unique perspective that convinces them they are right. In such cases, teachers should avoid arguing with the parents, instead raising their awareness by inviting them to observe their child in the classroom and review tests, assignments, and other evidence of actual performance.

More frequently than most teachers wish to admit, they work with punitive, abusive, and neglectful parents. It is difficult to avoid alienation from these parents, for psychological or physical child abuse raises teachers' feelings of anger and righteous indignation. Nonetheless, direct expression of these feelings is harmful to the child and the parent. Teachers who can control their anger are in a better position to help parents recognize the harmfulness of their behavior and encourage them to seek professional counseling. Many punitive parents have never learned to control their children in nonabusive ways; most likely they were abused as children. Punitive parents often suffer from severe pathologies that impede rational thinking and behavior.

In the United States, many people, through no fault of their own, lack the education, training, money, and other resources to provide for their children. Teachers must recognize that neglectful parents may have little choice but to neglect their children. These parents' primary need is practical help and guidance from the teacher.

SUMMARY

This chapter presents several formats for effective parent-teacher conferences: progress reports, problem-solving, and behavior management training conferences. The discussion focuses on the prerequisites for a successful conference in each case and details procedures that can help teachers plan and conduct the conferences. The chapter reviews the individualized education program meeting as a special type of conference and outlines parents' and teachers' roles. In addition, it discusses the advantages of home visits, which have become more common in recent years. Final sections of the chapter look at two conferencing issues: including the child in three-way conferences and coping with parents' anger and other negative reactions to conferences.

A major theme of the chapter is the importance of conferencing skills in the special education teacher's arsenal. Teachers need interpersonal skills as well as administrative and organizational skills to get maximum benefit from the conference.

EXERCISES AND DISCUSSION TOPICS

1. Plan, conduct, and evaluate a series of three progress report conferences. You may confer with the parent of an exceptional child you know or use a case in Appendix B.

2. With the members of your study group, discuss the "dos and don'ts" for teachers conducting a progress report conference. Do you

agree or disagree with the recommendations? Why? Can you add to the list?

3.   Plan, conduct, and evaluate a series of three problem-solving conferences. Apply one of the following models: behavior modification, communication, assertiveness. You may confer with the parents of an exceptional child you know or use a case in Appendix B.

4.   Plan, conduct, and evaluate a series of six behavior management training conferences. Train the parents of an exceptional child you know or use one of the cases in Appendix B.

5.   Conduct a psychosituational assessment interview with the parent of an exceptional child, or role play the interview using a case in Appendix B. With the parent's permission, ask a colleague familiar with the interviewing method to observe the interview and critique your performance.

6.   To familiarize yourself with the "Behavior Log Form," use it for one week to record a personal behavior of relatively high frequency. Graph your results. Explain the results to a colleague. Plan an intervention to change your behavior.

7.   Plan, conduct, and evaluate a home visit. You may visit the parents of an exceptional child you know or role play a visit using a case in Appendix B.

8.   Research the advantages and disadvantages of the three-way conference for child, parent, and teacher. Discuss or present your findings with the members of your study group.

9.   Plan, conduct, and evaluate a three-way conference. You may confer with a parent and child you know or role play the conference using a case in Appendix B.

10.   Carefully study the sections of this chapter on the IEP meeting, the sections on rights and responsibilities in Chapter Three, and the rules and regulations governing the IEP in your state, commonwealth, or province. Interview a special education teacher, a parent, an administrator, and/or a psychologist about the role of IEP committee members. Ask them to discuss with you their and others' roles "ideally" and "in reality."

11.   Plan, conduct, and evaluate an IEP meeting. You may confer with a committee familiar to you or role play meetings using a case in Appendix B.

12. Conduct a discussion of the following topics in your study group:

■ Negative reactions I have had as an interviewee

■ Negative reactions I have had as an interviewer

■ My role in my own and others' negative reactions.

REFERENCES

Bailard, V., and R. Strang. 1964. *Parent-teacher conferences*. New York: McGraw-Hill.

Bandura, A. 1969. *Principles of behavior modification*. New York: Holt, Rinehart and Winston.

Barsch, R. H. 1969. *The parent-teacher partnership*. Reston, Va.: The Council for Exceptional Children.

Bauer, A. M. 1981. *Program for parents of severely handicapped students— A plan*. Edwardsville, Ill.: Southern Illinois University.

Berkowitz, B. P., and A. M. Graziano. 1972. Training parents as behavior therapists: A review. *Behavior Research and Therapy* 10 (4):297–317.

Bersoff, D. N., and R. M. Grieger II. 1971. An interview model for the psychosituational assessment of children's behavior. *American Journal of Orthopsychiatry* 41 (3):483–93.

Blackard, M. K., and E. T. Barsch. 1982. Parents' and professionals' perceptions of the handicapped child's impact on the family. *Journal of the Association for the Severely Handicapped* 7 (2):62–69.

Carberry, H. H. 1975. Parent-teacher conferences. *Today's Education*, Jan./Feb., 67–69.

Crawford, D. 1978. Parent involvement in instructional planning. *Focus on Exceptional Children* 10 (7):1–5.

Croft, D. J. 1979. *Parents and teachers: A resource book for home, school, and community relations*. Belmont, Calif.: Wadsworth.

Duncan, L. W., and P. W. Fitzgerald. 1969. Increasing the parent-child communication through counselor-parent conferences. *Personnel and Guidance Journal* 47 (6):514–17.

Farr, R. 1977. When parents come to call. *Early Years,* Feb., 56–58.

Freeman, J. 1975. *Three-way conferencing. Teacher* 93 (4):40–42.

Gaines, E. 1976. Reinforce that home-school link. *Instructor,* Oct., 113.

Gillespie, E. B., and A. P. Turnbull. 1983. It's my IEP! Involving students in the planning process. *Teaching Exceptional Children* 16 (1):26–29.

Gilliam, J. E., and M. C. Coleman. 1981. Who influences IEP committee decisions? *Exceptional Children* 47 (8):642–44.

Glasser, W. 1969. *Schools without failure*. New York: Harper and Row.

Goldstein, S., and A. P. Turnbull. 1982. Strategies to increase parent participation in IEP conferences. *Exceptional Children* 48 (4):360–61.

Gordon, T. 1970. *Parent effectiveness training*. New York: Peter H. Wyden.

Hogan, J. R. 1975. The three-way conference: Parent, teacher, child. *The Elementary School Journal* 75 (5):311–15.

Hymes, J. L., Jr. 1974. *Effective home-school relations*. Sierra Madre, Calif.: Southern California Association for the Education of Young Children.

Instructional Materials Center. n.d. *Parent conference guidelines*. Springfield, Ill.: Instructional Materials Center, Office of the Superintendent of Public Instruction.

Kean, J. 1975. *Successful integration: The parents' role*. The Exceptional Parent 5 (5):35–40.

Kelly, E. J. 1974. *Parent-teacher interactions: A special educational perspective*. Seattle: Special Child Publications.

Kroth, R. L. 1972. Facilitating educational progress by improving parent conference. *Focus on Exceptional Children* 4 (7):1–9.

Kroth, R. L. 1975. *Communicating with parents of exceptional children: Improving parent-teachers relationships*. Denver: Love Publishing.

Kroth, R. L. and R. L. Simpson. 1977. *Parent conferences: A teaching strategy*. Denver: Love Publishing.

Long, A. 1976. Easing the stress of parent-teacher conferences. *Today's Education* Sept./Oct., 84–85.

Losen, S. M., and B. Diament. 1978. *Parent conferences in the schools: Procedures for developing effective partnership*. Boston: Allyn and Bacon.

Lusthaus, C., and E. Lusthaus. 1979. When is a child ready for mainstreaming? *The Exceptional Parent* 9 (5):R2–R4.

McAfee, J. K., and G. A. Vergason. 1979. Parent involvement in the process of special education: Establishing the new partnership. *Focus on Exceptional Children* 11 (2):1–15.

McAleer, I. M. 1978. The parent, teacher and child as conference partners. *Teaching Exceptional Children* 10 (4):103–5.

Marion, R. 1979. Minority parent involvement in the IEP process: A systematic model approach. *Focus on Exceptional Children* 10 (8):1–15.

Morgan, D. P. 1982. Parental participation in the IEP process: Does it enhance appropriate education? *Exceptional Education Quarterly* 3 (2):33–40.

Nardine, F. E. 1974. Parents as a teaching resource. *Volta Review* 76:172–77.

O'Dell, S. 1974. Training parents in behavior modification: A review. *Psychological Bulletin* 81 (7):418–33.

Parent-school conferences: Guidelines and objectives. 1979. *The Exceptional Parent* 9 (4):E19–E21.

The parent-teacher conference. 1973. *The Exceptional Parent* 3 (4): 40–44.

Patterson, G. R. 1969. Behavioral techniques based on social learning: An additional base for developing behavior modification technologies. In *Behavior therapy: Appraisal and status,* ed. C. M. Franks, 341–74. New York: McGraw-Hill.

Ross, A. O. 1972. Behavior therapy. In *Manual of child psychopathology,* ed. B. B. Wolman. New York: McGraw-Hill.

Rutherford, R. B., Jr., and E. Edgar. 1979. *Teachers and parents: A guide to interaction and cooperation.* Abr. ed. Boston: Allyn and Bacon.

Scanlon, C. A., J. Arick, and N. Phelps. 1981. Participation in the development of the IEP: Parents' perspective. *Exceptional Children* 47 (5):373–74.

Schopler, E., and R. J. Reichler. 1971. Parents as cotherapists in the treatment of psychotic children. *Journal of Autism and Childhood Schizophrenia* 1:87–102.

Shea, T. M. 1978. *Teaching children and youth with behavior disorders.* St. Louis: C. V. Mosby.

Shea, T. M., W. R. Whiteside, E. G. Beetner, and D. L. Lindsey. 1974. *Microteaching module: Psychosituational interview.* Edwardsville, Ill.: Southern Illinois University.

Shevin, M. 1983. Meaningful parental involvement in long-range educational planning for disabled children. *Education and Training of the Mentally Retarded* 18:17–21.

Stewart, D. 1973. How to get parents on your side. *Teacher* 91 (3):16–19.

Swick, K. J., C. Flake-Hobson, and G. Raymond. 1980. The first step—Establishing parent-teacher communication in the IEP conference. *Teaching Exceptional Children* 12 (4):144–45.

Truax, C. B., and D. Wargo. 1966. Human encounters that change behavior for better or worse. *American Journal of Psychotherapy* 20: 499–520.

University of New Mexico, Institute for Parent Involvement. 1979. *Tips for teachers conferring with angry parents—Dealing with aggression.*

Walker, J. E., and T. M. Shea. 1984. *Behavior management: A practical approach for educators.* 3d ed. St. Louis: C. V. Mosby.

Wallbrown, F. H., and F. B. Meadows. 1979. Working with angry parents. *The Directive Teacher* 2 (2):10, 29.

Winslow, L. 1977. Parent participation. In *A primer on individualized education programs for handicapped children,* ed. S. Torres. Reston, Va.: The Foundation for Exceptional Children.

Protocol Psychosituational Interview One

Mr. S arrives at the conference alone because his wife "wasn't feeling well" and did not wish to attend.

Teacher: Good afternoon, Mr. S.

Mr. S: Hello Mrs. M. How are you?

T: Fine, thank you. Glad to meet you. Sit down, please. I am Mark's special education teacher this year, and I'd like to ask you some questions about Mark. Let's see. He's nine years old and he's presently in Mrs. Lee's class, that's third grade.

Mr. S: Yes.

T: Mrs. Lee has told me that he does rather well in some of his subjects; he's particularly good in math. He enjoys that very much. He has a little bit of difficulty with reading and writing, however. And she says that she has some problems with his leaving his seat frequently. He's rather active in the classroom.

Mr. S: Yeah, she's not the only one that has problems with him.

T: I see.

Mr. S: He's a bad boy. We have trouble with him at home all the time.

T: Oh, you do.

Mr. S: Yeah, I'm . . . well, I know Mrs. Lee too because my wife tells me that Mrs. Lee calls and the principal calls about him and sending him home from school all the time. My wife should be here today. She really spends most of the time with Mark, but she didn't want to come, she wasn't feeling very good. I drive a truck and am on the road most of the time. I don't see much of him.

T: It was very nice of you to come today.

Mr. S: Well . . . thank you.

T: I'd like to ask you some more questions about Mark's behavior at home. You said that he seems to . . . you have some trouble with him, too. Would you explain that to me a little?

Mr. S: He fights all the time. He's just always getting in fights, and like I said, I'm gone a lot but my wife tells me that she has trouble with him all the time. Fights with his brothers and every once in a while he fights with the neighbors. He's just always getting into trouble—that seems to be about it.

T: Fighting seems to be the biggest problem.

Mr. S: Oh, yeah, he fights all the time—always in trouble.

T: Could you give me an example of how one of these fights occurs.

Mr. S: Well, my wife was telling me last night that he and the older boy were playing Chinese checkers and he lost. Mark lost and Bill picked up a handful of . . . not Bill, but Mark picked up a handful of marbles and threw them at Bill and went at him with his fists.

T: He became so agitated by losing that he started a fight.

Mr. S: He can't lose. He just goes . . . losing, he fights—that's just automatic, one, two. He just can't stand to lose. As long as he's winning, he gets along fine.

T: Are there any cases you can tell me about when he wins—how he acts?

Mr. S: Well, I take the boys fishing in the spring and in the summer.

T: That's nice.

Mr. S: Oh yeah, I like to fish. Actually it's comforting and it's lots of fun. We enjoy it being out, and usually Mark, when he goes with us, he catches most of the fish.

T: Oh, really.

Mr. S: Oh yeah, and yeah he has a good time then, bragging around and measuring, comparing the size of his fish and the other boys' fish and boasting about it. Yeah, he likes that.

T: He doesn't seem to fight much when you go fishing, does he.

Mr. S: Well, it all depends now if one of the other boys catches a bigger fish, or more fish, then he'll fight. He'll go at them, he'll hit them, holler at them—yeah, he can't stand to lose.

T: But if he's winning and especially when he's fishing, he must enjoy that . . . to go with you.

Mr. S: Yeah, he likes to go fishing. We have a good time.

T: Do you ever go with him by yourself?

Mr. S: We all go fishing. I tried to get my wife to go, but she doesn't care much for fishing. She doesn't like to bait the hook; you know how women are.

T: Oh yes. So fishing is one thing that Mark really enjoys, especially when he's winning, and then he's pretty good at it from what you say.

Mr. S: That's right.

T: He must have had some good training. Let's talk about the fighting that goes on at home. Could you tell me a little bit

	more about it? You said that if losing is involved, then he seems to fight.
Mr. S:	Yeah, that's right.
T:	One example was with the Chinese checkers and his older brother. Could you give me any other examples of . . . ?
Mr. S:	Yeah, if he thinks one of the other kids gets more ice cream, like his younger brother, he'll poke him and start a fight. You know. It's really bad. My wife says that she's on him all the time at home and she has to spank him or send him out of the house or send him up to bed and it keeps going on. He's really a bad boy at home.
T:	And you say he fights all the time. It probably seems like it's all the time because it's rather upsetting.
Mr. S:	She's always complaining about it.
T:	Yeah. Do you have any idea of how often exactly this happens? Once a night, twice a night, once a week?
Mr. S:	Well, it may be two or three times a week.
T:	Two or three times a week?
Mr. S:	Yeah, about two or three times a week. Mainly because he wins the other two or three days.
T:	Oh, I see.
Mr. S:	Yeah, he's pretty good.
T:	On the winning days, he's really not that much of a problem.
Mr. S:	No problem. As long as he's winning, he gets along with everyone really well.
T:	Let's talk about these fights a little. You mentioned that he gets into almost real fisticuffs. Do you mean that he actually punches?
Mr. S:	Not almost. He really does. Punches. And he keeps punching until the kid gives up.
T:	That's how the fight usually is settled?
Mr. S:	That's how it's settled unless one of the adults steps in and stops it.
T:	By one of the adults, I assume you mean yourself or your wife.
Mr. S:	My wife is home most of the time; she does this. When I'm home, I'm watching television, and if he starts a ruckus, I get in there and grab him and shake him and I stop it right away. I don't let anything go on. I stop it unless it's a tight inning, and then I may wait until the action's over and then I stop it. But it doesn't stop until I stop it.
T:	You mentioned shaking him to stop it.
Mr. S:	Yeah, I shake him.
T:	Does that seem to work?
Mr. S:	Well, you know, shake them till their teeth rattle; that straightens them out. That's what my daddy always said.
T:	Do you use any other forms of punishment besides shaking?

Mr. S: Well, if that doesn't work, yeah. Sure, I spank them when I feel that I should, and sometimes I just send them out of the house.

T: How long do these fights last? Just until . . . someone gives up? Maybe a minute, two, five minutes?

Mr. S: If an adult is not there, sometimes they'll go on five or ten minutes, fifteen minutes. If an adult is there, of course the adult stops it. Or an older kid can stop it, but they usually like to watch the fight.

T: Do you think what you're doing—this shaking and spanking—has changed his behavior any? Has it stopped the fighting?

Mr. S: It stops it then.

T: It stops it for that time?

Mr. S: Yeah.

T: When he loses, he fights, and when he fights, it's physical. It's dangerous to the other person.

Mr. S: Sometimes he yells and just hollers and screams at the other kids. One time he hit his older brother with a chair because he was losing the fight. And I mean he really gets violent. He really wants to win.

T: These fights, even though they are violent, last sometimes less than five minutes, sometimes up to fifteen minutes?

Mr. S: Yeah, that's about right.

T: And they seem to happen two or three times a week?

Mr. S: Yeah, that's about right.

T: But it seems like otherwise, the other four or five days a week, he's really pretty agreeable and easy to get along with. Things seem to go all right as long as he's winning.

Mr. S: As long as things are going his way and nobody steps on him or steps on his toes, he's all right.

T: Fine. Most of the time you're dealing with Mark, is it a pleasant interaction or are there problems? Let's say, for the most part.

Mr. S: See, I'm not home very much, and when I'm at home I like to do what I like to do. I like to watch television and sports and so forth, and you know of course we do go fishing in the spring and summer and then we get along fine, and you know, unless of course someone catches more fish than he catches. But when I'm home I like to watch television. I really don't pay that much attention to the kids. But my wife says that, you know, some days he can be very nice, but most of the time he's a bad, rotten kid.

T: Well, I think maybe we should start to work on this fighting behavior. Maybe I could help you with some suggestions.

Mr. S: Well, I'll tell you we'd appreciate anything you could suggest.

T: Well, one thing I think would be a good idea is if you and your wife could keep what we call a log. We train our teachers to keep this. All you do is write down each day what day it is and whether or not there was a fight. Then what time the fight occurred and what the behavior was just before the fight happened and how it was resolved. So an example of this, which was done by another parent, would show that, say, Monday there was a fight, Tuesday nothing, Wednesday nothing, but Thursday there were two fights. If you and your wife together would keep this kind of log . . .

Mr. S: Well, I know what a log is; that's what I do because I'm a truck driver. We keep a log, and I can show my wife how to do it, but I can't guarantee she'll do it . . . but I can show her how and . . .

T: That would be very helpful.

Mr. S: Yeah, fine.

T: I think that you can probably explain it better than I could.

Mr. S: Probably so, right.

T: Then maybe in three weeks we'll make another appointment for an interview and you and your wife can come together.

Mr. S: Well, I'm not sure that I'll be able to make it 'cause I'm on the road, but I think if my wife has something to talk about and hold onto, why she'll probably be willing to come and chat with you.

T: Let's see if we can't arrange it for the three of us.

Mr. S: All right.

T: I'll do it at your convenience.

Mr. S: Okay, right.

T: And if you will bring in the log for the next three weeks of behavior. How many times he fights. We won't worry about anything else, just the fighting behavior. Until that time, I'd also like you maybe to take some time with Mark alone and let me know how it works out when you deal with him individually, apart from his brothers. Just once in a while. I realize that you're very busy, but that may give us some insights.

Mr. S: Kinda father-son talks.

T: That kind of thing; that might work out well.

Mr. S: I'll try that.

Source: Shea, Whiteside, Beetner, and Lindsey 1974.

Protocol Psychosituational Interview Two

Mrs. G, a Mexican–American parent, is accompanied to the conference by her nineteen-year-old daughter, Rosa, who serves as interpreter, and her three-year-old daughter, Luisa.

T:	Hello, Mrs. G, Rosa. Hi, Luisa. Don't you look happy today!
Rosa:	Hi.
T:	Thanks for coming, Mrs. G. And thank you, Rosa, for coming again to help us out. I really appreciate it.
Rosa:	No problem.
T:	Would you like me to get some puzzles or picture books for the baby, Mrs. G?
Mrs. G:	No. She'll be a good girl.
T:	I'm happy to say that since we last talked, Raffie is becoming more and more independent. His self-help skills are really improving.
Mrs. G:	Raffie is a good boy. He tries.
Rosa:	What kind of things has he learned to do?
T:	He's getting away from using the spoon for all foods, and is using his fork more neatly and without us reminding him.
Mrs. G:	He's eating lunch with a fork?
T:	Yes. He still sometimes pushes the food onto the fork with his fingers, but he's getting much neater and trying to use his fork when he should.
Rosa:	Do you think we should start giving him a fork at home?
T:	That would be great. I think he's ready to generalize his skill.
Rosa:	Generalize?
T:	Yes, that's what we call it when a student takes something he learned in school and begins to apply it in other places, like home.
Mrs. G:	What is generalize?
	(Rosa explains in Spanish.)
T:	Is Raffie doing better with his meals at home, too?
Mrs. G:	He does okay, except when my husband is on him.
Rosa:	Yes, he seems to do better when my dad's not around.
T:	What happens? Can you tell me about a time when he had a problem when his father was around?
Rosa:	Well, like at dinner. Dad's really noticed that Raffie is now doing more and more things by himself. He wants him to do more, to be more like other kids. So he asks him to do things he can't do, and then Raffie blows it, and then Dad gets mad.
T:	What kind of things does he ask him to do?
Rosa:	Well, like last night, Raffie asked for more milk. Dad was really impressed, the way he said please and all. So Mama got him more milk.

Mrs. G: He said "More milk, please" so clear! I got him more milk right away, but my husband said, "See he can do things for himself. He can get his own milk. Let him pour his own."

T: Did Raffie get the milk and pour it into his glass?

Rosa: Sure, in the glass, on himself, and all over the table, too.

T: Then what happened?

Mrs. G: My husband, he got mad. Not yelling mad, just mad. He left the table and went out on the steps.

Rosa: It's like, before Raffie started doing things by himself, and Mama just sort of took care of him, Dad could handle that. But now that Raffie's starting to do things by himself, and gets out with the other kids and talks for himself, Dad's having a harder time figuring out what to do.

T: He seems to be proud of Raffie's accomplishments.

Mrs. G: He's happy Raphael is talking and doing by himself.

Rosa: Yeah, but he thinks that because Raffie is doing better, he should be able to do a lot more than he can. It's like, now Raffie isn't going to be a baby forever, so he should start acting his age.

T: How do you feel about the progress Raffie's made, Mrs. G?

Mrs. G: He's working hard. It's hard now, he wants to do "by myself." Before, I always got him on the bus on time. Now you say let him dress himself and feed himself breakfast. I have to wake him up at six-thirty!

Rosa: He's doing these things by himself, but like it's almost easier to do them for him.

T: So, we seem to be at an awkward time with Raffie. He's showing you at home the things that he's learned at school, but he's not doing them proficiently enough to really help out.

Mrs. G: Again?
       (Rosa and Mrs. G converse briefly in Spanish.)

Rosa: So what do we do?

T: I think one thing we might try, in helping Mr. G with Raffie, is to make sure that I let him know what things Raffie is able to do by himself and the things he just isn't quite ready for.

Mrs. G: My husband won't come to school. As long as Raphael is with those slow kids, he won't come to school.

T: I'll make up a list of the things Raffie can do by himself. Do you think your husband would look at it?
       (Rosa and Mrs. G converse in Spanish.)

Rosa: You'd write up a list?

T: Right.

Rosa: And address it to my Dad? He doesn't like secondhand notes.

T: Fine.
       (Rosa and Mrs. G converse in Spanish.)

Rosa: We'll give it a shot. Just make sure that you don't say anything about Raffie being retarded. Just say how good he's doing and what he can do now.

T: Do you think I could give Mr. G a telephone call?

Mrs. G: Don't call him at work. He can't talk on the phone at work.

Rosa: That might be okay. Just don't say you're a special ed teacher or anything. And tell him how good Raffie's doing.

T: Fine. The other problem, the one about his doing things by himself, but more slowly, is something we can work on together if you'd like.

Rosa: Great! It takes him ages to dress, and he gets mad if anybody tries to help.

T: We'll begin to keep track of how long it takes him to do things. Could you time him at home?

Mrs. G: Time him?

(Rosa and Mrs. G converse briefly in Spanish.)

Rosa: We don't have a timer or anything.

T: Could you keep track on the clock?

Rosa: Sure, we can watch the clock.

T: Okay. When we meet next week, do you think you could bring in a list of the amounts of time that dressing and breakfast are taking?

Rosa: Sure.

T: When we have that information, we can begin to look at ways to decrease the time Raffie requires to dress and eat breakfast.

Mrs. G: You mean speed him up?

T: Yes, we'll try it.

Mrs. G: Good. You speed him up.

Rosa: I think Ms. F means *we'll* speed him up—all of us, right?

T: Right, Rosa.

CHAPTER SEVEN

GROUPS

Teachers frequently use groups to foster parent–teacher communication. Carefully designed group activities can have significant value for the participants, with ultimate benefit to the exceptional child. When organizing groups, teachers should have a clear idea of their purpose and plan the size and structure accordingly. This chapter discusses general issues of planning and conducting large and small parent–teacher involvement groups as an introduction to the discussion of specific types of groups in Chapter Eight.

Parent–teacher groups require more planning and preparation and often greater personal involvement by parents and teachers than do written and telephone communications or parent–teacher conferences. Personal involvement varies with group purpose. For example, a group designed to provide social–emotional support to parents requires a greater personal investment than does a group designed to transmit information to parents. Time and energy requirements are considerable, for successful groups require planning, preparation, and scheduling, as well as participation in and evaluation of group activities.

GROUP SIZE

Parents and teachers meet together in group settings for three basic purposes: to tranfer information, to teach and learn instructional, behavior management, or interpersonal communication techniques, and to give and receive social-emotional support. Whatever its primary purpose, however, every group will to some extent include all three elements.

Both large or small groups are effective forums for transmitting information. However, a small group is preferable for exchanging personal or highly specific information. Small groups are also well-suited for providing social-emotional support. Either a small group or large group can effectively provide training and instruction as long as the larger group offers a small instructor-to-member ratio.

Group processes and procedures vary with the purpose of the group as well. Structured processes are most appropriate for instruction and information exchange. Less structured processes, those that encourage interpersonal communication, are most appropriate for a support group.

Participants in large groups tend to be passive recipients of information and instruction, for the limited amount of time available to each individual and the complexity of communication networks restrict active participation. Small groups, on the other hand, allow discussion, cooperative problem solving, and expression of feelings.

By necessity, control of large group activities rests with a few people or one person. Frequently, a few people plan, organize, and conduct activities for the entire membership. Without this concentration of control, a large group may disintegrate. Small groups permit and encourage shared control among members.

The large group has several advantages and disadvantages. It allows teachers to transmit information quickly and easily to a relatively large number of people; however, the depth and specificity of the information is generally limited. Quiet, shy people may be more likely to attend large group meetings than small group gatherings because pressures to participate are limited. Thus, large group meetings may get information to people who would otherwise not receive it.

The large group is also an excellent means of motivating people to seek additional information, training, or assistance in small groups or individual conferences. A dynamic speaker, dramatic audiovisual presentation, panel discussion, product or technique demonstration, or informal mingling before and after the meeting may all pique attendee's interest in further participation.

A major disadvantage of the large group format is its inability to respond to the needs of individual attendees. It is usually difficult to respond in depth to questions and comments. Another disadvantage is potential difficulty finding an adequate facility or scheduling dates and times acceptable to all participants.

The major advantage of the small group is its suitability for addressing participants' specific concerns. The informality and cohesiveness of small groups encourage interpersonal communication and allow flexibility in selecting locations and times.

On the negative side, small group activities require extensive planning and can be time-consuming. Small groups often find it difficult to obtain speakers because presenters are reluctant to devote time to a small audience. Perhaps the greatest danger is the formation of subgroups and cliques within small groups, which may work at cross-purposes to the majority of the members. Cohesiveness among members is an essential ingredient of small group success (Karnes and Zehrbach 1972).

When is a group small? When is it large? Small group size may range from three people, the parents and teacher, to perhaps twenty people. However, the parent-teacher ratio may be more important than the number of group members; small group processes appear most effective in groups maintaining a six-to-one parent-teacher ratio. Any group that exceeds a twelve-to-one parent-teacher ratio is really a large group. Group size depends on the group's purpose, the leader's strengths, and most important, the members' wishes and needs (Table 7–1).

This chapter and Chapter 8 focus on parent-teacher groups, but many community organizations offer opportunities for parents in large and small groups. The Association for Children and Adults with Learning Disabilities offers groups helpful to parents of exceptional children, as do the National Association for Retarded Citizens, the Down's Syndrome Congress, the National Society for Children and Adults with Autism, the Spina Bifida Association of America, the Parent Advocacy Coalition of Educational Rights, and others. These organizations offer parents information, training, and support through large- and small-group activities. A listing of organizations and agencies offering ser-

TABLE 7-1 *Large and Small Group Characteristics*

	Large Groups	Small Groups
Depth of information	General	Specific
Demands of participation	Limited	Extensive
Purpose	General informational and instructional	Specific informational, instructional, and social-emotional
Potential for interpersonal communication	Limited	Frequent

vices to the parents of children with special needs is presented in Appendix C.

LARGE GROUPS

Planning

Careful, systematic planning is the key to a successful parent-teacher large group meeting or series of meetings (Croft 1979). Kroth (1975) suggested organizing a parent advisory committee—as representative of the population of potential participants as possible—to work with teachers in planning and publicizing group activities. The advisory committee would plan and conduct three or four large group meetings during a school year. Planning begins the moment parents and teachers sit down with pencil and paper to determine the meeting's purpose. Kroth itemized the following committee objectives:

1. To identify potential members and assess their needs and interests

2. To establish general and specific meeting objectives

3. To design or select methods of attaining the group's objectives

4. To determine criteria and measurements for ascertaining the meeting's effectiveness.

The committee conducts a needs assessment before the group organizes formally or begins programming. Several approaches are possible: a survey questionnaire, an extensively publicized orientation meeting for potential participants, or preliminary small-group sessions for representatives of potential constituencies. The assessment process continues throughout a series of meetings. Meeting organizers can set aside time at the end of each session to discuss members' interests for future meetings.

The assessment will lead to group objectives. Planners should state objectives clearly, establishing what members will be able to do or will have gained at the end of the group. For example, at the conclusion of the meeting, parents will have knowledge of the federal and state laws governing educational services for exceptional children.

Group activities are "the highways and signposts" the members travel to reach the objectives (Croft 1979). Activities may include lectures, discussions, social events, visits, film viewings, reading assignments, workshops, work projects, and so on. After the meetings, the advisory committee may use tests, checklists, rating scales, attendance rates, opinion surveys, or other means to evaluate the program's effectiveness and to modify it or plan additional programs.

To be effective, a parent advisory committee must have sufficient freedom to accomplish its objectives. Teachers and other professionals should resist the impulse to dominate the committee. Once the committee is operational, the teacher serves as an adviser.

As a rule, three or four well-attended and well-received large group meetings per year are more desirable than eight or nine monthly meetings that are hurriedly planned, poorly attended, and on topics irrelevant to participants. The committee is wise to schedule only enough meetings to attain the group's objectives.

Guidelines for Conducting Large Group Meetings

Planning and preparation are of little value if the meeting is at an inconvenient time, poorly publicized, inaccessible, disorganized, or inhospitable. Several authors have suggested guidelines for conducting an effective large group meeting (Karnes and Zehrbach 1972; Kroth 1975; Bailard and Strang 1964).

Participants should receive proper notification of the meeting via bulletins, newsletters, written invitations, or person-to-person or telephone communication. The first invitation should go out three or four weeks before the meeting to allow people to plan their schedules. A follow-up telephone call or note three or four days before the meeting is a helpful reminder. Teachers should take care that meeting invitations truly invite parents to attend and avoid a coercive tone.

Meetings should begin and end on time. If a business session is necessary, it should be brief; it should also be at the end of the meeting if the discussion is not relevant to most attendees. Meeting organizers should avoid soliciting fees and funds at the meeting unless absolutely necessary or pressuring members of the audience to sign up for committees.

Meeting sites should be appropriate for the group's purpose and size, with furniture suitable for adults (no children's desks or bleachers). The meeting location should also be accessible to those wishing to attend, including handicapped children and adults. If transportation is not readily available, meeting organizers can organize carpools. The committee should consider transportation issues when they issue invitations.

Planners may want to provide child care services near the meeting room to draw parents reluctant to hire babysitters. (It is often impossible to find a qualified babysitter for an exceptional child, and babysitters are in short supply on school days.) Volunteer high school and college students can provide child care services at the meeting facility.

All communication during meetings must emphasize the fact that parents and teachers are equals. Teachers and presenters should use commonly understood language, avoid technical terms and jargon, and define those unfamiliar terms that are necessary. The program should be well thought out so that it speaks directly to the audience's needs.

Audiovisual aides and demonstrations often help underscore the message of the program in attention-getting ways.

To establish an informal, friendly atmosphere, teachers should greet parents as they arrive at the meeting room door. This greeting should be personal, including a positive comment about the parents and their child and recognizing the parents' efforts to come and their potential contributions. Teachers should invite parents to complete name tags and may want to give them a written agenda and pencil and paper for notes.

After the formal program, time should be available for questions and discussion. By requesting written questions, the meeting leader can encourage shy members of the audience to contribute. Recognition of everyone who helped with the evening's activities is a good way to close the meeting. This time is also good for soliciting immediate feedback on the meeting using an evaluation form that is easy to understand and complete (Figure 7–1). Meeting organizers should plan a time for informal socializing and refreshments after the meeting. (Parents are often willing to contribute refreshments.)

FIGURE 7-1
Meeting Evlauation
Form

Date: _____

Meeting Subject: _____

Please circle the responses that best reflect your feelings about this meeting.

1. The subject was:	Not relevant	Somewhat relevant	Relevant	Very relevant
2. The information was:	Not useful	Somewhat useful	Useful	Very useful
3. The manner of presentation was:	Poor	Fair	Good	Very good
4. Audio visual materials and handouts were:	Poor	Fair	Good	Very good

5. Would you like more information on the subject?   Yes   No

6. Comments:

Thanks! By letting us know how you feel, we can better meet your needs.

Your Advisory Committee

Occasionally, a large group disintegrates because of dwindling membership, overplanning, lack of interest, unnecessary and inappropriate programs, boring presenters and presentations, inadequate opportunities for meaningful involvement, or domination by a few people. When confronted with this problem, Smith (Olson et al. 1976) successfully reactivated a group by taking the following steps:

1. Sending a notice to all parents about the problem

2. Inviting parents to vote whether to continue or discontinue the group

3. Asking parents to indicate the contributions they were willing to make if the majority of parents voted to continue the group

4. After an affirmative vote, reorganizing the group in line with parents' wishes and establishing a council composed of parents, teachers, and an administrator

5. Asking the council to write limited organizational guidelines authorizing five working committees: community relations, learning materials, construction and repair, fund raising, and classroom helpers

6. Appointing parents chairpersons of all committees

7. Conducting meetings only when called by the council or required by an emergency.

As a result of this revitalization, the working committees, functioning with relative independence, accomplished many necessary tasks, and many parents became involved in activities meaningful to them and beneficial to their children.

SMALL GROUPS

Planning

Small group programs can be effective for a variety of informational, instructional, and social-emotional purposes. However, planners should be aware that small groups are sometimes inappropriate ways to meet parents' needs. Kelly (1974) cited the following cases in which small group activities are inappropriate:

1. If the child's problem is unique and the parents are unable or unwilling to discuss it in a group setting

2. If a group setting inhibits the parents' behavior and ability to communicate

3. If the child's problem is a symptom of the parents' personal or marital problems

4. If the probable solution to the child's problem is highly specific and inappropriate for other group members.

Once they have established that small group activities are indeed desirable, parents and teachers must consider many of the same factors they would consider for large group meetings: goals and objectives, the physical setting, meeting time, length and frequency of meetings, group size, program, attendance, materials and equipment, refreshments, leader or facilitator qualifications and preparation time, transportation, and child care services (Dinkmeyer and McKay 1976). For small groups, determination of group size, selection of the leader, program sequence, and physical comfort can be especially important, however, for they will determine the climate for sharing ideas.

Facilities that are either too large or too small are not conducive to free-flowing communication among members, for example. The facility should also be free of artificial physical barriers—such as fixed seats, bleachers, and desks and chairs—that may inhibit face-to-face communication. Quiet and privacy are important, for a group cannot function effectively with interruptions by traffic sounds, activities in adjoining rooms, or people passing through the meeting room.

Generally, evenings are the best times to find both mother and father free to attend meetings. Nonworking parents of school-age children may find it convenient to attend a meeting during the school day, and some parents of preschool children can attend meetings during the day as well if child care services are available.

Parents and teachers generally have busy schedules and can seldom devote more than an hour or two a week to a parent-teacher group meeting. However, the length of a meeting should reflect its content. A session to instruct parents in a behavior management or communication technique will be as long as the content demands; it is often easier to reorganize the instructional content into briefer lessons than to reorganize the schedules of a group of individuals, however. Once the session length is established, the leader should announce and discuss any exceptions in advance.

Frequency also reflects the group purpose and the members' schedules. As a rule, small groups should meet no more than once a week and no less than once a month.

The prudent planner determines the maximum allowable size of the group before organizing it. If the number of interested parents exceeds the limit, leaders must cut off enrollment or form another group. The group purpose, the competencies of the leader or leaders, and the parents' characteristics all determine the best size. Recruiting parents of similar interests, backgrounds, and concerns will enhance group cohesiveness. Members should be parents of children with similar developmental levels and exceptionalities (Webster 1977).

Planning lesson sequence is an important part of preparing for training, instructional, and information groups. Group leaders should distribute outlines, agendas, instructional materials, and texts to participants to alert them to the course content and the cumulative nature of the materials. In many cases, group planners must submit purchase orders and rental requisitions for instructional materials and equipment several weeks before the first meeting. If the teacher lacks the qualifications or time to lead the group, he or she must seek others who are competent to assume or share leadership responsibilities.

Refreshment plans must take place ahead of time also; frequently, members share this responsibility. Well-planned transportation and child care services will encourage group attendance.

The program planner must determine if attendance is to be mandatory or voluntary. When the program content is cumulative, attendance should be mandatory, unless the leader has time to offer individual instructon to absentees. Programs dependent on group interaction and the exchange of feelings will also be more cohesive if attendance is mandatory.

Structure

Webster emphasized the importance of structure and limits in parent-teacher small group programs: "While everyone enjoys participating in spontaneous events from time to time, it would be anxiety producing if everything in their lives were unplanned, unstructured, and unlimited" (1977, 49). Thus, structure helps both parties function purposefully. Webster suggested a verbal contract between parents and teachers as one way to establish an agreed-upon structure. The teacher opens the discussion of the contract, but all parties are responsible for negotiating its content and reaching consensus. Any verbal or written contract should be brief and concise, establishing meeting times, group purpose, participants, and activities. No party should enter into a program with a hidden agenda; thus, discussion of the group's purpose should be open, straightforward, and free of jargon. In discussing who will participate in the group, parents and teachers should decide whether they will work alone, with other parents and teachers, with the child, or with "experts." Finally, all parties should clarify expectations for the meetings themselves, clarifying meeting content and determining whether note taking, reading assignments, role-playing activities, and home assignments will be part of the program.

Meeting Effectiveness

Karnes and Zehrbach (1972) suggested the following guidelines for conducting effective small group meetings:

1. *Meeting content.* Content should relate directly or indirectly to the concerns expressed by the parent members. It should be challenging yet at a level that everyone can understand and assimilate.

2. *Planning and operation.* As the group matures, members should share responsibilities for planning and conducting meetings.

3. *Member preparation.* All members, including the leader, should prepare for the meeting by reading articles and chapters in books, listening to tapes, viewing films and videotapes, and digesting information in other ways.

4. *Members' needs.* Meetings should respond to the members' individual social, emotional, and intellectual needs.

5. *Atmosphere.* Meetings should take place in a relaxed, informal atmosphere. However, the atmosphere should further meeting goals, with all members observing social amenities.

6. *Meeting time.* Meetings should take place on agreed-upon dates and times. They should begin and end on time. A session should seldom, if ever, exceed two hours.

7. *Teachers' roles.* Teachers should participate in and facilitate but not dominate the meeting. They must avoid condescension and be alert to the needs of parents who have outgrown the group, suggesting a more appropriate group or an alternative activity in such cases. Teachers should remain alert to the members' changing social-emotional needs and offer them support and guidance as needed.

8. *Member support.* Members should have opportunities to help new members and reluctant participants become involved in group activities. This practice strengthens the group's cohesiveness.

Leadership Techniques

Small group leaders or facilitators have many responsibilities before, during, and after the meeting. These responsibilities include preparing themselves through study, preparing the setting and necessary materials, establishing the session tone, facilitating the group's activities, resolving problems within the group, and evaluating the meeting.

Small group leaders can select from a range of directive to nondirective techniques (Kroth 1975). Directive techniques, which assume parents need help to make effective decisions about their exceptional children, are generally most appropriate in information and training meetings. Nondirective techniques are more appropriate in small groups designed to provide social-emotional support to parents. The nondirective leader is primarily responsible for setting an atmosphere conducive to discussion. Nondirective techniques assume parents are capable of free choice about themselves and their exceptional children and will make effective decisions if given the opportunity.

Leading the Meeting. During the small group meeting, the leader's central function is to keep the group on the topic and progressing in an orderly fashion through the problem-solving, discussion, or training process. To accomplish this task, the leader must have several special skills (Hymes 1974; Dinkmeyer and McKay 1974, 1976; Shea 1978).

At the opening of the meeting, the leader reminds the members of the meeting purpose, perhaps linking the topic at hand to previously discussed topics. A skilled leader will also link the meeting content to members' stated concerns and interests. If the session is one of a series of meetings on a central theme, the leader reviews the group's progress so far and praises participants for their accomplishments.

Next the leader highlights the specific objectives of the meeting as clearly and precisely as possible. As necessary, he or she reviews the procedures and practices governing the meeting.

After these introductory comments, the leader issues an open invitation for members to begin the discussion. Buzz sessions, round robins, and brainstorming activities are helpful ways to stimulate discussion, especially among shy and quiet members.

During the discussion, the leader restates or represents participants' comments and opinions, avoiding negative judgments, and relates them to other members' comments. Dinkmeyer and McKay (1974) called this function *universalizing*. When questioning and commenting, the leader should use plural pronouns ("we," "us") to convey to members that he or she is speaking for and with the group.

The leader points out similarities and differences among participants' comments and helps redirect statements or questions to other group members. The leader should avoid dominating the group by personally responding to all comments.

Closed and open questions help keep the discussion moving. The leader asks closed questions to obtain specific information and open questions to facilitate the discussion (see Chapter 4).

Throughout the meeting, the leader gives the members feedback and encouragement. He or she reinforces the group as a whole and individual members for their participation and for their support of others. If the discussion bogs down, the leader encourages members to persist in their efforts to solve the problem.

Dinkmeyer and McKay suggested that the leader obtain from the members a commitment to apply what they learned in the meeting. The leader encourages participants and helps them develop an action plan, periodically seeking feedback on their commitment to act.

Occasionally during the meeting and, especially, at the conclusion of the meeting, the leader summarizes progress and, if necessary, restructures the discussion. This procedure keeps the group focused on its task. In the end-of-session summary, the leader relates the present discussion to previous and future discussions.

Some leaders must make a concerted effort to remain silent when other members are struggling with a problem. The effective leader does not become anxious when silences occur. Such times are necessary for members to receive, integrate, and evaluate information and to formulate opinions, phrase questions, or prepare comments.

Problems of Leadership. No small group functions smoothly all the time. Participants vary in personality, interests, attitudes, knowledge, experience, feelings, understanding, and social skills. They also express themselves in many ways—some productive, some counterproductive. The leader must recognize and redirect negative behaviors that hurt individuals or impede the group's functioning. Dinkmeyer and McKay (1976) cited the following common problem behaviors and suggested appropriate leader responses.

- *Behavior:* Monopolizing the discussion. *Response:* Intervene and redirect the group's attention to the topic; in extreme cases, ignore the monopolizer's inappropriate comments.

- *Behavior:* Challenging the leader's authority. *Response:* Be serious but casual in responding to the challenger; avoid defensive responses.

- *Behavior:* Talking too much or perseverating on a topic. *Response:* Interrupt the discussion and state clearly but courteously that the discussion of the topic is over and a new topic is now under consideration.

- *Behavior:* Resisting change. *Response:* Be patient and encourage the resisters to accept change.

- *Behavior:* Seeking a magical solution to the child's exceptionality. *Response:* Encourage interaction between the "miracle-seeking" parent and the parent who has experienced the difficult, frustrating, and time-consuming work of raising an exceptional child.

- *Behavior:* Rationalizing and intellectualizing problems. *Response:* Call attention to the intellectualizing and encourage parents to carry out an action program.

- *Behavior:* Enjoying and passively accepting problems. *Response:* Assist and encourage such parents to take command of their problems.

- *Behavior:* Stating exceptionality is normal. *Response:* Offer factual information about normal child growth and development and the problems and characteristics of the exceptionality.

In addition to problems introduced by individual members, the leader may confront group problems. Progress may come to a standstill, for example, or members may become bored, frustrated, and distracted. The leader should be alert to such problems and act immediately to restructure activities to draw the group back to its original purpose and objectives.

SUMMARY

This chapter explores the structure of parent-teacher involvement groups. It discusses the advantages and disadvantages of large and small groups and their most effective applications. Large groups are most appropriate for transmitting information efficiently; small groups are better suited to providing social-emotional support or intensive training. The chapter offers guidelines for conducting large and small group meetings, describes methods for revitalizing a disintegrating large group, and highlights leadership techniques for small groups.

Chapter 8 discusses several specific parent-teacher involvement group programs in detail, including informative, communication, problem-solving, discussion, and training groups.

EXERCISES AND DISCUSSION TOPICS

1. Research and write a brief paper on the relationship between a group's purpose and its size, processes, procedures, and leadership techniques.

2. Develop a checklist for planning, conducting, and evaluating a large group.

3. Develop a needs assessment instrument for a parent-teacher involvement group for use with your special class or a hypothetical class.

4. Discuss in your study group the composition, objectives, functions, and operations of an advisory committee for a parent-teacher involvement group.

5. Discuss in your study group the guidelines for conducting large group meetings.

6. Develop a checklist for planning, conducting, and evaluating a small group.

7. Research and write a brief paper on small group leadership.

8. Lead a study group discussion of a topic selected by your instructor. Discuss your leadership effectiveness with your instructor and members of your group.

9. Conduct a panel discussion in your study group on "The Trials and Tribulations of Group Leadership." Each person on the panel should research the topic before the discussion.

REFERENCES

Bailard, V., and R. Strang. 1964. *Parent-teacher conferences.* New York: McGraw-Hill.

Croft, D. J. 1979. *Parents and teachers: A resource book for home, school, and community relations.* Belmont, Calif.: Wadsworth.

Dinkmeyer, D., and G. D. McKay. 1974. Leading effective parent study groups. *Elementary School Guidance and Counseling* 9 (2):108–15.

Dinkmeyer, D., and G. D. McKay. 1976. *Systematic training for effective parenting: Leader's manual.* Circle Pines, Minn.: American Guidance Service.

Hymes, J. L., Jr. 1974. *Effective home-school relations.* Sierra Madre, Calif.: Southern California Association for the Education of Young Children.

Karnes, M. B., and R. R. Zehrbach. 1972. Flexibility in getting parents involved in the school. *Teaching Exceptional Children* 5 (1):6–19.

Kelly, E. J. 1974. *Parent-teacher interaction: A special educational perspective.* Seattle: Special Child Publications.

Kroth, R. L. 1975. *Communicating with parents of exceptional children: Improving parent-teacher relationships.* Denver: Love Publishing.

Olson, S. A., E. Gaines, J. H. Wilson, N. Volstad, and P. A. Smith. 1976. Reinforce that home-school link. *Instructor* 86 (2):112–14,119,166.

Shea, T. M. 1978. *Teaching children and youth with behavior disorders.* St. Louis: C. V. Mosby

Webster, E. J. 1977. *Counseling with parents of handicapped children: Guidelines for improving communications.* New York: Grune and Stratton.

GROUP MEETING MODELS

■ Teachers with skills in planning, conducting, and evaluating large and small parent–teacher involvement groups can select specific parent–teacher group models to fulfill their purposes. This chapter presents models for informative group meetings and for communication, problem-solving, discussion, and training groups. No single model will respond to all parents' needs. Consequently, teachers must use professional judgment in matching group processes to parents' needs, strengths, personal characteristics, and cultures.

INFORMATIONAL MEETINGS

Informational meetings are effective when teachers want to inform parents collectively of some aspect of their children's special education program (Kelly 1974; Hymes 1974). Kelly suggested that academic programs, special remedial and experimental programs, contemporary school-community problems (the effects of sex education, drugs, alcohol abuse, and other issues on exceptional children), behavior management, and the etiology, characteristics, and treatment of exceptionalities are all appropriate themes for such meetings. Hymes included program objectives, instructional methods and materials, and facilities and equipment in this list, and Kroth (1972, 1975) added classroom activities and their rationale, class and school schedules, the testing program, specialized training, and community services.

Bailard and Strang (1964) suggested that teachers hold a meeting to review the role and functions of the school staff, including principal, regular education teacher, special education teacher, program supervisor, counselor, psychologist, social worker, and others. Other possible themes are legal rights and responsibilities and federal and state rules and regulations governing special education and estate planning. In some cases, teachers may want to call a series of informational meetings devoted to various aspects of a single theme. If the meeting theme is not in the teacher's areas of expertise, a community or school professional with the needed knowledge and experience should be available to contribute to the meeting.

Informational meetings should be neither too democratic nor too dogmatic. Teachers should control the meeting enough to communicate the desired information yet provide opportunities for questions and discussions. They must answer parents' questions honestly and courteously, responding only briefly to off-target questions.

This section presents several representative informational group meeting models. They include a learning disabilities course for parents, an open house, toy workshops, worry workshops, and parent-child programs.

Learning Disabilities Course

Devereaux Day School offered one of the more formal group programs, a learning disabilities course aimed at direct instruction rather than active participation (McWhirter 1976). The course offered parents of exceptional children factual information on learning disabilities and emotional support through discussion with other parents and the instructor. The course comprised six sessions and three additional sessions if the parents so desired. The hour-and-a-half weekly sessions consisted of half-hour lectures followed by discussion. The course used printed materials, visual aids, and current reference materials to supplement lectures.

Similar courses could benefit parents of children with other exceptionalities. They are an efficient way to correct parents' possible misinformation.

Open Houses and Toy Workshops

Open houses and toy workshops are less formal group programs designed to enhance communication among parents and teachers. From the relatively restricted sharing of the open house, teachers may want to proceed to the informal, person-to-person sharing of the toy workshop.

The open house is an annual event in most special education programs. Its goals are to describe for parents the objectives of the special education programs and related services and to familiarize them with the accompanying instructional methods and materials (Jacobson 1974). Generally held in the fall, the open house is an excellent opportunity to introduce parents to the parent-teacher involvement program. It is helpful if other professionals and paraprofessionals associated with the program attend the open house to describe their roles in the program.

The open house is an opportunity to display students' academic work, art work, texts, workbooks, and other instructional materials. The special education teacher may wish to describe the classroom program briefly, including subject matter, psychomotor and physical education activities, and affective education programs. Parents will probably be interested in the behavior management techniques applied in the program as well. The teacher should invite parents' questions and comments.

Toy workshops are meetings during which parents can make inexpensive toys and games for their children (Huntinger and McKee 1978). The school provides toy and game patterns and materials. Teachers can solicit additional ideas and materials for projects from parents and staff. Generally, projects are simple enough to complete in one session. The meetings can be fun and unusual for parents, thereby encouraging an informal exchange of ideas, information, and feelings.

Worry Workshops

Worry Workshops for Parents (Downing 1974) require greater personal commitment than do courses, open houses, or toy workshops. Designed to both educate and counsel parents, worry workshops emphasize interpersonal interaction, self-exploration, and individual counseling. They link parents to school counseling programs, offering an eclectic mixture of parent education minicourses and individual and family counseling services.

Workshop planning begins with an assessment of community and school needs and resources. Mental health clinics, drug abuse centers, social welfare agencies, vocational rehabilitation offices, and public health departments often act as instructional, counseling, therapy, and referral resources. In addition, these agencies help publicize the workshops.

As part of the worry workshop, counseling service is available during school hours, afternoons, and two evenings a week. Individual counseling sessions are essential to the program as a means of serving parents uncomfortable in a group setting or parents wishing to discuss personal and highly specific concerns. In general, counseling services focus on the child's learning processes and the parents' contributions to the child's learning.

Parent education offerings emphasize interpersonal relations that influence a child's learning. These minicourses run three or four weeks, with groups meeting once a week for two or three hours. A counselor or school psychologist leads the groups, with other professionals contributing as resource people.

Parent Group/Child Recreation Program

In 1975, Flint and Deloach described an innovative parent group/child recreation program conducted at Memphis State University:

> The program was designed to provide information, mutual support, and improved communications among parents of handicapped children in the form of both small and large group sessions; recreation for the children themselves and their non-handicapped brothers and sisters; and career training for students of special education and rehabilitation (556).

While the exceptional children and their siblings participated in recreational activities—grouped by age and mobility, instructed by college physical education students, and supervised by special education students—parents attended large and small group meetings. The large group lecture-discussion session focused on social attitudes toward the exceptional, the triumphs and trials of raising an exceptional child, financial management, behavior management, demonstrations of related services, and other pertinent topics. Parents participated in eight to fifteen groups, with mothers and fathers separating to attend different groups. Group membership reflected a cross-section of parents with children of different ages and exceptionalities. Counselors served as group leaders.

Small group discussions emphasized mutual understanding and support and problem-solving skills. The goal of the small groups was to develop *contracts* among parents to organize action programs on behalf of their children.

In 1977, Shea published a detailed description of an evening/weekend camp program similar to the Flint/Deloach program. Evening/weekend camps, conducted in school or community recreation centers, involve exceptional children and their siblings in activities designed to improve psychomotor, leisure, social-personal, academic, and study skills. University special education trainees lead the activities under the supervision of special education teachers.

While the children are busy with their activities, parents participate in small group meetings with a school social worker and psychologist.

The meetings emphasize social-emotional support and problem solving.

COMMUNICATION GROUPS

Two commercial programs represent the communication group approach to helping parents of exceptional children. These programs—Parent Effectiveness Training (PET) and Systematic Training for Effective Parenting (STEP)—offer complete systems of instruction.

Parent Effectiveness Training

Parent Effectiveness Training (Gordon 1970) is designed to teach parents the communication skills they need to raise responsible children. Parents of any child—young or adolescent, normal or exceptional—can benefit from the PET course.

The program includes twenty-four hours of instruction in eight sessions of three hours. A trained instructor works with classes of twenty to thirty parents. Parents pay an instructional fee and purchase PET texts and workbooks.

Instructional methods include lectures, role playing, and discussion. Parents study the following topics:

1. parents are blamed but not trained,
2. parents are persons, not gods,
3. how to listen so kids will talk to you,
4. putting your active listening skills to work,
5. how to listen to kids too young to talk much,
6. how to talk so kids will listen to you,
7. putting *I-messages* to work,
8. changing unacceptable behavior by changing the environment,
9. inevitable parent-child conflicts: who should win?
10. parental power: necessary and justified?, *no-lose* methods for resolving conflicts,
11. parents' fears and concerns,
12. putting the *no-lose* method to work,
13. how to avoid being fired as a parent,
14. how parents can prevent conflicts by modifying themselves, and
15. the other parents of your children.

In an article on the need to design training programs responsive to the trainees, Gilliam (1975) cautioned teachers on the use of Parent Effectiveness Training with all parents. He suggested that the cost, reading and study requirements, and complexity of PET may make it most appropriate for parents who are professionals (physicians, teachers, managers) and less appropriate, without modification, for blue collar workers and nonliterate groups.

Systematic Training for Effective Parenting

Systematic Training for Effective Parenting (Dinkmeyer and McKay 1976) is an educational program to help parents raise responsible children and feel more adequate and satisfied as parents. Because of changes in society and in parenting practices, Dinkmeyer and McKay believe today's parents need training to be effective. Society has evolved from autocratic parenting practices to practices based on mutual respect between parent and child, equality, and individual rights and responsibilities. Many present-day parents were raised in an autocratic manner and lack understanding and experience in democratic parenting practices. STEP teaches parents the knowledge and skills needed to be a democratic parent.

Dinkmeyer and McKay do not recommend STEP for parents of troubled children, for it is not a form of therapy. However, Kroth and Kroth (1976) stated that STEP is valuable to parents of exceptional children because it helps improve communication skills among family members.

STEP is designed for use in small study groups of ten to twelve parents plus the group leader. The group meets for nine sessions of one and a half to two hours. Because the material is cumulative, attendance is mandatory.

STEP is a highly structured program of instruction. A leader's manual provides specific directions for each lesson. The STEP kit includes an invitational brochure and audiotape to publicize the program. Lesson materials, published in English and Spanish, include a leader's manual, parents' handbook, five audiotapes, six discussion guide cards, nine posters, and ten charts. In the group setting, parents share concerns and provide each other mutual support. They grow in self-awareness and awareness of their parenting effectiveness, learning they are not necessarily the cause of the child's difficulties. STEP teaches parents to communicate constructively with their children and how to reinforce acceptable behaviors and not reinforce unacceptable behaviors.

The STEP leader may be trained in psychology, social work, counseling, education, or another helping profession. A lay person willing to study the STEP materials may serve as group leader. The leader conducts each lesson guided by the STEP manual but must have the skills to facilitate discussion and set the tone or atmosphere for the group.

The leader's manual discusses the rationale for the program and instructs leaders on how to organize and conduct the program, how to lead the group, and so on. Clear and concise descriptions of nine lessons provide detail on materials, objectives, procedures, use of instructional aids, discussion topics, class exercises, home assignments, and reading assignments.

STEP's developers state that it is effective with any interested parent and can be taught by both lay and professional instructors. However, STEP is a complex program requiring considerable organizational and leadership skills. Thus, an instructor probably needs background and experience in child development, parenting, and the helping professions to effectively answer parents' questions and concerns. In addition, participating parents need skills in observation, discussion, and reading and writing to benefit from the program. Parents lacking these skills may not find it satisfactory. Other parents will be unable to participate because they cannot pay the fee.

PROBLEM-SOLVING GROUPS

According to Kelly (1974), parent–teacher problem solving is most effective when organized around a central theme that focuses members on the group's primary purpose of helping the exceptional child. This focusing device helps counter the tendency to stray into discussions of inappropriate topics, such as personal and marital problems.

Teachers should evaluate their personal capacities and competencies to lead parent problem-solving groups, for these groups require counseling skills unlike those teachers usually learn (Kelly 1974). Teachers lacking the competencies and confidence to counsel parents should enlist the services of an appropriately trained school counselor, social worker, or psychologist as group leader. The teacher retains the responsibility of helping the facilitator and members and should nonetheless participate actively in the group.

Rutherford and Edgar (1979) developed a problem-solving process model that provides logical and sequential procedures generally applicable to most problems, conceptual frameworks, and intervention strategies (see Chapter Six also). The four-step process provides a structure for facilitating group activities.

1. Defining the problem

2. Developing probable solutions

3. Implementing a solution

4. Evaluating the results.

In the first step, the group identifies the problem and specifies its parameters, determining the people, times, and settings related to the problem and reaching consensus on the desired outcome of the problem-solving process. At this stage, the group considers who owns the problem: the child, the parent, the teachers, or a combination of these people.

The second step, developing probable solutions, calls for the group to prepare a plan for solving the problem. Group members consider the who, what, where, when, how, and how many of the proposed solution, paying special attention to parents' and teachers' roles.

The third step is to carry out the proposed solution in line with the group's agreed-upon plan. During this stage, parents and teachers, as well as the child, need reinforcement for their efforts and successes. Changing a child's behavior may require that parents and teachers change their personal behavior. Frequently, a positive change in the child's behavior is sufficiently rewarding to sustain their efforts. However, when change is slow, parents and teachers become frustrated and discouraged and may discontinue their efforts. To avoid this consequence, an external reinforcement program may be necessary, whereby parents and teachers reinforce each other through periodic conferences, notes, or telephone calls.

The final step in the problem-solving process, evaluation, is a continuous process that takes place throughout implementation of the solution. The group assesses the impact of the intervention on the problem, and the efficiency and consistency of parents' and teachers' efforts. Collecting and graphing observation data on frequency, percent, or duration of the behavior help in evaluating the solution's effectiveness. Observations can ascertain the efficiency and consistency of interventions. The parents and teacher may want to observe each other's efforts and discuss their observations.

DISCUSSION GROUPS

In 1978, Shea described a model for parent-teacher discussion groups. These discussion groups have three objectives:

1. To communicate practical information to parents

2. To help parents solve problems related to their child

3. To provide a setting for parents to exchange support and understanding.

Shea's groups are parent-centered groups that focus on an agreed-upon information topic and on parents' immediate practical concerns and problems. The first part of each session is devoted to a ten-minute presentation by the teacher or a parent of a topic announced at the previous session. Thus, members have had an opportunity to read or, simply, think about the subject before the meeting. After the presentation, group members discuss the topic and relate it to their concerns and circumstances.

The group can select discussion topics in several ways. It can adopt a topic from a text on parenting, child development, behavior management, or exceptionality. Or the teacher can present the members with a list of ten to fifteen potential topics, which they rank in order of preference. Using a list of Dreikurs's and Soltz's child-raising principles (1964), Shea found that a group of fifteen parents and two teachers rated the following as their "top ten":

1. Being firm without dominating

2. Using natural and logical consequences

3. Stimulating independence

4. Withdrawing from conflict

5. Following through; being consistent

6. Encouraging the child

7. Talking with, not to, the child

8. Showing respect for the child

9. Having the courage to say no

10. Downgrading bad habits. (Shea 1978, 253)

During the discussion segments, parents and teachers discussed the following topics most frequently:

1. Difficulties in giving the child a choice

2. Laws governing services for the child

3. How to refrain from constantly evaluating the child's work and comparing it with others'

4. Physicians, treatments, and medications

5. How to tell children they are exceptional

6. The qualities of a good parent ("Am I a good mother or father?")

7. Sex education

8. Report cards (Why are exceptional children graded like nonexceptional children?)

9. How to protect the child from hurt

10. Punishment (especially physical punishment). (Shea 1978, 253)

Groups generally contain ten to twelve parents and one or two teachers. It is best if both mothers and fathers attend. Regular attendance is encouraged but not mandatory. Attendance increases if child care service is available. Teachers may want to organize a few members of the group into a subgroup responsible for reminding members of the next meeting. Car pools can help ensure that everyone who wishes can attend meetings.

Schools usually have a conference room available for group meetings. Conducting meetings in members' homes is generally undesirable for several reasons: preparing for the meeting can easily upset family harmony, parents lose the opportunity to get out for a few hours, and some parents consider their homes, furnishings, or neighborhoods inadequate.

Classrooms are also inappropriate for meetings unless adult-sized furnishings are available and artificial barriers can be removed. All sessions should begin and end at the agreed-upon time. The leader is unwise to remain after meetings for private discussions with individuals or small groups of parents. These activities should take place at another time.

When a group begins, the teacher functions as a directive leader. However, as the group progresses and cohesiveness grows, the teacher's role changes from direct leader to member and resource person. Then one or more parents can assume leadership functions. Table 8-1 presents a *cognitive map* of discussion group tasks and responsibilities.

To fulfill their functions, the members ideally initiate discussion, give and request information, give and request evaluation, restate and give examples of their perceptions of others' statements, confront and reality test suggested solutions, and clarify, synthesize, and summarize. However, many nonfunctional behaviors are likely to occur during group discussions as well, such as aggression, competition, confession, sympathy seeking, horsing around, withdrawal, domination, and negation. These behaviors, though unrelated to the task at hand, are often necessary to maintain group cohesiveness and affirm the integrity of individual members. They can also provide needed tension release after intense discussion. However, leaders cannot allow such behaviors to interfere with the group's productiveness.

According to Shea, an effective group will have the following characteristics, which help create a positive atmosphere:

1. Parents enjoy attending meetings.

2. Groups members are warm, accepting, and cordial toward each other.

3. The group is a nonthreatening environment in which each member feels free to express his or her problems and concerns.

4. Members attend meetings regularly, arrive on time, and are prepared for presentation and discussions.

5. Learning is a cooperative activity to which all members contribute.

Step	Task	Responsible Member
1	Presentation of purpose	Teacher
2	Definition of terms and concepts	Teacher
3	Development of discussion guidelines and general content	Teacher allows others to assume tasks
4	Selection and ranking of themes and subthemes	All members
5	Allocation of time	Teacher allows others to assume tasks
6	Discussion	All members
7	Integration of subthemes with major theme	Teacher
8	Planning of interventions	All members
9	Application of interventions	Concerned members
10	Evaluation of interventions	All members
11	Evaluation of the group process and function	All members

Source: Adapted from Hill 1969, 23.

6. Members view learning as the group's reason for existence and accept that learning requires effort.

7. All members participate actively in the discussion.

8. Members share leadership functions; no one dominates activities.

9. The exploration of topics is thorough and well-paced so that all members feel satisfied.

10. Members accept evaluation as an essential component of group activity.

TRAINING GROUPS

The professional literature covers a wide range of training programs for parents. This section highlights five of these programs, which represent the range and character of those available.

Living with Children

Living with Children (Patterson and Gullion 1968, 1969) is one of many books available for training parents in social learning theory and practices. This programmed text reviews principles of social learning theory; reinforcers and their use; techniques for observing, counting, and graphing behavior; and techniques for changing deviant behaviors such as fighting, negativism, overactivity, dependency, fear, and withdrawal.

As a form of programmed learning, *Living with Children* requires readers to participate actively by writing responses, receiving feedback, recording and graphing data, and planning intervention strategies. The program has effectively trained parents and teachers, as well as psychiatric residents, nurses, and undergraduates in psychology, child development, and education. Suggested interventions have successfully changed child problems of severe behavior deviancy, speech, reading, and normal social learning.

People with seventh- to eighth-grade reading ability can use the text successfully; slow readers and retarded people need some help to benefit from the material. The text is most useful as a catalyst for parent-teacher training. At least two members of each child's family should participate in training, preferably including both mother and father. The typical parent group consists of four or five families plus a teacher. The group meets for five to fifteen weekly two-hour sessions. Before studying the text, families receive training in behavior observation, during which period the professional stays in frequent contact with the parents.

Families (Patterson 1975) extends the theory and practices presented in *Living with Children* by focusing on "the details, the technology as it were, of how a person goes about changing his own behavior and the behavior of the people around him" (v). It describes how to use behavior modification procedures with both normal and severely behavior-disordered children and adults, including the punishment concepts and techniques, contingency contracting, *time-out* strategies, and token exchanges.

Managing Behavior

Managing Behavior: A Parent Involvement Program (McDowell 1974) instructs parents in behavior modification principles and practices. Parents participate actively in the process of changing behavior by selecting a target behavior, collecting and charting baseline data, and selecting and implementing an intervention. Through a variety of activities—observing, listening, viewing audiovisuals, charting, and conducting home behavior change programs—parents learn to use behavior modification to help their children.

The McDowell program proceeds logically and sequentially, offering clear, concise instructions for planning and conducting group sessions. A program kit includes three fifteen-minute filmstrips with audiotapes, a leader's manual, and a parents' workbook. The leader's manual offers guidelines for workshop preparation, presentation, and evaluation.

The program consists of four sessions, one of which is a follow-up session. Meetings run approximately one-and-a-half hours. Each unit includes a didactic presentation, skill practice activities, and a discussion period. Group size may vary from three or four to fifteen or sixteen parents, depending on the professional-to-parent ratio. Mc-Dowell recommends a ratio of approximately four sets of parents to each staff person, or an eight-to-one ratio.

Behavior Modification in Families

In *Training in Child Management: A Family Approach,* Brockway (1974) integrated didactic presentations, role-playing activities, and home assignments into a ten-week behavior modification course for small groups of parents. Each session comprises two segments, with a brief break between them. The first segment offers a brief review of the previous session, a lecture by the instructor, role-playing activities, and an examination. The second segment focuses on home management activities; parents develop and conduct two home management programs during the course.

The text for the course contains text for each lecture, which leaders may read to the group or use as a basis for their own lectures. The text includes an agenda, handouts, and an examination for each session, which leaders can reproduce and distribute to participants. Text material for each session includes role-playing and behavioral rehearsal vignettes. Course content includes learning theory, positive and negative reinforcement, rules for behavior change, methods of teaching new behaviors and changing inappropriate behaviors, role playing, and home management. Anybody with moderate knowledge of learning theory and child development can serve as instructor.

The course provides several evaluation tools: pre- and post-tests, weekly examinations, an observation scale for assessing role-playing skills, and criteria for success in home management programs.

A Practical Approach to Parent Training

Walker and Shea (1984) presented a behavior modification training program for parents in their text *Behavior Modification: A Practical Approach for Educators.* The program has two primary objectives: to train parents in the theory and application of behavior modification principles and practices and to help parents systematically modify selected behaviors of their exceptional children. Although not a primary objective of the program, the opportunity to receive support and understanding from the teacher and other parents is often an additional benefit for many parents. The program proceeds in three phases.

Preparation Phase. The teacher interviews each parent or couple one or more times before the training begins to determine the parents' needs, interests, and readiness to participate in a formal training program and to identify at least one child behavior the parents wish to change. These interview sessions are an excellent time for the teacher to discuss the program objectives, organization, and requirements and to invite the parents' participation.

Instructional Phase. The instructional phase of the parent training program includes eight weekly sessions. The one-and-one-half-hour sessions break into two forty-minute segments and a ten-minute recess.

In the first forty-minute segment, the teacher offers brief formal presentations on the principles and practices of behavior modification and then opens the segment to a question-and-answer session, group discussion, and practice exercises and activities. The ten-minute break is an opportunity for informal discussion, perhaps over coffee, tea, milk, soft drinks, and snacks furnished by the parent educator and the parents.

The second forty-minute segment focuses on planning, implementing, and evaluating the parents' behavioral intervention programs. Interventions aim to change the behaviors the parents selected during the preparation interviews. During this second segment, parents report on their interventions, and the other members question, discuss, and make suggestions for improving the interventions. The teacher has the responsibility for keeping the discussion positive and helpful throughout this segment.

Group membership is limited to twelve to fourteen people, plus the teacher. Teachers of the children under discussion can become group members. As in most parent involvement activities, participation by both parents is desirable.

Regular attendance is important because of the cumulative nature of the material. Parents unable to attend a particular session should receive an update from the teacher; however, absences should be discouraged for the sake of group cohesiveness and the teacher's time.

The teacher functions as both instructor and group facilitator. However, the teacher can offer opportunities for parents to make instructional presentations. And the teacher's function as group facilitator should diminish as the instructional phase of the program progresses and individual parents begin to assert leadership.

Occasionally a team of two teachers presents the training program, a format that is particularly effective if one acts as instructor and the other as facilitator. Of course, success in team teaching assumes personal-professional compatibility as well as fundamental agreement on the subject matter and instructional methods.

Any person who is knowledgeable about behavior modification, child behavior, and group leadership can serve as instructor-facilitator. Thus, regular and special education teachers, college instructors, counselors, psychologists, nurses, social workers, and other helping professionals are good candidates.

Instructional materials include the Walker and Shea text and worksheets. Each participant should have a copy of the text, which suggests instructional aids for each lesson.

The training program includes eight sessons:

Session 1:   An introduction to behavior modification
Session 2:   The consequences of behavior
Session 3:   Potentially effective reinforcers
Session 4–5: Strategies to increase behavior
Session 6–7: Strategies to decrease behavior
Session 8:   Ethical and effective applications.

The text presents detailed lesson plans that specify goals, content, instructional methods, group and individual activities, instructional resources and aids, evaluation techniques, and home assignments. (See Figure 8-1 for a sample lesson.)

Follow-up Phase. Teachers should maintain contact with parents after the eight-week training program. Walker and Shea suggest that the teacher develop a follow-up plan, maintaining periodic contact with the group and with individual parents to reinforce their efforts and help

---

LESSON 1: AN INTRODUCTION TO BEHAVIOR MODIFICATION

Goals

1. To familiarize students with the models of causation of human behavior and with the behavior change process

2. To enable parents to exemplify each of the principles of behavior modification

3. To enable parents to complete two or more target behavior selection checklists correctly

4. To enable parents to accurately observe and record a target behavior

Content

1. Models of causation of human behavior

2. Principles of behavior modification

3. Overview of the behavior change process

4. Selecting target behaviors

5. Observing and recording target behaviors

(cont.)

FIGURE 8-1
Sample Lesson Plan

Instructional Methods

1. Lecture

2. Discussion

3. Demonstration

4. Completion of a target behavior selection checklist

5. Recording the target behavior rate or frequency

Activities

1. Segment A (40 minutes)

   a. Introduction of the parent educator(s) and individual parents

   b. Overview of the course organization and content

   c. Brief lecture on theories of causation of human behavior

   d. Brief overview of the behavior change process

   e. Lecture on the principles of behavior modification; each participant requested to cite a personal example of each principle (may be written)

   f. (1) Examples of target behaviors and explanation of the target behavior selection process;

      (2) Demonstration of how to complete a target behavior selection checklist;

      (3) Each participant requested to select a target behavior selection checklist.

   g. Procedures for observing and recording target behaviors presented, exemplified, and discussed

2. Break (10 minutes)

3. Segment B (40 minutes)

   a. Target Behavior 1 (home behavior)

      (1) Each participant (or mother and father) presents to the group the target behavior selected during the psychosituational assessment interview of the course preparation phase. Participants also present and discuss the data that they recorded on the behavior log form.

      (2) Each participant completes a target behavior selection checklist on Target Behavior 1.

      (3) Each participant transfers the data on the behavior log form to an appropriate tally form.

Resources

1. Segment A

   a. Parent educator and individual participants

   b. Chapter Six: Preparation phase of program and lesson titles

   c. Chapter One: Models of human behavior

   d. Chapter Three: Entire chapter

FIGURE 8-1
(cont.)

(cont.)

   e. Chapter Two: Principles of reinforcement

   f. Chapter Three: Selecting a target behavior
      Target behavior selection checklist

   g. Chapter Three: Collecting and recording baseline data

2. Break

3. Segment B

   a. Target Behavior 1

      (1) Behavior log form

      (2) Target behavior selection checklist

      (3) Chapter Three: Collecting and recording baseline data

Evaluation

1. Quiz on or written examples of the principles of reinforcement

2. Completed behavior log form, target behavior selection checklist, and tally form

Home Assignments

1. Observe and record baseline data on Target Behavior I

2. Read

   a. Chapter Two: Consequences of behavior; schedules of reinforcement

   b. Chapter Three: Collecting and recording baseline data

(Walker and Shea 1984, 182–84)

them plan and implement additional interventions. Individual interviews, telephone conversations, and monthly group meetings are several follow-up methods. This periodic reinforcement increases the probability that the skills learned during the training program will not fall into disuse.

Parenting Course in Behavior Modification

Parenting: Strategies and Educational Methods (Cooper and Edge 1978) is an eight-session behavior modification course for a small group of parents. The course teaches parents the skills to change the behavior of their children. The Cooper and Edge text, designed for instructors, provides very specific directions for developing, conducting, and evaluating the parent course.

   The first section of the text reviews the theory and practices of behavior modification, discusses several problems of planning and conducting parent group activities, and presents detailed lesson plans for the eight sessions. The potential problems it discusses include leader preparation activities; parent compliance with course requirements; intragroup relations; enrollment, attendance, and tardiness; meeting time, date, and location; and home assignments.

The second section discusses how to apply the knowledge and skills presented in the course. The authors present 122 strategies in a case study format for changing behaviors common to family settings. The cases are actual incidents occurring in the home, ranging from mild to severe problems.

The text includes many useful checklists, forms, tests, graphs, and other instructional aids. The authors field tested the materials in the text for six years before publication.

Training for the IEP Process

The vast majority of parents of exceptional children would profit greatly from training in the IEP process. Katz et al. (1980) designed an adult education course to help parents improve their effectiveness in the IEP meeting. The course includes three two-hour training modules, or lessons. However, Katz and associates indicated that other formats, such as three miniworkshops or a one-day workshop, could be equally effective. One strength of the program is its wide applicability, for participants require only limited reading, writing, and verbal skills.

The first module, "Parents' Role and Rights Under Public Law 94–142" provides information on the history, purpose, and components of the law. In addition, it reviews due process procedures and explains how to find the local special education agency responsible for services for exceptional children.

The second module explores the parents' role in evaluating and observing their exceptional children. After a brief review of the first lesson, the group leader conducts a discussion to help parents share common experiences with and feelings about their exceptional children and their families' adjustments. Next, the group leader describes the assessment and evaluation methods used by the school's professional staff, including cumulative records, formal and informal tests, psychological evaluations, and classroom observations. At the end of the second lesson, parents receive worksheets and instructions to help them observe their child's strengths and needs more objectively and systematically. The parents record their observations on the worksheets for the next session.

The final module prepares the parent for the meeting itself. After reviewing their "homework," parents discuss with the group the goals they have established for their children. Also during this lesson, the group leader shows parents how to organize a file of all the information they have about their children. The instructor suggests several ways for parents to prepare for and participate in the IEP meeting. Finally, in the third module, the group conducts a simulated IEP meeting to practice skills.

SUMMARY

This chapter concludes the discussion of parent-teacher involvement groups by reviewing several models for informational communication, problem-solving, discussion, and training groups. Working in groups requires parents' and teachers' time, energy, and commitment beyond those demanded by written, telephone, and conferencing activities. The models described in this chapter are teacher resources to be adapted to group purpose and the unique needs of the parent participants. The next chapter presents several classroom, school, home, and community parent-teacher involvement activities to benefit exceptional children.

EXERCISES AND DISCUSSION TOPICS

1. Plan an informational meeting for a large group of parents (thirty to thirty-five people) on the etiology, course, treatment, and prognosis of a form of exceptionality with which you are familiar. Present your program to your study group. Invite the group members to critique your program and performance from the perspective of a parent of an exceptional child.

2. Plan a series of at least four informational meetings for a small group of parents (six to eight people). Select a different topic from the one you discussed in the first exercise. Present one meeting from this series to your study group. Invite group members to critique your program and performance from the perspective of a parent of an exceptional child.

3. Instruct your study group in the use of Parent Effectiveness Training (PET), Systematic Training for Effective Parenting (STEP), or another commercially available parent education program.

4. Conduct a panel discussion in your group of the cognitive map of tasks and responsibilities in Table 8-1.

5. Research the literature and write a brief paper on "discussion group atmosphere."

6. Plan a series of behavior management training lessons for a small group of parents (ten to twelve people) using a theoretical model of

your choice. Present one lesson to your study group. Invite the members of the group to critique your performance from the perspective of the parent of an exceptional child.

7. Write a lesson or series of lessons for training parents to increase their effectiveness in the IEP meeting.

REFERENCES

Bailard, V., and R. Strang. 1964. *Parent-teacher conferences.* New York: McGraw-Hill.

Brockway, B. S. 1974. *Training in child management: A family approach.* Dubuque, Iowa: Kendall/Hunt Publishing.

Cooper, J. O., and E. Edge. 1978. *Parenting: Strategies and educational methods.* Columbus, Ohio: Charles E. Merrill.

Dinkmeyer, D., and G. D. McKay. 1976. *Systematic training for effective parenting: Leader's manual.* Circle Pines, Minn.: American Guidance Service.

Downing, C. J. 1974. Worry workshop for parents. *Elementary School Guidance and Counseling* 9 (2):124–31.

Dreikurs, R., and V. Soltz. 1964. *Children: The challenge.* New York: Hawthorn Books.

Flint, W., and D. Deloach. 1975. A parent involvement program model for handicapped children and their parents. *Exceptional Children* 41 (8):556–57.

Gilliam, G. 1975. Parent training. *Health Education* 6 (5):11–12.

Gordon, T. 1970. *Parent effectiveness training.* New York: Peter Wyden Press.

Hill, W. F. 1969. *Learning through discussion.* Beverly Hills, Calif.: Sage Publications.

Huntinger, P. L., and N. McKee. 1978. Toy workshops for parents: Bridging a gap. *ICEC Quarterly* 27 (4):3–4.

Hymes, J. L., Jr. 1974. *Effective home-school relations.* Sierra Madre, Calif.: Southern California Association for the Education of Young Children.

Jacobson, I. 1974. A plan for open house. *The Pointer* 19 (1):74–75.

Katz, S., J. Borten, D. Brasile, M. Meisner, and C. Parker. 1980. Helping parents become effective partners: The IEP process. *The Pointer* 25 (1):35–45.

Kelly, E. J. 1974. *Parent-teacher interaction: A special educational perspective.* Seattle: Special Child Publications.

Kroth, R. L. 1972. Facilitating educational progress by improving parent conferences. *Focus on Exceptional Children* 4 (7):1–9.

Kroth, R. L. 1975. *Communicating with parents of exceptional children: Improving parent-teacher relationships.* Denver: Love Publishing.

Kroth, R., and J. Kroth. 1976. Evaluation of parent training materials. *Journal of Learning Disabilities* 9 (10):620–23.

McDowell, R. L. 1974. *Managing behavior: A parent involvement program.* Torrance, Calif.: B. L. Winch and Associates.

McWhirter, J. J. 1976. A parent education group in learning disabilities. *Journal of Learning Disabilities* 9 (1):16–20.

Patterson, G. R. 1975. *Families: Applications of social learning to family life.* Rev. ed. Champaign, Ill.: Research Press.

Patterson, G. R., and M. E. Gullion. 1968. *Living with children: New methods for parents and teachers.* Champaign, Ill.: Research Press.

Patterson, G. R., and M. E. Gullion. 1969. *A guide for the professional for use with Living with children.* Rev. ed. Champaign, Ill.: Research Press.

Rutherford, R. B., Jr., and E. Edgar. 1979. *Teachers and parents: A guide to interaction and cooperation.* Abr. ed. Boston: Allyn and Bacon.

Shea, T. M. 1977. *Camping for special children.* St. Louis: C. V. Mosby.

Shea, T. M. 1978. *Teaching children and youth with behavior disorders.* St. Louis: C. V. Mosby.

Walker, J. E., and T. M. Shea. 1984. *Behavior management: A practical approach for educators.* 3d ed. St. Louis: C. V. Mosby.

SCHOOL, HOME, AND COMMUNITY PROGRAMS

■ Throughout the nation, thousands of parents are volunteering services in the classrooms and schools. Others, unable to go to school, demonstrate interest in their children's formal education by contributing time and effort to committee work and special projects. Some parents act as advocates for exceptional children in the community. Others participate in their children's education through home-teaching programs.

This chapter discusses several ways to involve parents and help them be effective in classroom, school, home, and community services for exceptional children. To act as paraprofessionals, aides, instructors, volunteers, and home teachers, parents need special skills. This chapter discusses techniques for training them in these roles, such as observation, demonstration, role playing, instructional coaching, and modeling. Teaching packages and resource centers are also important aids that supplement parents' efforts to educate their exceptional children.

The effectiveness of parent involvement in the classroom, school, home, and community depends in large part on teachers' and parents' attitudes and expectations for the activities. Brown (1978) and Croft (1979) suggested several premises for positive, productive parent-teacher involvement:

1. Both parents and teachers are concerned about the education and general welfare of the exceptional child. Each group must understand their importance, as well as the importance of the other, as active members of the child's educational team. Parents and teachers will participate in cooperative programming as their living and working conditions and personal abilities and skills allow. The first step toward effective involvement is to recognize, understand, and accept the concerns and expectations that each group brings to the cooperative efforts.

2. Both parents and teachers are effective treatment providers. Each party must recognize the other's areas of expertise in fostering the exceptional child's education. Each must recognize that the other has much to offer, yet much to learn about, exceptional children.

3. Parents and teachers must recognize and change as necessary the social-emotional and physical environment in which they work with the exceptional child. Neither can function effectively in an environment lacking needed facilities, furnishings, equipment, and materials.

4. Parents and teachers must recognize the importance of each other's goals for the child and themselves and consider both sets of goals in planning. Consensus on common goals is essential for effective collaboration.

5. Parents and teachers must have training in the processes of collaboration and in the skills and knowledge needed to participate in activities. Through training sessions carefully organized to present the needed skills and knowledge, parents and teachers grow in confidence and are better able to help the exceptional child.

6. Parents and teachers function more comfortably and effectively when they have well-defined rules of operation. Each must know the when, where, how, who, what, and why of their collaborative activities.

7. Both parties need encouragement and positive reinforcement. They need firm yet kind supervision to increase their effectiveness.

8. Finally, parents and teachers must be persistent and patient in their efforts to become effective in helping the exceptional child.

PARENT TRAINING
TECHNIQUES

Adults do not naturally possess the knowledge and skills to be effective teachers. Most parents need training to be effective in teaching their exceptional children.

Learning instructional skills involves several stages (Blackard 1976; Haring 1976): Parents must acquire the skills and become proficient in using them for instruction and behavior management. They must maintain the skills in conditions similar to those in which they learned them, and they must learn to generalize and adapt the skills to new or different conditions.

This section reviews several techniques for training parents to teach their exceptional children, including observation, instructional coaching, modeling, and role playing. These techniques are useful for classroom and school aides, tutors, volunteers, teacher assistants, and home teachers. Because research on the effectiveness of these techniques in parent training is scant (Clements and Alexander 1975), teachers should carefully monitor and evaluate their effectiveness in specific settings.

Observation

Practitioners in parent education recommend that parents receive training in objective observation of classroom procedures and behavioral incidents (Karnes and Zehrbach 1972; Miller 1975; Shea 1978; Croft 1979). Croft emphasized that such training should be a prerequisite for active involvement in the classroom, and Miller (1975) thought it especially important for parents learning to be behavior modifiers.

Training in observation helps parents overcome personal biases when observing interpersonal interactions, increasing their awareness of their own interactions in the process. Parents' observations can also help teachers responsible for explaining to the parents their child's therapeutic and instructional objectives and programs. Careful observation during periodic visits may better equip parents to evaluate their children's progress and to adapt specific techniques for use at home.

Croft (1979) developed two checklists to help parents develop their powers of observation (Figures 9-1 and 9-2). One focuses on student motivation, language development, emotional conditions, academic learning program, and opportunities for creative expression. The second guides parents in evaluating their children's physical environment, materials and equipment, personnel, and instructional program. Parents benefit most from these and similar observation schedules when they can discuss their observations with a teacher either during or immediately after the observation period. The teacher can then clarify parents' perceptions and misperceptions of what they saw.

Shea (1978) suggested the following guidelines for training parents to observe specific behaviors:

Name of Observer: _____   Date: _____

Instructions: Please sit down in an unobtrusive place where you can see most of the classroom. In order to observe objectively it is best to limit your interactions with the children. If they should approach you and talk with you, answer them, but do not encourage a lengthy conversation. If they want you to do something with them, refer them to the teacher.

　　Give yourself time to take in the total environment. Absorb the general atmosphere, look all around the room, listen to the sounds, and generally acquaint yourself with the surroundings and the people. When you are comfortable, begin to focus on more specific aspects of the curriculum.

　　In this classroom we want to:

1. Increase the Child's Awareness and Knowledge about the Physical World

　　　　　　　　　　　　　　　　　　　　　　　　　　　　　　　　　　Check

Does the program encourage the development of curiosity through materials and displays that lead a child to explore?　　　　　　　　　　　_____

Do you hear children asking questions?　　　　　　　　　　　　　_____

Do the teachers encourage children to ask questions?　　　　　　　_____

Are the children free to touch and explore and actively experiment with materials in the classroom?　　　　　　　　　　　　　　　　　　_____

Do the teachers foster a child's interest in new things?　　　　　　_____

Are there opportunities for freedom of choice in a variety of learning activities?　_____

2. Develop Language Abilities

Are the children encouraged to express themselves verbally?　　　_____

Are there a variety of language-motivating materials available to the child? (Records, books, puppets, dramatic play materials?)　　　　　　_____

Do you hear children expressing ideas and feelings?　　　　　　　_____

Do the activities encourage verbal interaction between and among the children?　_____

Do the teachers introduce new concepts and terminology?　　　　_____

Do the teachers name objects and verbalize clearly about procedures to the children?　　　　　　　　　　　　　　　　　　　　　　　　_____

3. Foster Mental and Emotional Health

Do the children appear comfortable in the classroom?　　　　　　_____

Do the children seem self-confident?　　　　　　　　　　　　　_____

Are the teachers respectful of the child who is different?　　　　　_____

Do the children seem secure in the routines and methods used by the teachers?　_____

Are disciplinary methods fair and reasonable?　　　　　　　　　_____

Are the teachers sufficiently firm and flexible?　　　　　　　　　_____

Do you see examples of building a child's strong self-concept?　　_____

Do teachers value individual children?　　　　　　　　　　　　_____

Are children learning responsibility for their actions and choices?　_____

Are children learning to care for others?　　　　　　　　　　　_____

4. Teach Cognitive Skills

Are there materials designed to teach children concepts like large and small, geometric shapes, numbers, colors, letters?　　　　　　　　　_____

(cont.)

FIGURE 9-1
Observation Check Sheet

Are there small group and individual instruction times set aside during the day? _____

Is plenty of time allotted for working with learning materials? _____

Do the children get immediate feedback about the correctness of the concepts they are learning? _____

Are children allowed to learn at their own pace? _____

Do teachers use praise to encourage children? _____

5. Encourage Creative Expression

Are there many art materials and opportunities for creative expression available? _____

Are there opportunities for dramatic play and imaginative involvement? _____

Are there music and creative movement activities? _____

Are children encouraged to use their imaginations? _____

Is the individual child given space and time to daydream or simply to be alone? _____

   This observation form is intended to provide a framework for looking more closely at various aspects of the curriculum. You can expand on these as you work with us in our program. We value your comments and invite your suggestions.

Comments and Suggestions:

FIGURE 9-1
(cont.)

(Croft 1979, 176–78)

FIGURE 9-2
*What to Look for in a
School Visit*

Name of Observer: _____   Date: _____

1. Physical Aspects

                                                                          Check

Ample indoor and outdoor space? (A minimum of thirty-five square feet indoors and fifty square feet outdoors per child.) _____

Space for running and plenty of large-muscle activities? _____

Variety of physical activities encouraged through good design? _____

Isolation quarters? _____

Place for quiet contemplation? _____

Supervision taken into account in overall design? Can children be easily seen and supervised, or are there many areas not easily covered at all times? _____

Hygienic conditions? (Clean sinks, toilets, safe conditions, heating facilities, drafts, fire extinguishers well located, well lighted, children appear healthy?) _____

(cont.)

2. Equipment

Sterile equipment leads to limited and sterile responses. Are children able to get many different ideas in use of materials, and are they free to explore and question and work out their curiosity? Can most equipment be used in many ways? _____

Are there enough equipment and materials to go around? _____

Is all equipment in good condition? (Painted, sanded, no sharp or broken edges?) Do puzzles have all pieces? Are books in good repair? Is most equipment readily available for children? _____

3. People

Do you get the feeling the school is friendly? _____

Is it too quiet or too hectic? _____

Do you hear lots of "No, No"? _____

Do the teachers seem interested, relaxed, but busy? _____

Are the needs of children cared for, or are there some who seem left out and ignored? _____

What is the ratio of adults to children? (Recommended minimum of one adult to ten children. A better ratio is one to five or six depending on age of children.) _____

Are visitors apparently welcome at any time, or is it necessary to make an appointment? _____

Are children free to express themselves verbally and explore physically without constant direction from adults? _____

Does there appear to be a mutual trust and respect among staff and children? _____

Do the teachers have plenty of physical contact (hugging, holding) with children? Or do they seem to be too busy setting up and cleaning up? _____

4. Program

Does the daily routine offer a comfortable balance between free play and organized activities? Does it allow for flexibility within an organized routine? _____

Do the various areas show adequate preplanning? _____

Are the areas inviting and appealing to children? _____

May children move freely within well-supervised areas? Or do they have to all do the same things at the same time? _____

Are there "escape hatches" for those who do not want to participate with the group? _____

Do art work and creative play areas seem stereotyped? That is, are materials precut; are children required to all make the same thing to take home; are some activities special and not always available whenever children want them? _____

Is there a good variety of small- and large-muscle activities available—music, stories, nature studies? Do tools and materials (such as carpentry) provide for successful experiences rather than frustration and failure? _____

Are there well-planned, cognitively oriented activities with appropriate teaching guidance by an adult? _____

Are there many self-help, self-correcting tasks to engage the children so they can learn at their own pace? _____

(Croft 1979, 178–80)

1. Parents' first observations should not be in their children's classrooms, unless an observation booth or one-way viewing mirror is available. They should observe another child, teacher, or classroom group. This restriction prevents parents' emotional responses to their children from interfering with objectivity (Susser 1974).

2. Parents' first observations should be brief (ten to fifteen minutes) and focus on a specific behavior or behaviors (attending, out-of-seat, hand raising, and so on). Parents should count the frequency or duration of the selected behavior. As their observational skills increase, parents can broaden their focus and increase the length of their observations.

3. Parents should first observe with a teacher or paraprofessional. The staff person can explain the activities under way in the classroom and discuss children's and teachers' behaviors with parents. As parents' skills develop, they can observe independently, but a staff person should remain available to discuss observations and respond to parents' questions and concerns.

Instructional Coaching

Clements and Alexander (1975) found that parent training programs often use instructional coaching to train parents. This procedure precisely specifies how parents are to instruct their children, either through oral directions, written lesson plans, audiovisual aids, programmed materials and texts, or a combination of these (Karnes and Zehrbach 1972).

In a research study comparing the effectiveness of instructional coaching, instructional coaching with cues, and modeling, Green et al. (1976) found that instructional coaching (written and verbal directions) combined with auditory cueing was more effective than instructional coaching or modeling. The cue, provided by a professional observing the parent and child working together, helped the parent learn exactly how and when to use specific techniques. Green and associates also found that those parents initially trained with both verbal and written directions and cues could respond effectively to new types of behavior without cues. Thus, cues appear to be a significant initial training aid.

Whatever aids augment instructional coaching procedures, Clements and Alexander suggested the following general guidelines for parent trainers:

1. Provide the parents with clear, concise, and specific directions

2. Begin by working with highly specific behaviors and actions

3. Reinforce parents' efforts as well as their successes

4. Offer the parents immediate or near-immediate feedback on their performance

5. Ask parents to discuss their perceptions of the training program and their performance to enhance their understanding and motivation.

Modeling

Modeling, a process of observation and imitation, is one of the most common forms of human learning. Theorists have described modeling variously as observational learning, identification, copying, vicarious learning, social facilitation, and contagion (Walker and Shea 1984).

> This method of parent training may be employed in vivo (where the teacher engages in the task or demonstrates the activity in the actual situation and environment in which the parent[s] is to perform, while the parent observes) or in individual or group training sessions with only the teacher and parents present (Clements and Alexander 1975, 7).

To teach a skill using modeling, parents and teacher repeat the following three steps until the parent has mastered the skill:

1. The teacher, a paraprofessional, or a trained parent demonstrates the target skill or activity with an exceptional child as the parent trainee observes. The demonstrator offers verbal or written instructions before the demonstration and follows it with a discussion.

2. The parent practices the activity with the child while the trainer observes.

3. The parent and trainer critique the parent's performance.

In their research, Green et al. found that modeling produces "very rapid and dramatic changes in both parent and child behaviors" (1976, 16). However, the study did not indicate whether improvements in children's behavior resulted from the model's effect on the child, from changes in parent behavior after observing the model, or from a combination of both. Because of the complexity of modeling, Clements and Alexander (1975) suggested that it be carefully evaluated. Among the variables the teacher using modeling should monitor are the persons involved (child, parent, and teacher), the specific skill or activity being learned, the instructional setting, and the instructional method.

Role Playing and Behavioral Rehearsal

Role playing is "the acting out or demonstration of situations" (Webster 1977, 73). It is a technique that takes into account both the cognitive and emotional components of the incident being acted out.

For role playing to be effective, the teacher and parents, together, must agree on its purpose, whether in a group setting or family conference, and agree on the situation to be enacted. Role playing is most effective when used for these purposes:

1. To teach new behaviors and skills

2. To select the most effective behavior or skill for a given situation

3. To determine the behavior or skill the parent will be most comfortable using in a given situation

4. To explore the emotional components of a situation.

Webster (1977) divided role playing into three phases: selecting and clarifying the situations and roles to act out, acting out the roles, and discussing the thoughts and feelings evoked by the process.

Brockway (1974) used role playing with families learning effective behavior modification. She suggested that teachers introduce parents to role playing slowly and with great caution, using modeling and desensitizing parents to public performance before beginning the exercise. The following seven-step process is an effective approach:

1. The teacher demonstrates the incident to be played and discusses the performance with family members.

2. A family member models the teacher's performance, and the teacher and other family members discuss the exercise.

3. Family members play several roles related to child management.

4. After each simulation, role players critique their own performances, while the teacher notes the emphasis on the performances' strengths and weaknesses and how they can be improved.

5. The teacher summarizes the performers' critiques and adds constructive criticism.

6. The teacher asks for other family members' opinions and suggestions, emphasizing constructive criticism.

7. All participants receive positive reinforcement for their contributions to the role playing.

Behavioral rehearsal is a variation on role playing in which "parent(s) actually engage in the activity or task in other environments or situations than those in which they will be expected to perform. Role-playing may be utilized, in which the teacher or another parent assumes the role of the child if appropriate to the activity the parent is to engage in. This is not a prerequisite to behavioral rehearsal, however, and in numerous activities, it may be more expedient to have the parent 'walk through' the activity both physically and verbally under the direction and guidance of the teacher. Behavioral rehearsal may also be covert, in which case the parent imagines the situation, task, or activity and cognitively rehearses his behavior in a sequential or systematic way" (Clements and Alexander 1975, 7). Another variation is simulation training, which allows parents to learn in an arranged environment approximating as closely as possible the realities of their lives with their children and others. Through simulation techniques, parents not only learn the "nuts and bolts" of specific techniques, but they also learn to interact productively.

In simulation training, parents act both as players and observers. Members of the training group suggest simulation topics that are significant to them. Audiovisual and videotaping methods can provide useful feedback during the training.

Because simulation training can respond to parents' individual needs and interests, Wagonseller and Mori (1977) recommended its use in small groups of parents of exceptional children. It enhances parents' motivation, encourages both cognitive and affective self-evaluation, and adapts to parents' speeds, levels, and styles of learning. Perhaps most important, simulation allows parents to try out interactions in a safe environment, where they need not fear harming or embarrassing their children or themselves.

PARENT ROLES

Parents as Paraprofessionals

Parents can improve their behavior management and instructional skills in a variety of classroom and school functions. While improving their personal competencies, parents can also be instrumental in improving classroom and school services for exceptional children (Shea 1978).

Paraprofessionals in the classroom relieve the teacher of many routine but necessary tasks, freeing the teacher to plan, coordinate, and supervise instruction. With the extra time, teachers can also personalize and individualize the exceptional child's educational program (Greer 1978).

Wood (1975) recommended that parents be trained as *support teachers* for severely emotionally disturbed children. In this role, parents are responsible for a broad spectrum of helping activities, including the instruction of children under supervision. Karnes and Zehrbach (1972) also recommended that parents be trained to instruct exceptional children in the classroom setting. Serving as instructors, they not only support the teacher's efforts to individualize the children's programs but also acquire teaching skills they can use at home.

Soar and Kaplan (1976) developed a taxonomy of the activities teachers and paraprofessionals can share in the classroom (Figure 9-3). A comprehensive list of classroom activities, the taxonomy offers a common basis for teachers' and professionals' discussions. They can then assign or take on responsibilities according to their training, experience, competency, and legal and ethical responsibilities. Parents and teachers may want to add or delete activities in the taxonomy to fit the children and setting in which they are functioning. When completing the taxonomy, parents and teachers should perform the following tasks independently:

1. Study the activities in the taxonomy and decide which should be modified, added, or eliminated.

2. Place a check mark (√) by those activities for which they take responsibility.

3. Write S next to those activities they feel are shared responsibilities.

4. Leave unmarked those activities whose assignment is unclear.

After marking the form individually, the teacher and paraprofessional can meet for the following tasks:

1. Discuss each activity to ensure mutual understanding of the parameters of the activity and each person's responsibility.

2. Reach consensus on each shared (S) and unmarked activity.

3. Complete the form and post it in the classroom or office for reference.

FIGURE 9-3
Classroom Activities

Teacher	Paraprofessional (Parent)		Both
		Housekeeping Activities	
_____	_____	Dusting, cleaning, and so on	_____
_____	_____	Helping children with clothing	_____
_____	_____	Arranging furniture	_____
_____	_____	Keeping order	_____
_____	_____	Posting items on the bulletin board	_____
_____	_____	Monitoring children on the bus, during lunch and snacks, in the lavatory, and during recess	_____
_____	_____	Other: _____	_____

Clerical Activities

_____ _____ Collecting money   _____
_____ _____ Collecting papers   _____
_____ _____ Taking attendance   _____
_____ _____ Duplicating and distributing materials   _____
_____ _____ Filling out routine reports   _____
_____ _____ Administering tests   _____
_____ _____ Taking inventory   _____
_____ _____ Maintaining an instructional materials file   _____
_____ _____ Keeping records   _____
_____ _____ Other: _____   _____

Materials Activities

_____ _____ Locating materials   _____
_____ _____ Making bibliographies   _____
_____ _____ Setting up displays and demonstrations (preparing ma- _____
            terials)
_____ _____ Other: _____   _____

Instructional Activities

Teaching

_____ _____ Tutoring   _____
_____ _____ Organizing play activities   _____
_____ _____ Selecting and developing materials   _____
_____ _____ Large or small group teaching   _____
_____ _____ Disciplining   _____
_____ _____ Organizing groups for instruction   _____
_____ _____ Making judgments   _____
_____ _____ Other: _____   _____

Planning

_____ _____ Planning and organizing meetings   _____
_____ _____ Planning bulletin boards   _____
_____ _____ Planning small or large group lessons   _____
_____ _____ Other: _____   _____

Evaluation Activities

_____ _____ Grading papers   _____
_____ _____ Keeping anecdotal records   _____
_____ _____ Making systematic observations   _____
_____ _____ Organizing case studies   _____
_____ _____ Evaluating materials   _____
_____ _____ Making tests   _____
_____ _____ Interpreting test results   _____
_____ _____ Other: _____   _____

(Adapted from Soar and Kaplan 1976, 77)

Soar and Kaplan suggested that parents and teachers review the taxonomy three or four times annually to assure that they are meeting their responsibilities. This review allows changes in responsibilities that may be necessary to respond to changes in the student population, personnel training and experience, instructional materials, student objectives, and work setting. Teachers should not assign all routine, unstimulating activities to parents. Both parties should share desirable and undesirable classroom activities.

Greer (1978) identified two categories of paraprofessionals: teacher assistants and teacher aides. In general, the teacher assistant offers direct support to a teacher, therapist, or other professional and assumes, under supervision, those activities designated by the professional. The teacher assistant has limited decision-making authority. In contrast, the teacher aide does not act independently and has no decision-making authority. The aide performs assigned routine functions under supervision.

Greer suggested that teacher assistants perform the following activities; stars indicate those activities suitable for teacher aides as well.

1. Reinforcing positive behavior★

2. Assisting in instructing large groups

3. Tutoring individuals and small groups of children

4. Correcting home and seat work

5. Checking standardized and informal tests

6. Observing and recording behavior★

7. Collecting materials and preparing displays, teaching centers, and similar instructional activities★

8. Assisting children with make-up work as a result of absence from school or class

9. Assisting students with oral and written communication

10. Participating in reading and story-telling activities

11. Assisting with hands-on activities★

12. Assisting with fine and gross motor activities, physical development, and lifetime physical and recreational activities★

13. Providing a model with whom the children can identify★

14. Recording written materials for children who have visual or other learning disabilities★

15. Assisting children with extended-day activities

16. Helping children solve personal conflicts with other children

17. Assisting on instructional field trip activities★

18. Assisting children with self-care activities★

19. Assisting with feeding and toileting★

20. Working with audiovisual equipment★

21. Assisting the teacher with noninstructional tasks★

22. Assisting in classroom organization and management. (1978, 4)

Parents who function as paraprofessionals need training. Croft (1979) suggested the following sequence of activities for training parents in their duties as teacher assistants and aides:

1. *School orientation.* This training session offers general background information about the school program, its practices and procedures, and provides an informal welcome and get-acquainted time, a tour of the school and facilities, refreshments, and a question-and-answer period.

2. *Small group meetings.* In these sessions, parents discuss their feelings and expectations and learn their roles and duties. An experienced parent paraprofessional currently teaching in the school can lead the discussion.

3. *Practice observations and visits.* Trainees, as individuals or in a small group, observe classroom procedures and discuss their observations with a teacher or qualified professional or paraprofessional.

4. *Classroom assistance.* After training with a supervisor, who may be a trained parent paraprofessional, parent aides follow the daily routine in their assigned classrooms. At the end of the session, supervisor and trainee evaluate and discuss the trainee's performance.

5. *Group meeting.* After all parents have had at least one opportunity to assist in the classroom and discuss their experiences, they meet together to reassess and clarify their duties as paraprofessionals.

6. *Revision of work schedule.* Periodically, professionals and paraprofessionals meet as a group to evaluate and revise as necessary the parent-teacher relationship in the classroom.

Informal discussions and individual conferences may supplement these formal training sessions if they will benefit the trainees.

Greer (1978) presented an agenda for a five-day training workshop for paraprofessionals. This training program covered these topics:

1. An overview of special education

2. The paraprofessional's role in special education

3. The paraprofessional's duties in the classroom and school

4. The paraprofessional's responsibilities

5. Personnel procedures, payroll, administrative organization, communication, and so on

6. An overview of community agency resources and interagency cooperation

7. The support services available within the school system, such as art and music therapy, social work, counseling, and psychological services.

The training program also included visits to schools, special education facilities, community agencies, and classrooms.

In addition to serving as teacher assistants and aides, parents of exceptional children can serve as aides for field trips, parties, and special events; library aides; clerical aides; lunchroom or cafeteria aides; and playground and physical education aides. They can help various specialized personnel also, such as music and art teachers, physical and occupational therapists, psychologists and counselors, social workers, and others.

PARENTS AS INSTRUCTORS

Frequently, educators in both regular and special education settings overlook parents' skills and talents in their children's formal educational process. Often, parents' vocations or avocations prepare them to contribute significantly to their children's instructional programs. Much depends on the students' instructional objectives and the teacher's ability to integrate the lesson content into the curriculum.

With minimal guidance, parents can become effective instructors. They can prepare and conduct brief lessons or more extended minicourses related to their occupations, hobbies, and other interests. Many programs already use parents as instructors.

Hicks (1977) invited parents into the classroom "to do their thing" in a series of half-hour lessons. Parents learned about this *Parents' Day* program at a regular parent group meeting, at which time they could ask questions and sign up to conduct sessions.

Hicks scheduled lessons on the same day of the week throughout the school year; parents could select either a morning or afternoon session. Parents received a reminder letter two weeks before their scheduled appearance (Figure 9-4).

Parents' lessons varied greatly during the year, generally focusing on occupations, avocations, travel, and special interests. On occasion, the children visited the parent's home or work place as part of the lesson.

PARENTS' DAY

Date: _____

Dear _____:

The students and I are looking forward to your presentation on _____,
                                                                   (Day)
_____. Please complete the applicable portions of the form below and
(Date)
return it to me at least one week before your presentation. This will help me plan
and schedule your lesson.

The students and I appreciate your time and effort.

Morning parents only

I will present at: (check one)
_____ 9:00–9:30 AM
_____ 10:00–10:30 AM
_____ 11:00–11:30 AM

Afternoon parents only

I will present at: (check one)
_____ 12:30–1:00 PM
_____ 1:30–2:00 PM

All parents

Lesson topic or title: _____
_____

Please write a brief explanation of your lesson plan:
_____
_____
_____

All parents (check those appropriate)

_____ I will require one-half hour.
_____ I will require more than one-half hour.
        (The estimated time is _____.)
_____ Everything is planned.
_____ Call me so that we can plan in more detail.
        (Telephone number: _____)
_____ I will bring all the necessary materials and equipment.
_____ I will need _____
_____
_____ I will have some expenses. I would like to be reimbursed.

        Thank you.

(Hicks 1977, 54)

FIGURE 9-4

Parents' Reminder Letter

Grunbaum (1975) offered a similar program in a first-grade classroom, inviting parents to lead vocational preview lessons and craft minicourses. Parents visited the classroom and discussed their work, why they chose it, their training, their likes and dislikes in their work, and their hours, benefits, vacation days, and salaries. Children could ask questions at the end of the presentation and occasionally visited the parents' work places.

Parents also conducted minicourses, one afternoon a week for five weeks, in such crafts as knitting, crocheting, macrame, embroidery, first aid, puppet making, baking, flower arranging, and ceramics. Some courses took place in the parents' homes.

Granowsky et al. (1977) suggested a vocational preview program for more advanced students in which parent instructors discussed such occupations as homemaking, business, volunteer work, auto mechanics, nursing, and teaching. The program included field trips.

PARENTS AS VOLUNTEERS

Parent volunteers can contribute significantly to the quality of the services offered to exceptional children. Along with teachers and paraprofessionals, they can become an integral part of the exceptional child's educational team.

The National School Volunteer Program cited four reasons for using volunteers in the classroom and school (Greer 1978):

1. Relieving the professional staff of nonteaching duties

2. Providing needed services to individual children to supplement the work of the classroom teacher

3. Enriching the experiences of children beyond that normally available in school

4. Building better understanding of school problems among citizens and stimulating widespread citizen support for public education. (4)

Although parents are the most frequent volunteers, siblings, older elementary and secondary school students, college students, senior citizens, business and professional people, members of church and civic groups, and other members of the community also volunteer in the schools. The major prerequisite is a willingness to help exceptional children. Volunteers should also be personable in their relationships with others, dependable in discharging assigned duties, and willing and able to follow instructions.

The special education parent volunteer works under the direct supervision of a professional teacher, therapist, administrator, or other qualified staff person, and occasionally under a teacher assistant. Volunteers generally work on task-specific activities, either individually or in small groups. For example, volunteers may check a child's home or class assignments, assist during field trips and special events, serve as a companion or guide for a child, reinforce acceptable behavior and work, or prepare instructional materials and equipment (Greer 1978).

Volunteers should participate in a brief preservice training program, as well as in on-the-job training. Preservice training workshops introduce volunteers to special education, school, and classroom processes and procedures, and spell out their roles and functions. The training emphasizes the importance of confidentiality and attendance and offers an opportunity to discuss the program with experienced volunteers and to visit the classroom to observe and discuss the program with the teacher. On-the-job training is a continuous process in which volunteers learn the specific activities for which they will be responsible.

The prudent teacher matches tasks with the volunteers' abilities, interests, and special skills. A questionnaire completed by potential volunteers during recruitment or preservice training can help teachers assign tasks and develop schedules (Figure 9-5). Individual interviews can supplement questionnaire data if necessary.

FIGURE 9-5
Parent-Volunteer
Questionnaire

Date _____

Parents' Names _____

Child's Name _____ Telephone Number _____

Teacher's Name _____

Parents! We need your help. Please consider helping with the activities and projects listed on this questionnaire. Check all those activities for which you can volunteer service. Your participation will help us provide an interesting, stimulating, individualized educational program for your children.

Mother   Father

_____ _____ I would like to assist in the classroom on a regular basis. The times I have available are:

                              Days   Hours
                              _____   _____
                              _____   _____

_____ _____ I would like to assist *occasionally* in the classroom.

                      (check one)
                      a.   Contact me _____
                      b.   I will contact the school _____

_____ _____ I would like to assist from my home.

                                                              (cont.)

In-Classroom Activities

_____ _____ Read a story to the children.

_____ _____ Assist children in a learning center.

_____ _____ Assist individual children with learning and remedial tasks.

_____ _____ Assist with the music program.

_____ _____ Assist with the art program.

_____ _____ Assist with the movement activities program.

_____ _____ Work puzzles and play table games with the children.

_____ _____ Help with cooking projects.

_____ _____ Assist with writing activities.

_____ _____ Assist with carpentry projects.

_____ _____ Assist with homemaking projects.

_____ _____ Assist with the care of classroom pets.

_____ _____ Assist with gardening and horticultural projects.

_____ _____ Assist children during recess, snack time, lunch, and free time.

_____ _____ Take a child for a walk.

_____ _____ Assist with field trips.

Home-Based Activities

_____ _____ Make instructional materials: games, flash cards, puppets, costumes, charts.

_____ _____ Type.

_____ _____ Help with costumes for dress-up events.

_____ _____ Cut out and catalog pictures from magazines, catalogs, and newspapers for instructional use.

_____ _____ Help repair classroom furnishings and instructional materials and equipment.

_____ _____ Help construct new furnishings and equipment for the classroom.

_____ _____ Organize parties for birthdays and holidays.

_____ _____ Babysit for parents who are volunteering their service to the classroom.

_____ _____ Care for classroom pets during vacations.

_____ _____ Make props and sets for plays, parties, and special events.

_____ _____ Make room and bulletin board decorations.

_____ _____ Make posters.

_____ _____ Assemble and staple materials.

FIGURE 9-5
(cont.)

(cont.)

_____ _____ Research and organize field trips.

_____ _____ Help plan and conduct parent activities, such as meetings, educational training programs, and conferences.

_____ _____ Research and contact sources for free instructional supplies (computer cards and paper, wood scraps, boxes, carpet, print shop discards, spools, pencils, paper).

_____ _____ Make items to sell for fund raising.

_____ _____ Assist with fund-raising activities.

_____ _____ Plan and organize social events.

What other activities could you help with?

A. In the classroom:

B. At home:

What other family members or friends are interested in volunteering services to the children?

A. _____

B. _____

Your comments, concerns, and questions are welcome.

Rockwell and Grafford (1977) suggested five ways that parent volunteers can help:

1. Act as "room parents"

2. Help children in the classroom during school hours

3. Help in the school during school hours

4. Help in the classroom and school after school hours

5. Help at home.

Table 9-1 lists activities in each of these categories suggested by several authors (Rockwell and Grafford 1977; Benson and Ross 1972; Cory 1974; Granowsky et al. 1977; O'Brien 1977; Sayler 1971; Shea 1978; Stahl 1977).

Parent partner programs offer other volunteer opportunities. Teachers may be able to pair parents to help each other with their exceptional children. For example, parents may go shopping together, share the names of physicians and dentists who treat exceptional children, attend

TABLE 9-1 Parent Volunteer Activities

Room Parents

• Foster working relationships among classroom, school, home, and community workers

• Coordinate parent volunteer program
  —Recruit volunteers
  —Help in preservice and on-the-job training programs
  —Schedule volunteers

• Oversee classroom, school, and community committees

• Coordinate parties, field trips, special events, student performances, and parent meetings

Classroom Volunteers during School Hours

• Serve as managers of learning centers
  —Schedule, supervise, and assist children
  —Prepare materials and equipment

• Assist with arts and crafts, music, carpentry, sewing, gardening, cooking, science, and so on

• Assist with recreational activities, large group activities

• Assist individual children in reading, writing, spelling, and arithmetic

• Organize and supervise snacktime, freetime, and so on

• Supervise personal hygiene activities (handwashing, toileting)

• Prepare and operate audiovisual equipment

• Assist with routine evaluation of home and class assignments

Parent Volunteers

• Parent volunteer activities in the school *during* school hours may include the following:
  —Serve as bulletin board and display designers and constructors
  —Assist in researching, organizing, and supervising field trips
  —Supervise cafeteria, lunchroom, playground, hallways
  —Locate reference materials and other resources needed by the professional staff
  —Assist in the library, audiovisual center, physical education equipment center, and office
  —Accompany teachers on home visits
  —Serve as interpreter for non-English-speaking parents
  —Serve as manager of all-school learning center
  —Coordinate all-school special event, festival, and holiday activities
  —Assist in the evaluation of materials, curriculum, and equipment
  —Serve as clerical assistant (typing, filing, duplicating, counting and depositing money, taking attendance, lunch count, answering the phone, sorting mail, scheduling appointments

• Parent volunteer activities in the classroom and school *after* school hours may include the following:
  —Create and construct learning materials (games, flashcards, individual project charts, study carrels, filmstrips, movies, slide presentations)
  —Conduct and supervise tutoring programs
  —Care for equipment, materials, furnishings, physical facilities
  —Clean, paint, and repair materials, equipment

TABLE 9-1 *(continued)*

251 ∎

CHAPTER NINE
SCHOOL, HOME, AND
COMMUNITY
PROGRAMS

—Confer with other parents and community persons related to school and classroom programs
—Serve on various education-related committees

• Parent volunteer activities *in the home and community* may include the following:
    —Organize and operate tutoring centers
    —Construct and repair instructional materials
    —Coordinate and supervise Saturday and evening field trips and special events
    —Locate community resources for utilization in school and classroom programs
    —Organize and conduct fund-raising activities
    —Serve as members and officers in various community organizations, agencies, boards, and committees bearing on the welfare of exceptional children
    —Participate in groups that lobby at the local, regional, state and federal levels for the benefit of exceptional children

Sources: Rockwell and Grafford 1977; Benson and Ross 1972; Cory 1974; Granowsky et al. 1977; O'Brien 1977; Sayler 1971; Shea 1978; Stahl 1977.

meetings together for mutual support, or just simply talk about their progress and problems in raising their children.

Teachers should take care to train the partners and supervise their relationship in a partner program. Partner training should remind parents to share but not attempt to solve the other parent's problems, to use active listening skills, to maintain objectivity, and to guard confidentiality. Teachers should also meet with parent partners at least once a month to ensure they are exchanging accurate informaton and building a healthy relationship.

Parents can help train other parents in more direct ways as well. Hall, Grinstead, Collier, and Hall (1980) used parents to implement their "Responsive Parenting" program. In this program, parents who had successfully completed at least one behavior change project, had demonstrated a grasp of the principles and practices of behavior modification, and had shown enthusiasm became apprentice group leaders. As apprentices, they took on increasing responsibilities for a small instructional group. If they attended meetings regularly, gave appropriate instructions and feedback to the members, and helped each member produce workable behavior change programs, they became group leaders. After directing three successful groups, parents could apprentice as program directors.

Hall and associates suggested several advantages of this approach. Parents can relate to parent trainers as people who have "been there." In addition, parents are less likely to be in awe of a parent trainer than of a professional and are less likely to reject a program as impractical if another parent has used it successfully. Using parents as trainers also helps ease the personnel shortage and reduce the cost of the training program.

However, Hall and associates cautioned against the indiscriminate use of parents as trainers. Their program was geared to middle-class parents with strong academic and social skills, who already possessed many skills for leading groups. Another study of a program using parent trainers yielded inconsistent results (Edgar, Singer, Ritchie, and Heggelund 1981). In this study, some group participants rated parent communication skills low, though they accepted information they received from parent trainers as correct.

PARENTS ON COMMITTEES

Parent participation as chairpersons or members of classroom and school committees can contribute significantly to the exceptional child's education. Through committee work, parents not only contribute to the classroom and school but also receive indirect training in serving exceptional children's needs through program development, operation, staffing, and evaluation. They develop appreciation for staffing concerns, curriculum development, fiscal exigencies, materials and equipment needs, and other demands of instructional programming.

Karnes and Zehrbach (1972) and Granowsky et al. (1977) encouraged teachers to establish classroom and school parent advisory committees. These committees of three or four parents meet regularly with the teacher or other professionals to discuss current programs, problems and plans for the future. A school advisory committee should represent all constituencies, for it focuses on issues affecting the total school or special education program.

An advisory committee can serve as a liaison between school or classroom and home and community, functioning as a permanent parent-to-parent communications committee to announce meetings, special events, legislative happenings, personnel changes, and so on. The school or classroom advisory committee can assume responsibility, in cooperation with the professional staff, for organizing and directing several ad hoc or temporary committees.

Ad hoc committees, like advisory committees, should be broadly representative of the parents in the classroom or school. They form to accomplish specific tasks and disband once they have attained their objectives and have reported to the advisory committee. Ad hoc committees are essentially "working" (Shea 1978) or "action" (Pasanella and Volkmor 1977) groups with limited functions and short lives. Service on ad hoc committees is ideal for busy parents with limited time to devote to committee work.

Berger (1981) conducted an informal survey of 350 parents that duplicated a 1977 Gallup poll of public attitudes toward public schools.

Of the respondents, 82 percent indicated a willingness to serve on one or more of the following committees:

1. Curriculum

2. Discipline and related problems

3. Teacher evaluation

4. Student-teacher relations

5. Home study and work habits

6. Extracurricular activities

7. Student assessment and test results

8. Educational innovations

9. Community use of school buildings

10. Career education

11. Athletic programs

12. Handicapped students

13. Public relations of schools

14. Work-study programs

15. Student dropouts

16. Educational costs and school finance

17. School facilities

18. School transportation

19. Education for citizenship

20. Progress of recent graduates.

A number of other activities are suitable for parent committee work:

1. Fund raising

2. Special projects (parties, open house, field trips, dramatic presentations)

3. Curriculum evaluation

4. Textbook and instructional materials review

5. Program evaluation

6. Newsletter

7. Public relations

8. Local, state, and federal liaison

9. Parent education and training

10. Transportation for special events

11. Refreshments

12. Parent-teacher relations

13. Report cards and grading

14. Community resources

15. Legal and counseling referrals

16. Respite care services

17. Child care and babysitting services

18. Parent library.

Whether serving on a classroom or school advisory or ad hoc committee, committee members can benefit from the following guidelines (Pasanella and Volkmor 1977):

1. Remember the committee's purpose and objectives. Stick with the task at hand.

2. Remember that people's attitudes toward exceptionality change slowly. Be patient.

3. Be confident in the committee's ability to accomplish the assigned task. Approach the task positively.

4.. Start small. Take one step at a time.

5. Function within the system. Become an integral part of the classroom or school.

6. Seek financial, administrative, informational, and other assistance when necessary.

7. Use committee expertise at home first. Once the task is accomplished, the committee can help other schools, classrooms, and communities.

8. Do not impede progress by becoming unnecessarily aggressive or antagonistic. However, do not be too passive.

PARENTS AS HOME-BASED TEACHERS

In recent years, teachers have increasingly advocated home programs for exceptional children. Programs to train parents as home-based teachers vary greatly in structure, content, and personnel requirements, however. Some programs offer highly structured, systematically conducted activities designed to train parents and supervise and evaluate their instructional activities at home (Shearer 1974; Gordon and Breivogel 1976). Others are more loosely structured to help parents with tutoring and home study (Barsch 1969; Kelly 1974; Spadafore 1979; Gang and Poche 1982).

Programs may simply teach parents how to monitor their children's work on teacher-assigned projects, or they may train parents to teach highly specific readiness skills and academic knowledge to supplement or reinforce school instruction. Content may emphasize parent-child interpersonal interactions or may focus on instruction in specific skills.

The exceptional child's teacher organizes and supervises some home-based programs that involve only the parent, child, and teacher. Others may employ professionals, paraprofessionals, or other parents specifically trained for home-based instructional programs. In general, however, structured home-based parent involvement programs have several common dimensions (Levitt and Cohen 1976).

1. *Preservice orientation and training of liaison personnel.* Training may range from a two- or three-hour orientation to an extensive course of instruction lasting several days or weeks. Many training programs come with printed instructional materials, procedural manuals and guidelines, and audiovisual presentations prepared specifically for the program.

2. *Parent orientation.* Most programs offer parent orientation sessions to present program goals, objectives, methods, materials, and procedures. Sessions may be small group meetings or individual conferences in the home, at school, or at a clinic. Frequently, printed and audiovisual aids supplement verbal explanations.

3. *Professional leaders.* Few special education programs use paraprofessionals as parent instructors or as liaison personnel in home-based programs. Although teachers usually consult parents, they are ultimately responsible for establishing instructional objectives and prescribing teaching content and methods. Programs allow the teacher varying degrees of latitude in curricular decisions.

4. *Demonstrations.* The most common training method is teacher or paraprofessional demonstration of the instructional technique while the parent observes. The teacher then observes the parent as he or she uses the technique with the child and critiques and discusses the parent's performance. Participants repeat this procedure until they are satisfied with the result.

5. *Performance monitoring.* All home-based programs incorporate procedures for monitoring acceptable parent performance over time.

6. *Reinforcement.* All programs also include procedures for systematically reinforcing parents' efforts and successful performance.

7. *Evaluation.* The teacher only, or the teacher in cooperation with a paraprofessional, assumes responsibility for evaluating the exceptional child's progress and the parents' performance.

8. *Parent input.* Teachers consult parents about the activities, materials, and equipment used in home-based teaching. For a program to be effective, parents must see the sense of it for their children.

In a follow-up study of parents who had completed the Read Project, a program to train parents to be more effective teachers of their retarded children, Baker, Heifetz, and Murphy (1980) found that almost half continued to teach their children at home, one year later. The parents identified several limitations to home teaching: time, the child's learning ability, the parents' teaching ability, and professional support. Teachers considering training parents as home-based teachers should account for these potential problems in their planning.

Project PACE

Project PACE (Parent Action in Childhood Education) (Crozier 1976) takes professional preschool services into exceptional children's homes. The program serves children up to six years old with Down's syndrome, cerebral palsy, speech delay, hyperactivity, and behavior disorders.

PACE trains parents to teach their children. A professional home teacher visits the child's home for one and one-half hours each week and presents one to five lesson plans to the parent for the following week's work. Each lesson plan includes specific learner objectives, precise instructional procedures, and activity cards with spaces for the parents' comments and evaluation. PACE lessons focus on socialization, speech, academics, self-help skills, motor skills, and other special instructional topics for exceptional children. The daily lessons last fifteen to thirty minutes. During each home visit, the teacher explains and demonstrates the lessons and then gives the parent an opportunity to practice the lesson while the teacher observes and critiques the practice session.

PACE home teachers perform other supportive services as well:

1. Answer questions about the child's exceptionality, the educational program, and other parent concerns

2. Bring specialized consultants into the home to confer with the parents and work with the child

3. Provide reading materials responding to the parent's needs and requests

4. Accompany parent and child to doctor's appointments and to diagnostic centers as advocates

5. Explore educational placements for the child and discuss them with parents

6. Represent the child's and parents' interests to teachers, administrators, and other professionals in schools and treatment centers.

Although PACE is designed primarily for preschool populations, many of its concepts and procedures are equally useful with older exceptional children and their parents.

Project PEECH

Home-based teaching is one of several components of Project PEECH (Precise Early Education for Children with Handicaps) (Karnes and Franke 1978). In this program, professional teachers visit the home to train parents to instruct the exceptional child. Lesson plans include instructional objectives, instructional materials, teaching procedures, reinforcement techniques, and evaluation criteria (Figure 9-6). The teacher follows established guidelines in conducting the program:

FIGURE 9-6
Project PEECH
Lesson Plan

SHAPE LOTTO

This activity will help the child:
1. Learn the names of basic geometric shapes.
2. Match shapes that are the same.
3. See form in his environment.

You will need:
1. Three pieces of stiff paper or cardboard—about 12" x 16"
2. Ruler, scissors, crayons.
3. Large envelope.

TO MAKE THE SHAPE LOTTO:

1. Using a black crayon and ruler, divide one piece of cardboard into eight equal spaces. Draw a shape in each space, following the diagram. This is the game card.

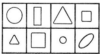

2. Draw the same shapes on each of the other two pieces of cardboard. Cut them out. These are the individual shape pieces used in playing the game. There should be 16 pieces.

EMPHASIZE THESE WORDS:

1. Shape.
2. Circle.
3. Square.

4. Triangle
5. Rectangle
6. Oval.

TO USE THE SHAPE LOTTO:

The First Day: Place the game card on a table in front of your child. "Look at all the shapes." Point out each shape, helping your child trace it with his finger. Talk about each one as he traces it. "This shape goes around and around. See how this shape has corners." Ask your child to repeat the word "shape." Then, referring to one set of the individual shapes, say, "All of these shapes have names. Let's talk about their names." Hold up a circle. "This shape is a circle. Say circle with me. Now feel the circle. Can you find a circle just like this one on the game board? Put this one on top of it." Repeat this procedure until each shape has been named and placed on the game board. Then say, "Now, let's put the game back in the envelope. First, give me the circles." Ask for each shape by name, helping your child find the right one.

The Second Day: Let your child hold the game board. Review the shape names. "Yesterday we talked about

(cont.)

the names of these shapes. Let's see if you remember them. Show me the circle. Say, 'This is a circle.' Now, find the square." Repeat this procedure for all of the shapes. Give your child time to find the right shape but be ready to help him if he is not sure. After each shape has been named, give him both sets of individual shapes. "I will watch while you play the game. Put these shapes where they belong on the game board." Show your child what you mean by selecting one of the shapes and placing it on top of the matching shape on the game board. Encourage your child to name the shapes as he works.

The Third Day: Place one set of individual shapes in front of your child; help him name them. "Let's play a new game with the shapes. First, you choose a shape; then we'll look all around the house to see how many things we can find that have the same shape." Repeat the game with the remaining shapes.

The Fourth Day: Place one set of individual shapes in front of your child and ask him to name them as you point to each one. Collect the shapes. "Let's play a guessing game with the shapes." Have your child put his hands behind his back. Put a shape in his hand and ask him to identify the shape by feeling it. After

he has guessed the names of the shapes. lay them in a row on the table. "Look carefully at the shapes because in a minute I will take one away and you will have to tell me which one is missing." Ask your child to hide his eyes while you remove a shape. Repeat this activity with several other shapes.

The Fifth Day: Place both sets of shapes in a pile in front of the child. "The shapes are all mixed up. Can you find all the shapes that are the same and put them together?" Show your child what you mean by finding all the circles and putting them in a group. Then put them back with the other shapes. "Now you do it by yourself." As soon as your child finishes, ask him to name the groups of shapes.

OTHER WAYS YOU CAN HELP YOUR CHILD:

1. Point out shapes in the environment: plates, glasses, knobs, and clocks are circles; windows and tables are squares; doors are rectangles.
2. Help your child make designs from the shapes.

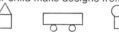

3. Help him draw and cut out shapes.
4. Let him find shapes in picture magazines.

(Karnes and Zehrbach 1972, 15)

1. Select lesson objectives responsive to the child's needs and readily attainable by the parent teacher

2. Encourage parents' understanding and interest in the program by planning and discussing lessons with them

3. Provide needed instructional materials and equipment or select materials available in the home

4. Demonstrate the lesson for parents, request that they conduct the lesson, and critique their performance

5. Reinforce parents' efforts and successes

6. Establish a system for parent-teacher communication about the home teaching program

7. Discuss and evaluate the home teaching program with the parent at regularly scheduled conferences.

The home teaching program, along with other components of Project PEECH, can serve exceptional children in a variety of educational and clinical settings.

Portage Project

259 ■

CHAPTER NINE
SCHOOL, HOME, AND
COMMUNITY
PROGRAMS

Portage Project

The Portage Project (Shearer 1974) is a home-based parent training program that uses precision teaching methods to help parents work with their preschool exceptional children. The program operates on the following premises:

1. Parents care about their children and want them to attain their maximum potential, however great or limited that potential may be.

2. Parents can, with instruction, modeling, and reinforcement, learn to be more effective teachers of their own children.

3. The socio-economic and educational or intellectual levels of the parents do not determine either their willingness to teach their children or the extent of gains the children will attain as a result of parental instruction.

4. The precision teaching method is the preferred learning model since feedback is provided daily to parents and weekly to staff, thereby reinforcing both when goals are met. Moreover, the method provides a continual data base for curriculum modification, thus maximizing the likelihood of success for parents and children (49).

A *home teacher*—either a trained professional or paraprofessional—visits parents to instruct them how to teach their exceptional child. Each teacher is responsible for serving approximately fifteen families. Teachers visit each family weekly for one and a half hours.

The exceptional child's individualized curriculum may focus on language, self-help, cognitive development, motor skills, or social-emotional behaviors. Each week the teacher selects three objectives for the child to learn, taking care to choose objectives that parents and child can achieve comfortably. The home teacher collects baseline data to check the child's readiness for the activities.

During the week, parents complete the learning activities with their children and maintain appropriate records. On the next visit, the home teacher collects additional data to determine if the child has learned the prescribed skills and is ready to proceed to the next activities.

The goals of the home visits are to instruct parents on what to teach, how to teach it, what behaviors to reinforce, what behaviors to extinguish, and how to observe and record behavioral data. The Portage kit offers the home teacher and parent a variety of programming and instructional aids:

1. *Activity cards and checklists.* A checklist itemizes 580 sequenced behaviors in all curricular areas. The cards describe activities for each of the checklist behaviors. Each card identifies the instructional topic, the title of the activity, the appropriate range for activity, a

behavior objective, specific teaching methods, instructional materials needed, and cross-references to cards with correlated activities (Figure 9-7).

2. *Activity chart.* The home teacher and parents complete an activity chart to record the child's progress (Figure 9-8). The teacher fills in the child's and home teacher's names, the week of activity, the behavior or objective, and the directions or methods the parent will use to instruct the child. The parent completes the remainder of the chart at the end of each learning session.

3. *Weekly progress report.* Parents complete a progress report during the week and review it with the home teacher at the next visit (Figure 9-9).

4. *Behavior evaluation form.* As the exceptional child attains instructional goals, the teacher or parent completes a behavior evaluation form, recording the accomplishment and the date the child achieved it (Figure 9-10).

Parent–Supervised Home Study

Special education teachers frequently assign home study projects and ask parents to supervise their child's study. This activity often causes

FIGURE 9-7
Portage Project Activity Card

```
Portage Project
                                CARD NO. 76              MOTOR
AGE 3–4

TITLE:
  Walks up stairs, one foot on each step.

BEHAVIORAL DESCRIPTION:
  The child will climb steps alternating feet with each step while holding on to the
  handrail.

SUGGESTED ACTIVITIES AND MATERIALS:
1. Help the child accomplish the task by standing in back of him and moving his
   feet up to the next step, skipping the step his other foot is now on.
2. When he can do this with reduced physical help, just touch the leg to be moved.
3. Hold onto the child's other hand and help him walk up the steps alternating;
   then reduce the help.
4. Have one of the child's shoes tied with red string, the other with green and
   place colored yarn, red and green on alternating steps going up. Praise the
   child and reward each improvement in skill (red shoe goes on red step, green
   shoe goes on green step).
5. See Card No. M64,M56.

S76                        ©1972 C.E.S.A. No. 12
```

(Bluma et al. 1976)

FIGURE 9-8
*Portage Project Activity
Chart*

Activity Chart

PORTAGE PROJECT

CREDIT: ✓ yes _____ no

Child's Name _____ *Richie* _____

Home Teacher's Name _____ *Susan* _____

Week of _____ *Oct. 7* _____

> This is a completed Activity Chart.

BEHAVIOR:

*Richie will point to
3 colors named red,
yellow, blue,
5 trials per day,
no model.*

ACTIVITY CHART

DIRECTIONS:

*Place the 3 colored circles
6" apart on the table.
Tell Richie to put his
finger on the color you
name. Then name a color. When Richie points to
the correct color reward him with a hug, smile,
praise, cereal, and a color chip the same color he
pointed to correctly. Repeat the correct color after
him. Record the number of times Richie points to
each color correctly with an x. Change position of
circles frequently. Gradually start reducing the
amount of rewards so that by Sunday he is
working for verbal praise and the color chip.*

(Bluma et al. 1976)

confusion, frustration, and conflict at home, eventually proving counterproductive. Several authors have suggested ways to make home study
an enjoyable and productive time for both students and parents (Barsch
1969; Kelly 1974; Feder 1974; Marcovich 1975; Spadafore 1979):

1. Teachers should limit the amount of homework assigned each day.
   They may wish to vary the subject matter from day to day, as-

FIGURE 9-9
Portage Project Progress
Report

WEEKLY PROGRESS REPORT

PORTAGE PROJECT   Date ___Dec. 14___

Child's Name ___Brenda___   Home Teacher ___Jean___

I. Child's Progress

Developmental Area	Prescribed Activity (Behavior Description)	Original Baseline	Week's Post Basal	Credit
Language	The child will make the initial sound of W as in water w/aid, 3 trials each day.	1/3	3/3	*
Cognitive	The child will hand 1, 2, 3 items on request, 3 trials each	2/9	6/9	
Motor	The child will jump w/feet together from bottom stair step (w/phys. cue of pressing hands)	2/5	5/5	*

II. Prescription for Coming Week

Developmental Area	Activity (Behavior Description)	Baseline	Reinforcement	New or Continued
Language	Speech exercises - games		Piece of cereal and praise	Cont.
	1) Blow feather across table	2/3		
	2) Lick honey from outside of lips	1/3		
	3) Blow ping-pong ball up inclined plane	1/3	Sips of juice + praise	
Motor	Tricycle riding (motor aid)	2/4		New

(cont.)

III. Home Visit Activities

Developmental Area	Activity (Behavior Description)	Review Prescribed or not Prescribed	Baseline	Post Basal	Credit
Lang. P-C	Reviewed prescribed activities Worked on prescriptions Read story to Brenda	N. P.	0/1	1/1	*

IV. Teacher-Child Relationship

Brenda was very cooperative but she tired easily. This may be due to her new medication.

V. Parent's Comments

Brenda had a good week. She worked well & liked doing her work. Am glad we're working on speech sounds.

VI. Log Information

(Dr. appointments, clinic appointments, other important information)

Clinic appointment on December 18

(Bluma et al. 1976)

signing mathematics on Monday, spelling on Tuesday, reading on Wednesday, and so on. The student should be able to complete the home assignment within a specified period appropriate for the child's ability and attention span.

2. Parents should establish a daily study time convenient to both child and parent. Study time should take place before the student becomes involved in playtime, television watching, or other leisure activities. These activities become rewards if scheduled after the study period.

3. Parents should establish a study area in the home and use it each day. The study area must be quiet, well-lit, away from household traffic, and isolated from radio, television, and nonstudying siblings and parents. The child's room is appropriate if it contains a desk or table; the kitchen table is another possibility. The parent should be nearby to help out when necessary.

FIGURE 9-10
Portage Project Behavior
Evaluation Form

BEHAVIOR EVALUATION

Child __Jim__   Period __9-3 – 10-16__
Teacher __Jean__

Special Goal	Date	Cognitive	Communicative	Motor	Self-Help	Socialization	Parent/Child
attends to tasks – 10 min.	9/3					10/2	
places O+□ in foamboard w/help	9/3	9/10		9/10			
" " " no trial + error	9/10	9/17		9/17			
strings 5 beads in 2 min – no aid	9/10			9/17			
stands on one foot 5 sec. w/support	9/10			9/17			
" " " " no support	9/17			10/2			
names 7 action pictures in imit.	9/17		9/24				9/24
" " " no model	9/24		10/2				
names picture using 3 word phrase	9/24						
put on pants – no aid	10/2				10/9		
hops on one foot in place w/support	10/2			10/9			
unbuttons 4 buttons – pushed halfway through hole	10/2			10/16	10/16		
" " – no aid	10/9			10/16	10/16		
traces letters M + N w/finger	10/9	10/16					
draws letters M + N by connecting dots	10/9	10/16					
draws □ by connecting 4 dots	10/16	10/23		10/23			
buttons 4 buttons – pushed 1/2 way through holes	10/16						
draws □ in imitation of model	10/16	10/23		10/23			
Total							

(Bluma et al. 1976)

264

4. The study session must begin positively. Parents may want to use an egg timer to time the session. A special table cloth on the study table can indicate to younger children that it is time to study. All materials should be ready in the study area.

5. The teacher should prepare a lesson plan for the parent stating the lesson objective, recommended teaching methods, necessary materials, and evaluation procedures. At the beginning of the study time, the parent should review the assignment with the child and make sure the child understands the directions. If the directions remain unclear to both parent and child, they should do the best work possible and send a note to the teacher explaining the confusion. Such notes save the child embarrassment about incomplete or inaccurate work.

6. The parent should check the child's work for general quality and accuracy, reviewing it with the child and correcting it. If parents cannot work out the correct answer, they should send a note to the teacher.

7. Parents should maintain a record of the child's home study assignments, logging the assignment, the work sessions, the child's effort, work completed, work accuracy, and rewards.

8. The parent should reinforce the child's effort and accuracy. Social reinforcement is more desirable, supported by occasional tangible rewards when necessary.

9. Before returning the home study assignment to the teacher, parents should sign and date it.

10. Parents and teacher should meet for a preprogram orientation session so that the teacher can explain the purpose of home study and relate the assignments to the student's educational objectives. They should meet periodically thereafter to discuss the home study program. Monthly or bimonthly evaluation sessions allow parents and teacher to discuss the student's progress, to discuss whether home study is proceeding as planned, whether it is effective, and whether it should continue, change, or end.

Vantour and Stewart-Kurker (1980) developed a lending library to motivate parents and children in home study programs. They rewrote the instructions in commercially available instructional materials to make them easy to use by parents and children at home. Teachers wrote *prescriptions* to specify the book, cards, games, and other materials the child should take home from the library. The system allowed teachers to coordinate library materials with classroom lessons.

PARENT RESOURCES

The Parent Resource Center

Establishing a parent resource center is an effective way to meet the informational and social–emotional needs of the parents of exceptional children (Edmister 1977; Karnes and Franke 1978). The center staff should select materials and equipment carefully to respond to the parent users' needs.

Borrowers can use materials, such as the following, at the center or borrow them for home or classroom.

1. For parents: books, pamphlets, periodicals, filmstrips and audiotapes, cassettes, films, and teaching packages on a broad range of topics related to raising exceptional children

2. For teachers: textbooks and journals on exceptionality, parent education, and training materials and kits

3. For exceptional children: toys, books, periodicals, records, and educational games.

The center can also provide important services to parents, exceptional children, and teachers, serving as a facility for individual study, small group meetings, conferences, informal discussions, and social activities. If located in a standard classroom, staff can furnish it with library facilities such as bookcases, storage cabinets, audiovisual equipment, and tables and chairs. One area of the room can serve as an audiovisual viewing area, another as a small group discussion center, and another as a private place for individual conferences or study activities. The center can also include a play or discovery area for children.

Edmister (1977) recommended that the center contain the following equipment:

■ Film projector and screen

■ Filmstrip and slide projectors

■ Videotape monitor

■ Cassette recorder and tapes

■ Typewriter

■ Record player

■ A desk and chair for the staff person and storage

■ File cabinet

■ Library tables and chairs

■ Display stands.

The center may share this equipment with school personnel. Regularly scheduled hours, including some late afternoon and evening hours for parents and teachers unable to visit the center during traditional working hours are important, as is a standard lending policy. The center might lend books and pamphlets for two weeks, for example, toys and games for one week, and films, videotapes, and filmstrips for two days. Ideally, a parent-professional committee supervises the center, with day-to-day operation the responsibility of parent volunteers.

Teaching Packages

Interest is growing in using *teaching packages* to replace or supplement more traditional ways of training parents to help their children, such as expert trainers and printed materials (Stowitschek and Hofmeister 1975). Reavis, Rice, and Hamel defined a teaching package in this way:

> A teaching package is a set of systematic materials and a prescribed procedure for delivering content and process to learners. The term "teaching package" implies careful programming of the instructional events and the contingencies of reinforcement. Teaching packages are self-contained and exportable. They can be used independent of the professional who developed and validated the package. (1976, 45)

Teaching packages offer several advantages in educating exceptional children:

1. They expose parents to quality instructional programs and methodologies

2. They offer a quality teaching program for parents without regular access to professional services because of location, inadequate transportation, poor availability of professionals, inability to employ a babysitter, or other reasons.

3. They are a cost-effective way to provide professional expertise to many parents.

Although paper-and-pencil packages are most common, teaching packages frequently include photo slides, audiotapes, videotapes, and films as well. More and more packages are becoming available for use on home computers. Packages must be economical to produce in multiple copies and must be amenable to easy transportation and mailing.

Teachers wishing to develop their own teaching packages for parents should seek expert advice on their content and methodology, field test the package with a selected population of parents, and revise the package before producing and distributing it for general use. A well-presented package includes the following:

1. Step-by-step instructions for conducting the teaching session

2. All materials needed to conduct the lesson

3. Student materials such as worksheets, games, or flashcards

4. Materials for monitoring and recording the child's progress, such as charts, graphs, and checklists

5. Feedback or evaluation forms to inform the teacher of the child's progress and the parents' evaluation of the package.

Packages can help parents teach academic and preacademic skills, such as addition, subtraction, multiplication, and division; number recognition; phonic skills; writing; recognition and vocalization of letters, words, and phrases; spelling; recognition of colors, shapes, and sizes; and sorting and classification. They can also guide instruction in self-care skills, such as personal hygiene, feeding, dressing, and toileting; and in behavior management techniques, such as positive reinforcement, shaping, a token economy, and desensitization (Latham and Hofmeister 1973).

Parents should use teaching packages consistently to benefit fully from them. Brief daily work sessions of ten or fifteen minutes are most effective. The package content and instructional methodology must be interesting, motivating, and relevant to the parent and exceptional child. Packages are especially useful if parents and children learn techniques they can generalize to other skills and instructional settings.

Teaching Aids

Technological advances and new teaching ideas have increased the arsenal of aids available for use in parent training programs. Cassette tapes, open-ended visuals, and videotapes are three tools that can supplement such traditional instructional aids as written and verbal directions, programmed texts, photoslide presentations, and films.

Cassette Tapes. Karnes and Zehrbach (1972) recommended cassette tapes, prepared by either parents or teachers, as effective ways to transfer knowledge or foster positive attitudes in individual or group study sessions. Tapes, which may cover such topics as parent education, exceptionality, behavior management, instructional techniques, and exceptional people's rights, offer several advantages:

1. Their recorded message is consistent over time.

2. Parents can review them as often as they want to learn the message.

3. Parents can listen to them at their convenience.

4. Recording and duplicating the tapes are relatively simple, and they are inexpensive. Schools or others can purchase or rent recorders and players at relatively low costs.

Open-Ended Visuals. Rossett (1975) developed a parent course using open-ended visuals, provocative materials designed to stimulate learning. Visuals are important not so much for themselves but for the group reactions and interactions they trigger. Properly applied visuals stimulate group members to seek facts, express feelings, and plan actions (Figure 9-11). A counselor, psychologist, teacher, or other professional or parent should coordinate the use of visuals and encourage group members to exchange ideas.

In a course for parents of deaf children, Rossett presented forty-nine open-ended visuals to parents for discussion. Visuals are equally useful for parents of children with other exceptionalities, as long as they reflect course content and respond to the group's concerns. Visuals can encourage group discussion of such common issues as diagnosis, placement, etiology, education and treatment, services, program selection and evaluation, parent responses to exceptionality, other people's responses, and legal rights.

FIGURE 9-11
Open-Ended Visual

Do you think she has to sleep with those?

Videotapes. "The human eye is limited" (Marinoff 1973, 66). People cannot take in all the actions and objects that contribute to an event. Videotapes help overcome this human limitation.

In parent education, videotapes have several uses. They can demonstrate an instructional technique or behavior management method. Teachers can use them repeatedly in different settings. They are an efficient way to show common behaviors and possible responses.

Videotapes can also offer useful feedback to parents practicing instructional methods or techniques. Recording a parent's interaction with a child or role-playing exercise preserves the incident for later parent, parent-teacher, or group evaluations of the parent's performance. Moreover, the ability to see, hear, and time the interaction strengthens the critiquing process.

Video equipment is available to parents and professionals in many schools. Tapes are relatively inexpensive and can run many times.

SUMMARY

This chapter discusses ways for parents to participate in classroom, school, home, and community programs. Parents should receive training before they work in the school or teach their children at home. The chapter discusses several training techniques, including observation, instructional coaching, modeling, and role playing. Parents can play many roles at school and at home. They can work as paraprofessionals, instructors, and volunteers in the classroom; serve on classroom and school committees; and participate as home-based instructors and home study supervisors. The chapter describes appropriate activities for each role and identifies programs and techniques available to help parents be effective in each setting.

The final pages of the chapter discuss resources for parent training, including parent resource centers and such teaching aids as cassette tapes, open-ended visuals, and videotapes.

The next and final chapter assembles the material in Chapters Five through Nine into a sample parent-teacher involvement program in a classroom of exceptional children.

EXERCISES AND DISCUSSION TOPICS

1. Observe a teacher and paraprofessional working in a classroom or resource room for exceptional children. Note each person's role and function; then interview both about their views of their roles. Using the information from the observations and interviews, develop a taxonomy of classroom or resource room functions. Compare your taxonomy to the Soar and Kaplan taxonomy in Figure 9-3.

2.   Develop an agenda for a parent paraprofessional training program for your classroom or a hypothetical classroom. Present the agenda to your study group for discussion and evaluation.

3.   Develop and administer a questionnaire to several parents on their instructional and volunteer contributions to a classroom program. Develop a plan for incorporating the results into a training program.

4.   Using data on a specific child and parent, develop a series of five lessons for parents to teach their children at home.

5.   Develop a package to help parents teach a skill to their exceptional children. Ask at least three parents to use the package. Revise the package to incorporate changes suggested by their experiences.

6.   Develop a plan for using parent committees in your classroom and school. Determine each committee's purpose, role, function, composition, and operation. Critique your plan with your study group.

7.   Research and write a brief paper on "parents in classroom, school, home, and community education programs."

8.   Using data on a specific child and his or her parents, simulate an individualized education program meeting. Assign members of your study group to play the roles of the child, parent, an interpreter, the special education teacher, a psychologist, and a school principal who is also a special education supervisor.

REFERENCES

Baker, B. L., L. J. Heifetz, and D. M. Murphy. 1980. Behavioral training of parents of mentally retarded children: One year follow-up. *American Journal of Mental Deficiency* 85 (1):31–38.

Barsch, R. H. 1969. *The parent teacher partnership*. Reston, Va.: The Council for Exceptional Children.

Benson, J., and L. Ross. 1972. Teaching parents to teach their children. *Teaching Exceptional Children* 5 (1):30–35.

Berger, E. H. 1981. *Parents as partners in education: The school and home working together*. St. Louis: C. V. Mosby.

Blackard, K. 1976. Introduction to the family training program: Working paper, 1–15. Seattle: Experimental Education Unit, Child Development and Mental Retardation Center, University of Washington.

Bluma, S. M., M. S. Shearer, A. H. Frohman, and J. M. Hilliard. 1976. Portage guide to early education: manual. Portage, Wisconsin: Co-operative Educational Service Agency #12.

Brockway, B. S. 1974. *Training in child management: A family approach.* Dubuque, Iowa: Kendall/Hunt Publishing.

Brown, S. L. 1978. A structure for early parent involvement. In *Parents on the team,* eds. S. L. Brown and M. S. Moersch, 113–22. Ann Arbor: University of Michigan Press.

Carter, B., and G. Dapper. 1974. *Organizing school volunteer programs.* New York: Citation Press.

Clements, J. E., and R. N. Alexander. 1975. Parent training: Bringing it all back home. *Focus on Exceptional Children* 7 (5):1–12.

Cory, C. T. 1974. Two generations of volunteers: Parents. *Learning,* Oct. 3 (2):76–79.

Croft, D. J. 1979. *Parents and teachers: A resource book for home, school, and community relations.* Belmont, Calif.: Wadsworth.

Crozier, J. 1976. Project PACE: Parent Action in Childhood Education—Ages 0–6. *The Exceptional Parent* 6 (4):11–14.

Edgar, E., T. Singer, C. Ritchie, and M. Heggelund. 1981. Parents as facilitators in developing an individual approach to parent involvement. *Behavioral Disorders* 6 (2):122–27.

Edmister, P. 1977. Establishing a parent education resource center. *Childhood Education* 54 (Nov.–Dec.): 62–66.

Feder, B. Y. 1974. A shared learning time. *The Pointer* 19 (1):71.

Gang, D., and C. E. Poche. 1982. An effective program to train parents as reading tutors for their children. *Education and Treatment of Children* 5 (3):211–32.

Gordon, I. J., and W. F. Breivogel, eds. 1976. *Building effective home-school relationships.* Boston: Allyn and Bacon.

Granowsky, A., A. Hackett, J. Hoffman, A. Keller, J. Lamkin, F. Morrison, J. Rabbitt, M. Schumate, S. Schurr, E. Stranix, and J. Woods. 1977. How to put parents on your classroom team. *Instructor* 87 (4):54–62.

Green, D. R., K. Budd, M. Johnson, S. Lang, E. Pinkston, and S. Rudd. 1976. Training parents to modify problem child behaviors. In *Behavior modification approaches to parenting,* eds. E. J. Mash, L. C. Handy, and L. A. Hamerlynck, 3–18. New York: Brunner/Mazel Publishers.

Greer, J. V. 1978. Utilizing paraprofessionals and volunteers in special education. *Focus on Exceptional Children* 10 (6):1–15.

273 ■

CHAPTER TEN
PROGRAMMING FOR
PARENT
INVOLVEMENT: AN
ILLUSTRATION

Grunbaum, E. 1975. Welcome volunteers: Parental involvement. *Instructor* 84 (7):72.

Hall, M. C., J. Grinstead, H. Collier, and R. V. Hall. 1980. Responsive parenting: A preventive program which incorporates parents training parents. *Education and Treatment of Children* 3 (3):239–59.

Haring, N. G. 1976. *Systematic instructional procedures: An instructional hierarchy*. Final report of a program project for the National Institute of Education. Washington, D.C.

Hicks, J. 1977. Parent's Day. *Early Years* 8 (2):53–54.

Karnes, M. B., and B. Franke. 1978. *Family involvement*. Urbana: Institute for Child Behavior and Development, University of Illinois.

Karnes, M. B., and R. R. Zehrbach. 1972. Flexibility in getting parents involved in the school. *Teaching Exceptional Children* 5 (1):6–19.

Kelly, E. J. 1974. *Parent-teacher interaction: A special educational perspective*. Seattle: Special Child Publications.

Latham, G., and A. Hofmeister. 1973. A mediated training program for parents of the preschool mentally retarded. *Exceptional Children* 39 (6):472–73.

Levitt, E., and S. Cohen. 1976. Educating parents of children with special needs: Approaches and issues. *Young Children* 31:263–72.

Marcovich, S. J. 1975. Waiting in the window for teacher. *American Education* 11 (6):9–12.

Marinoff, S. L. 1973. When words are not enough—Videotape. *Teaching Exceptional Children* 5 (2):66–73.

Miller, W. H. 1975. *Systematic parent training: Procedures, cases and issues*. Champaign, Ill.: Research Press.

O'Brien, K. 1977. Parent power: Household aides. *Early Years* 8 (2):52, 53, 56.

Pasanella, A. L., and C. B. Volkmor. 1977. *To parents of children with special needs: A manual on parent involvement in educational programming*. Los Angeles: California Regional Resource Center, University of Southern California.

Reavis, H. K., J. M. Rice, and K. Hamel. Home teaching packages for parents. *Audio Visual Instruction* 21:45, 62.

Rockwell, R. E., and K. J. Grafford. 1977. *TIPS (Teachers Involve Parent Services*. Edwardsville, Ill.: School of Education, Southern Illinois University.

Rossett, A. 1975. Parenting of the preschool exceptional child. *Teaching Exceptional Children* 7 (4):118–21.

Sayler, M. L. 1971. *Parents: Active partners in education.* Washington, D.C.: American Association of Elementary-Kindergarten-Nursery Education.

Shea, T. M. 1978. *Teaching children and youth with behavior disorders.* St. Louis: C. V. Mosby.

Shearer, M.S. 1974. A home based parent training model. In *Training parents to teach: Four models,* ed. J. Grim. Vol. 3,*First Chance for Children,* 49–62. Chapel Hill: Technical Assistance Development System, North Carolina University.

Soar, R. S., and L. Kaplan. 1976. Taxonomy of classroom activities. In *Building effective home-school relationships,* eds. I. J. Gordon and W. F. Breivogel. Boston: Allyn and Bacon.

Spadafore, G. 1979. A guide for the parent as tutor. *The Exceptional Parent* 9 (4):E17–E18.

Stahl, N. A. 1977. 25 ways to harness parent power. *Early Years* 8 (2):56.

Stowitschek, J. J., and A. Hofmeister. 1975. Parent training packages. *Children Today* 4 (2):23–25.

Susser, P. 1974. Parents are partners. *The Exceptional Parent* 4 (3):41–47.

Vantour, J. A. C., and E. A. Stewart-Kurker. 1980. A library for exceptional children promotes home-school cooperation. *Teaching Exceptional Children* 13 (1):4–7.

Wagonseller, B., and A. Mori. 1977. Applications of the simulation technique as a training instrument for teachers and students. *Focus on Exceptional Children* 9 (5):10–12.

Walker, J. E., and T. M. Shea. 1984. *Behavior management: A practical approach for educators.* 3d ed. St. Louis: C. V. Mosby.

Webster, E. J. 1977. *Counseling with parents of handicapped children: Guidelines for improving communications.* New York: Grune and Stratton.

Wood, M. M., ed. 1975. *Developmental therapy: A textbook for teachers as therapists for emotionally disturbed young children.* Baltimore: University Park Press.

PROGRAMMING FOR PARENT INVOLVEMENT: AN ILLUSTRATION

■ Meeting the needs of several parents and their exceptional children in a parent-teacher involvement program requires careful planning and organization. This chapter offers a detailed, step-by-step illustration of the parent-teacher involvement program model. This illustration, which pulls together the material presented in Chapters Four through Nine, is not a model or ideal program because each program must focus on participants' special needs. However, it does show how teachers can go about planning and carrying out a program using the ideas in this text.

The illustration assumes a hypothetical group of exceptional children in a self-contained special education class; however, the procedures and activities are readily applicable, with limited modifications, to other special educational service programs, such as resource rooms or special day schools. The planning and scheduling framework is an August-to-May school calendar.

THE CLASS

The hypothetical classroom serves eight exceptional children in a non-categorical program for children classified as behavior disordered, learning disabled, educable mentally handicapped, and combinations of these exceptionalities. Two children are from one-parent families; one child is in foster care; the others live with their natural parents or step-parents. Parents in three families work full-time outside the home. The families represent a range of socioeconomic levels and ethnic backgrounds.

One teacher (Mrs. Paul) and one full-time paraprofessional (Mr. Kevin) work in the classroom. The teacher assistant, Mr. Kevin, has legal certification to substitute in the teacher's absence. Mrs. Paul is competent in several skills that are important to a comprehensive parent-teacher involvement program, such as interviewing and leading groups. Both Mrs. Paul and Mr. Kevin are committed to encouraging parent involvement. Although not active in the program, the school principal (Mr. Hanes) supports the teacher's and assistant's efforts.

The parents of two children (Mrs. Daniels and Mr. and Mrs. Ming) serve as examples throughout the chapter. They are generally representative of the class's parents.

PROGRAM INTRODUCTION

Mrs. Paul and Mr. Kevin meet in late August to begin planning the parent-teacher involvement program. They decide that, at a minimum, they will offer the following services to the parents of the children in the class:

- A welcome letter and follow-up telephone call (Chapter Five)

- A parent orientation meeting (Chapter Eight)

- An intake and assessment interview (Chapter Four)

- An optional home visit, with an opportunity for the child to participate (Chapter Nine)

- Periodic report cards, including task analysis forms (Chapter Five)

- An individualized education program conference (Chapter Six).

In addition, they decide to recruit parents for a class advisory committee to help organize and schedule individual and group activities for parents. And they decide to determine parents' interest in serving as instructors and volunteer aides. Mrs. Paul and Mr. Kevin expect other parent-teacher activities to develop from the individual intake and assessment interviews.

Two weeks before the first day of school, Mrs. Paul mails a personalized letter to each family welcoming parents to the class and inviting them to the orientation meeting (Figures 10-1 and 10-2).

After about a week, Mrs. Paul calls each home to follow up on the written invitation and to determine approximate attendance. This attendance estimate helps Mrs. Paul and Mr. Kevin to prepare sufficient materials and refreshments for the group. Mrs. Paul is careful not to pressure the parents to attend the orientation meeting. If parents say they cannot attend the orientation meeting, she makes an appointment for an intake and assessment interview.

277 ■
CHAPTER TEN
PROGRAMMING FOR
PARENT
INVOLVEMENT: AN
ILLUSTRATION

August 20, 19__

Dear Mrs. Daniels:

I was very happy to learn that Mary is in our class again this year. The gains we saw in Mary's skills and behaviors last year promise another successful year together.

This year we plan to continue Mary's individualized program, emphasizing behavior management and socialization. We will continue work on self-help skills, language and communication, reading, and arithmetic. The children will again attend physical education each day with Mr. Lansing.

To begin the school year, we are planning a parent orientation meeting on August 31, 19__, at 7:00 PM I would really enjoy visiting with you and sharing some information you may find useful this school year. During the meeting, I will introduce the school staff, and we will tour the building.

In the near future, I would like to meet with parents individually to discuss their child's individualized educational program and to review the goals and objectives we established last May. During the conference, we will discuss expectations for Mary this year.

Parent-teacher involvement programs will continue this year. I think you will agree that this cooperative programming contributes a great deal to Mary's success. I will telephone you about these matters in a week or two.

Both Mr. Kevin, our teacher's assistant, and I are looking forward to another rewarding and productive school year. With your support and assistance, we are sure Mary will make significant progress. Please feel free to contact us at Springvalley School (555-8477).

Sincerely,

Sarah Paul
Teacher

FIGURE 10-1
Welcome Letter for
Parents of a Returning
Student

August 20, 19__

Dear Mr. and Mrs. Ming:

I am very happy to welcome you and John to Springvalley School for the 19__ – __ school year. Your child is a member of the special education program here at Springvalley and has been assigned to our special class. He will attend regular class part-time as soon as we determine the best type and amount of participation for him.

Let me introduce myself. I have taught exceptional children at Springvalley for four years. Mr. Kevin, our teacher's assistant, has been at Springvalley School for two years. In our class, we provide individualized programming for each child. The program stresses behavior management and socialization. In addition, the children work on self-help skills, language and communication, reading, and arithmetic. John will also participate in physical education each day with Mr. Lansing, the school physical education teacher.

To begin the school year, we are planning an orientation meeting for parents on August 31, 19__, at 7:00 PM. We would enjoy visiting with you and sharing information you may find useful this school year. During this meeting, you will meet the school staff, and we will tour the building.

In the near future, I'll be meeting with parents to discuss their child's individualized educational program and to review the year's goals and objectives. During this conference, we will discuss the expectations for John this school year.

As parents new to our class, you may be particularly interested in our parent-teacher involvement program. This program helps us get to know each other and conduct activities to help John. It is also a good way for you to learn more about John's educational program. I will telephone you about these matters in a week or two.

Both Mr. Kevin and I are looking forward to a rewarding and productive school year. With your support and assistance, we are sure John will make significant progress. Please feel free to contact us at Springvalley School (555-8477).

I look forward to seeing you on August 31.

Sincerely,

Sarah Paul
Teacher

FIGURE 10-2
Welcome Letter for
Parents of a New
Student

Before the orientation meeting, Mrs. Paul and Mr. Kevin prepare a file folder for each family. They will record each family's contacts and activities during the year on the "Parent Involvement Log" in the file (Figure 10-3). The file will also store all letters, notes, and messages the parents receive from and send to the school during the year, as well as pre- and post-conference notes.

279 ■

CHAPTER TEN
PROGRAMMING FOR
PARENT
INVOLVEMENT: AN
ILLUSTRATION

Parent Name(s) _____

Child's Name _____ Birthdate _____

Home Phone Number _____ Work Phone Number _____

Date File Opened _____

Activities	Date

I. INTAKE AND ASSESSMENT
    A. Intake and Assessment Conference(s)   _____
     _____

    B. Intake and Assessment Completed   _____
     _____

II. SELECTION OF GOALS AND OBJECTIVES
    A. Parents' Needs Form Returned   _____
    B. Parents' Activities Form Returned   _____
    C. Goals and Objectives Conferences   _____
     _____

    D. Parent-Teacher Involvement Plan Completed   _____

III. ACTIVITY ATTENDANCE
    A. Individual Conferences
        1. Home Visit   _____
        2. Child Evaluation Conference   _____
        3. IEP Conference   _____
        4. _____   _____
        5. _____   _____

    A. Group Meetings
        1. Orientation Meeting   _____
        2. _____   _____
        3. _____   _____
        4. _____   _____
        5. _____   _____

IV. EVALUATION
    A. Evaluation Form Returned   _____
    B. Evaluation Conference   _____

Phone Contacts

Date	Reason/Results
_____	_____
_____	_____
_____	_____
_____	_____
_____	_____

FIGURE 10-3
(cont.)   *Parent Involvement Log*

FIGURE 10-3
(cont.)

Other Contacts (Letters, notes, and so on)

Date	Description	Reason/Results
_____	_____	_____
_____	_____	_____
_____	_____	_____
_____	_____	_____

PARENT ORIENTATION MEETING

At the orientation meeting, Mrs. Paul's main goal is to communicate information to parents. However, she also plans a discussion and question-and-answer period to allow parents to air immediate problems and to dispell new parents' concerns about their child's placement in special education.

The meeting agenda includes the following items:

1. A description of the special education program and class, its purpose and objectives, and the integration of children into regular classes

2. A description of the parent-teacher involvement program

3. A formal introduction of the special education program and the school staff, including the special education teacher and teacher's assistant, appropriate regular class teachers, principal, psychologist, social worker, nurse, school secretary, and others

4. Presentation and handouts on "who to call for what": information on transportation, food service, lunch program, absences, Parent Teacher Association, health services, occupational and physical therapy, testing, and so on

5. A tour of the classroom and school, including visits with staff people at their work stations

6. A discussion and question-and-answer period

7. Refreshments and informal discussion in the classroom.

The day after the orientation meeting, Mrs. Paul mails a "nice to have seen you again" or "sorry you couldn't make it" note to each family, enclosing meeting handouts in the latter. In the notes, Mrs. Paul lets parents know she will contact them within a week to make an appointment for an intake and assessment conference.

INTAKE AND ASSESSMENT

281 ■

CHAPTER TEN
PROGRAMMING FOR
PARENT
INVOLVEMENT: AN
ILLUSTRATION

The welcome letter and orientation meeting have introduced parents to the parent-teacher involvement program. Now it is time to enter phase I of the parent-teacher involvement model, the intake and assessment.

During this phase, Mrs. Paul meets individually with parents in one or more conferences. Through interviewing techniques, she determines parents' perceptions of their needs and interests in their exceptional child's program.

Mrs. Paul plans carefully for this phase. She lists the fourteen parents of her students, establishing priorities for intake and assessment. She decides to interview the two families new to the program first, for she anticipates that these parents will need at least two conferences for intake and assessment. She expects one conference to be adequate for parents of returning children.

Mrs. Paul plans to confer with all parents before mid-September; and she establishes a calendar schedule for these conferences and other activities she and Mr. Kevin have planned for the month. For example, they plan to send home a newsletter toward the end of the month, have each parent complete a "Parents' Needs Form" and a "Parents' Activities Form," and hold an informational group meeting on "Rights and Confidentiality."

Mrs. Paul develops the following agenda for intake and assessment conferences:

1. Review the child's diagnostic findings and the reason for special education placement

2. Review the roles classroom and support staff will play in the child's education

3. Review the parents' role and functions in the child's education

4. Interview parents using Sloman and Webster's (1978) format (Chapter Four)

5. Administer the Vineland Adaptive Behavior Scales (Sparrow, Balla, and Cicchetti 1984) if the child is new to the program (Appendix A)

6. Explain the "Parents' Needs Form" and "Parents' Activities Form" and ask parents to complete and return the forms within one week (Appendices D and E)

7. Respond to parents' questions and concerns.

Parents of children returning to the program will be familiar with some of the information, so Mrs. Paul will not need to discuss items 1, 2, and 3 in great depth. Parents of children new to the program will require more detailed discussions of most items.

SELECTION OF GOALS AND OBJECTIVES

After completing the intake and assessment conferences, Mrs. Paul schedules conferences to select goals and objectives for the parents' involvement. By this time, Mrs. Paul has received the needs and activities forms from seven of the eight families. The "needs" and "activities" forms completed by Mrs. Daniels and Mr. and Mrs. Ming, our representative parents, are presented in the Supplementary Material section at the end of this chapter. In a telephone conversation, she learns that one parent cannot participate in parent-teacher activities because of family, work, and community commitments. She accepts the parent's reasons and lets her know that she is welcome to join the program at a later date and that she will receive periodic report cards, newsletters, an invitation to the IEP conferences, and occasional notes and telephone calls during the year.

Before each goals and objectives conference, Mrs. Paul and Mr. Kevin review all available information on each family, including the forms they completed. To help organize this large quantity of information, Mrs. Paul summarizes and enters the information on "Program Development Forms" (Figures 10-4 and 10-5). She and Mr. Kevin discuss each parent's needs and prepare a tentative list of goals and objectives that seem appropriate.

At the beginning of the conference, Mrs. Paul reviews the information she has on parents' needs and interests and asks the parents if they have any additions, corrections, questions, or comments. She asks parents which items are most important to them and then states the items most important to her as the child's teacher. Mrs. Paul and the parents then compare and discuss their ideas until they reach a consensus on their common goals for involvement. Thus, she and the parents work as equal partners for the child's benefit. Mrs. Paul writes her goals and the parents' goals on the "Program Development Form."

Once they agree on goals, Mrs. Paul and the parents write specific objectives designed to accomplish each goal, again discussing both parties' ideas and reaching a consensus. Mrs. Paul records the agreed-upon objectives on the "Program Development Form."

During this process, both parents and teacher are aware that they cannot accommodate all their personal needs and interests in a single school year. Thus, they defer work on some low priority goals and objectives.

ACTIVITY SELECTION AND IMPLEMENTATION

Next, Mrs. Paul works with parents to select or design activities to meet the objectives (phase 3 of the model). She may accomplish this task during the goals and objectives conference or during a special con-

Parent's Name Luane Daniels

Child's Name Mary Daniels

Teacher's Name Sarah Paul

Date 9-13-

I	II	III	IV
Assessment	Goals and Objectives	Activities	Evaluation
Sloman and Webster Vineland Needs Assessment Form	Goals: I To apply behavioral techniques and instructional methods at home as in school II To develop my own skills for dealing with Mary's behaviors III To continue communication between school and home	Objective IA: —Appropriate reading directed by teacher —Classroom observation by babysitter Objective IIA: —Directed reading Objective IIIA: —Passport —Monthly phone calls	Process: IA, IIA Were readings available to Mrs. Daniels and the sitter? IIA Did Mrs. Burden observe in the classroom? IIIA Was the passport used between home and school? IIIA Did the teacher make monthly phone calls?
—Gives up too easily —Is independent and reliable once she knows she can do something —Uses instructional methods at home —Works with babysitter for consistency	Objectives: IIA To use a problem-solving technique independently IIIA To continue using the passport to maintain communication and consistency between home and school IA Mrs. Burden (Mary's sitter) to demonstrate one new behavioral technique in dealing with Mary's behavior		Content: IA Did the readings help in developing one new behavior management technique? IIA Can Mrs. Daniels now use a problem-solving technique? IIIA Was communication between home and school adequate?

FIGURE 10-4
Program Development
Form for a Returning
Student

FIGURE 10-5
Program Development
Form for a New Student

Parents' Names ___James & Lynn Ming___   Teacher's Name ___Sarah Paul___

Child's Name ___John Ming___   Date ___9-6-84___

I	II	III	IV
Assessment	Goals & Objectives	Activities	Evaluation
Sloman and Webster	Goals:	Objectives:	Process:
Vineland	I To increase general informa-tion about John's exceptionality	IA Individual conferences with teacher, parent, and special ed-ucation supervisor	IA Did conferences take place? Did Mr. and Mrs. Ming observe in the classroom?
Needs Assessment Form	II To increase knowledge about John's rights, confidentiality, and reasons for placement	Observation of teacher in classroom	IIA Did Mr. and Mrs. Ming attend the group meeting?
	III To increase skills in disciplin-ing John and in behavior management	IIA Group meeting Objective IIIA Individual conference	IIIA Did Mrs. Ming work with the teacher in the classroom?
	IV To increase John's participa-tion in the family	Observation of teacher in classroom Work with the teacher in classroom	IIIB Did Mr. and Mrs. Ming partici-pate in behavior management groups?
		IIIB Behavior management parent groups	IVA Were parent partners available to the Mings?
		IVA Parent partner	
			Content:
-Perceive John as demanding	Objectives:		IA Verbal reporting to teacher
-Concerned John doesn't ex-press affection	IA To define behavior disorders and describe reasons for placement		IIA Verbal reporting to teacher
-John's poor self-help skills cause stress to family	IIA To understand the rights of handicapped children		IIIA Behavior counts: has John's hit-ting decreased?
-Both parents express the need to discuss feelings	IIIA To decrease John's hitting behavior at home		IIIB Teacher observation
-Want information on exception-ality and placement	IIIB To demonstrate two tech-niques useful in dealing with John's behaviors		IVA Report of parent partner
	IVA To perform one social-com-munity activity with John per month		

ference focusing specifically on activities. Mrs. Paul schedules remaining conferences so that phase 3 activities will be complete by mid-October.

285 ■

CHAPTER TEN
PROGRAMMING FOR
PARENT
INVOLVEMENT: AN
ILLUSTRATION

To prepare for the conference, Mrs. Paul develops a list of activities that will meet the target objectives, be consistent with the information on the "Parents' Activities Forms," and fit with parents' personalities, life-styles, and desired level of participation. At the beginning of the conference, Mrs. Paul and the parents review their objectives and the information on the "Parents' Activities Form." They then devote the remainder of the conference to selecting the activities, negotiating and being willing to compromise if necessary. Mrs. Paul then enters the activities on the "Program Development Form."

When the activities are selected, Mrs. Paul prepares a parent-teacher activities plan for the remainder of the school year. She and Mr. Kevin enter all group and individual activities on monthly calendars, which they will modify during the school year as necessary.

From program development forms and her notes, Mrs. Paul writes a summary of the individual and group activities all parents will participate in during the year. She records the following activities:

■ Newsletter (all parents)

■ Periodic report cards with task analysis forms (all parents)

■ Informational meetings (all parents)

■ Monthly telephone calls (Mrs. Daniels, Mr. and Mrs. Lang, Mr. and Mrs. Pulley)

■ Biweekly telephone calls (Mrs. and Mrs. Martinez)

■ Passport (Mrs. Daniels, Mr. and Mrs. Ryan)

■ Individual conferences (Mr. and Mrs. Ming)

■ Behavior management training group (Mr. and Mrs. Ming, Mr. and Mrs. Lang, Mr. Webster)

■ Directed readings (Mrs. Daniels and Mary's babysitter)

■ Parent partners (Mrs. and Mrs. Ming with Mr. and Mrs. Ryan)

■ Observations in classroom (Mary Daniels's sitter, Mr. and Mrs. Ming)

■ Daily report cards (Mr. and Mrs. Martinez)

■ Classroom assistance (Mr. and Mrs. Ming)

■ Parent Advisory Committee

While completing the calendar, Mrs. Paul attempts to balance parents' individual needs with those of the group. Consequently, she plans as many activities as possible that respond simultaneously to several parents' objectives. To facilitate scheduling, the teacher completes a calendar for each month of the year. Examples are shown in the Supplementary Material Section at the end of this chapter.

EVALUATION

With scheduling completed, Mrs. Paul turns her attention to evaluation, phase 4 of the parent-teacher involvement model. She evaluates both the process (availability of activities and participation) and the content (knowledge, practices, and skills learned) of the parent program. The evaluative criteria should be objective. To evaluate process, she considers the following questions, among others:

■ Are the activities available?

■ Are the activities taking place or scheduled as planned?

■ Do the parents (teacher) attend the activities?

■ Do the parents (teacher) participate in the activities?

Mrs. Paul's content evaluation responds to the following questions:

■ Did the desired behavior change occur?

■ Are the participants demonstrating the designated level of skill or knowledge?

■ Is the activity content responding to participants' needs?

Mrs. Paul writes her process and content evaluation techniques—determined with parents during the activities conference—on the "Program Development Form."

Mrs. Paul will evaluate individual parent-teacher activities in a conference in which she and parents will discuss their progress toward their objectives and ways to improve their progress if they are dissatisfied. She may use the annual IEP conference for this evaluation. To evaluate workshops and group meetings, Mrs. Paul designs and distributes evaluation forms for participants to complete and return.

Mrs. Paul periodically evaluates the overall impact of the parent-teacher involvement program, asking herself and parents two key questions:

■ Is the program meeting parents' (teacher's) goals and objectives?

■ Do parents (teacher) feel positive about the program?

To answer the first question, Mrs. Paul develops a summary sheet of goals and objectives and invites parents' help in judging the program's effectiveness in meeting them. To assess parents' perceptions of the program, she decides to use an anonymous questionnaire (Figure 10-6). Parents indicate which activities they liked or disliked, and which they viewed as meaningful or irrelevant. The questionnaire also requests program ideas for the next school year.

287 ■
CHAPTER TEN
PROGRAMMING FOR
PARENT
INVOLVEMENT: AN
ILLUSTRATION

SUMMARY

This text presents a broad spectrum of parent-teacher involvement activities, each activity selected for its potential value to parents and teachers sharing a commitment and responsibility for educating exceptional children. These suggested activities are but printed symbols on paper unless they motivate others to action.

Parent and teacher involvement begins with:

■ *You, the reader.* You are responsible for helping the exceptional child grow and learn. Involvement begins with a good heart and a sincere wish to provide the best possible education for exceptional children. It begins with openness and acceptance of parents' and children's special needs and preferences.

■ *Study.* Involvement begins with a critical study of this text and other literature on parents and teachers working together. Involvement requires a commitment to continuously seek new or more effective activities and techniques.

FIGURE 10-6
*Parent Involvement
Program Evaluation
Form*

May 24, 19__

Dear _____:

The Parent-Teacher Involvement Program is your program, designed with you and for you. We want it to meet your needs and the needs of your child. Thus, it is important to know what you like and dislike about the program and what activities you would and would not participate in next year.

To help in the planning of next year's program and to make it more responsive to your needs, we invite you to complete and return the attached questionnaire. Please be frank. If you wish to remain anonymous, do not sign the form. Anonymous or signed, your responses will be held in the strictest of confidence.

Thank you for your help.

Sincerely,

Sarah Paul
Teacher

FIGURE 10-6
(cont.)

Please make an X in the appropriate columns to the right of each activity listed in the left column. Indicate whether you participated in the activity and how you felt about it. For meetings and workshops, please indicate if you wanted to attend but were unable to. Comments and suggestions are welcome.

ACTIVITY	I was involved in this activity.	I wanted to participate but could not.	I would participate again next year.	My rating of this activity is:			
				Excellent	Good	Fair	Poor
Intake/Assessment Conferences							
Parent Orientation Meeting							
Open House							
Rights and Confidentiality Meeting							
Newsletter							
Passport							
Telephone Calls							
Individual Conferences							
Parent Partners							
Behavior Management Group							
Other:							
Other:							

Use the space below to comment on this year's program and make suggestions for next year.

289 ■

CHAPTER TEN
PROGRAMMING FOR
PARENT
INVOLVEMENT: AN
ILLUSTRATION

- *Analysis.* Involvement begins with objective analysis of your personal needs, the child's needs, and parents' needs.

- *Planning.* Planning a parent-teacher involvement program requires full consideration of the goals and objectives of involvement, the resources available, the most desirable activities, and the potential barriers. The teacher's professional judgment is the most powerful planning tool.

- *Knowledge of exceptional children and parents.* Involvement means recognizing and working with professional strengths and weaknesses when selecting and carrying out activities.

- *Action.* Involvement begins with one activity, then another, and another, until a comprehensive program of services for parents of exceptional children is realized.

EXERCISES AND DISCUSSION TOPICS

1. Plan a comprehensive parent-teacher involvement program for the parents of the children assigned to your program (or to a hypothetical program). The program may be at the preschool, elementary, or secondary level, categorical or noncategorical, self-contained or resource based.

2. Apply the parent-teacher involvement model in your plan.

REFERENCES

Sloman, L., and C. D. Webster. 1978. Assessing the parents of the learning disabled child: A semistructured interview procedure. *Journal of Learning Disabilities* 11 (2):73–79.

Sparrow, S. S., D. A. Balla, and D. V. Cicchetti. 1984. The Vineland Adaptive Behavior Scales. Circle Pines, Minn.: American Guidance Service.

Confidential   Date: **Sept. 4**

Parent's Name ___**LUANE DANIELS**___

Child's Name ___**MARY DANIELS**___

Introduction:

Listed below are several statements describing concerns common to the parents of exceptional children. The items may or may not concern you at this time. Please complete only those items that currently concern you.

The information on this form is used *only* to help plan and implement a parent-teacher involvement program. All information is held in strict confidence.

Directions:

1. Read each statement carefully.
2. Circle the number on the 1–5 scale that most closely approximates your current need in each area. Circle *1* to indicate a low priority need and *5* to indicate a high priority need.
3. Below the 1–5 scale are several statements suggesting ways you may prefer to meet your stated needs. Please check only *two* of the four statements listed below each item.
4. You may write additional comments in the space provided.

I. I need the opportunity to discuss my feelings about my exceptional child and myself with someone who understands the problem.

(Circle the appropriate number.)

①	2	3	4	5
Low Priority				High Priority

(Check *only* two statements.)

_____ I prefer to talk to a professional.

_____ I prefer to talk to the parent of an exceptional child.

_____ I prefer to be referred to another agency for counseling.

_____ I prefer to read articles and books discussing the reactions of parents of exceptional children.

✓ I prefer **JUST TALKING TO YOU EVERY NOW AND THEN. I FEEL FINE ABOUT MARY AND WHAT SHE'S DOING.**

II. I would like to talk with other parents and families who have exceptional children.

(Circle the appropriate number.)

①	2	3	4	5
Low Priority				High Priority

(Check *only* two statements.)

_____ I prefer to be in a discussion group.

_____ I prefer to participate in social gatherings (picnics, parties, potluck dinners).

✓ I prefer to meet informally.

_____ I prefer to participate in general meetings, workshops, lectures, demonstrations, and other informational gatherings.

_____ I prefer _____

291 ■

CHAPTER TEN
PROGRAMMING FOR
PARENT
INVOLVEMENT: AN
ILLUSTRATION

III. I would like to learn more about my child's exceptionality.

(Circle the appropriate number.)

1	②	3	4	5
Low Priority				High Priority

(Check *only* two statements.)

✔ I prefer to obtain information through reading.
_____ I prefer to observe teachers and other professionals working with my child and then discuss my observations.
✔ I prefer individual parent-teacher conferences.
_____ I prefer a parent-teacher discussion group.
_____ I prefer _____

IV. I would like to learn more about how children develop and learn, especially exceptional children.

(Circle the appropriate number.)

1	②	3	4	5
Low Priority				High Priority

(Check *only* two statements.)

✔ I prefer to obtain information through reading.
_____ I prefer to participate in a formal behavior management training course.
_____ I prefer a parent-teacher discussion group.
_____ I prefer individual training in my home by a teacher or other professional.
_____ I prefer to attend meetings at which specialists present information on behavior management.
✔ I prefer TO MEET WITH YOU ABOUT MY SPECIFIC QUESTIONS.

VI. I would like to work with a teacher or other professional so that I can use the same instructional methods at home that the school uses.

(Circle the appropriate number.)

1	2	③	4	5
Low Priority				High Priority

(Check *only* two statements.)

_____ I prefer to observe my child in school.
_____ I prefer to attend a training program in observation.
_____ I prefer to attend a course in instructional methods.
_____ I prefer to work with the teacher in my child's classroom.
✔ I prefer in-home training by a teacher or other professional.
✔ I prefer to learn through readings, newsletters, telephone communication, and similar resources.
_____ I prefer _____

VII. I would like _____

(Circle the appropriate number.)

1	2	3	4	5
Low Priority				High Priority

(Write the appropriate statements.)

_____ I prefer _____

_____ I prefer _____

Comments: I'M AFRAID WITH MY JOB AND ALL, I CAN'T GET TO SCHOOL THAT OFTEN. I'D REALLY LIKE TO KEEP UP OUR WRITTEN LOG AND PHONE CALLS. MAYBE THIS YEAR WE CAN GET MARY'S SITTER INVOLVED.

Thank you.

Confidential   Date: Sept. 4

Parent's Name ___LUANE DANIELS___

Child's Name ___MARY DANIELS___

Introduction:

Listed below are thirty-five topics and activities generally believed of interest to the parents of exceptional children. Not all parents are interested in any single item, nor is any parent interested in all the items.

Your response to this questionnaire is used *only* to assist in planning and implementing a parent-teacher involvement program for you. All information is held in strict confidence.

Directions:

1. Read the entire form carefully.
2. In Column A check 15 items of interest to you.
3. In Column B rank 5 of the 15 items you checked in Column A. Number the item of highest priority to you 5, the next highest 4, and so on.
4. You may write additional comments in the space provided.

A	B	
✓		1. Help my child learn.
✓		2. Build my child's self-confidence.
		3. Select activities to help my child learn (books, games, toys, projects, experiences).
✓	3	4. Teach my child to follow directions.
✓		5. Help my child enjoy learning.
		6. Assist my child in language development.
✓		7. Teach my child problem-solving skills.
		8. Fulfill my role as (father) (mother) to my child.
✓		9. Avoid emotional involvement in my child's emotional outbursts.
✓		10. Protect my child from getting hurt.
		11. Care for my child when he or she is sick or injured.
✓	4	12. Discipline my child.
✓		13. Deal with my child's misbehavior.
✓		14. Teach my child respect for people and property.
✓	5	15. Teach my child to express feelings in a socially acceptable manner.
		16. Teach my child to show love, affection, and consideration for other family members.
		17. Teach my child to live in harmony with the family (television, bedtime, meals, sharing, responsibilities).

293 ■

*CHAPTER TEN
PROGRAMMING FOR
PARENT
INVOLVEMENT: AN
ILLUSTRATION*

_____ _____ 18. Develop a positive and productive relationship with my child.

___✓___ ___2___ 19. Develop my problem-solving skills.

How can I obtain information on the following topics affecting my child:

_____ _____ 20. Art activities

_____ _____ 21. Creative dramatics

_____ _____ 22. Educational games and activities

_____ _____ 23. Exercise

_____ _____ 24. Health and hygiene

_____ _____ 25. Music

_____ _____ 26. Nutrition and diet

_____ _____ 27. Puppetry

___✓___ _____ 28. Recreation

___✓___ _____ 29. Sleep

_____ _____ 30. Toys

Other topics and activities of interest to me are:

___✓___ ___1___ 31. HELPING MARY'S BABYSITTER DEAL WITH HER.

_____ _____ 32. _____

_____ _____ 33. _____

_____ _____ 34. _____

_____ _____ 35. _____

Thank you!

Confidential   Date: Sept 6

Parent's Name _James and Lynn Ming_

Child's Name _John Ming_

Introduction:

Listed below are several statements describing concerns common to the parents of exceptional children. The items may or may not concern you at this time. Please complete only those items that currently concern you.

The information on this form is used *only* to help plan and implement a parent-teacher involvement program. All information is held in strict confidence.

Directions:
1. Read each statement carefully.
2. Circle the number on the 1–5 scale that most closely approximates your current need in each area. Circle *1* to indicate a low priority need and *5* to indicate a high priority need.
3. Below the 1–5 scale are several statements suggesting ways you may prefer to meet your stated needs. Please check only *two* of the four statements listed below each item.
4. You may write additional comments in the space provided.

I. I need the opportunity to discuss my feelings about my exceptional child and myself with someone who understands the problem.

(Circle the appropriate number.)

1	2	3	4	(5)
Low Priority				High Priority

(Check *only* two statements.)

__X__ I prefer to talk to a professional.
__X__ I prefer to talk to the parent of an exceptional child.
_____ I prefer to be referred to another agency for counseling.
_____ I prefer to read articles and books discussing the reactions of parents of exceptional children.
_____ I prefer _____

II. I would like to talk with other parents and families who have exceptional children.

(Circle the appropriate number.)

1	2	3	4	(5)
Low Priority				High Priority

(Check *only* two statements.)

_____ I prefer to be in a discussion group.
_____ I prefer to participate in social gatherings (picnics, parties, potluck dinners).
_____ I prefer to meet informally.
_____ I prefer to participate in general meetings, workshops, lectures, demonstrations, and other informational gatherings.
__X__ I prefer *to talk to people in very small groups.*

III. I would like to learn more about my child's exceptionality.

(Circle the appropriate number.)

1	2	3	(4)	5
Low Priority				High Priority

(Check *only* two statements.)

_____ I prefer to obtain information through reading.
__X__ I prefer to observe teachers and other professionals working with my child and then discuss my observations.
__X__ I prefer individual parent-teacher conferences.
_____ I prefer a parent-teacher discussion group.
_____ I prefer _____

IV. I would like to learn more about how children develop and learn, especially exceptional children.

(Circle the appropriate number.)

1	(2)	3	4	5
Low Priority				High Priority

(Check *only* two statements.)

__X__ I prefer to obtain information through reading.
_____ I prefer to participate in a formal behavior management training course.
_____ I prefer a parent-teacher discussion group.
__X__ I prefer individual training in my home by a teacher or other professional.
_____ I prefer to attend meetings at which specialists present information on behavior management.
_____ I prefer _____

295 ■

CHAPTER TEN
PROGRAMMING FOR
PARENT
INVOLVEMENT: AN
ILLUSTRATION

VI. I would like to work with a teacher or other professional so that I can use the same instructional methods at home that the school uses.

(Circle the appropriate number.)

1	2	3	④	5
Low Priority				High Priority

(Check *only* two statements.)

__X__ I prefer to observe my child in school.
_____ I prefer to attend a training program in observation.
_____ I prefer to attend a course in instructional methods.
__X__ I prefer to work with the teacher in my child's classroom.
_____ I prefer in-home training by a teacher or other professional.
_____ I prefer to learn through readings, newsletters, telephone communication, and similar resources.
_____ I prefer _____

VII. I would like _more information about why John is in this class._

(Circle the appropriate number.)

1	2	3	4	⑤
Low Priority				High Priority

(Write the appropriate statements.)

__X__ I prefer _to talk to you and someone in charge._
_____ I prefer _____

Comments: _We need more information about why John changed rooms. At the I.E.P. they said it would help him. We'll do anything that will help, but would like to know what we can do to make it possible for him to go back to his old school and not be in a special room._

Thank you.

Confidential   Date: _Sept 6_

Parent's Name _James and Lynn Ming_
Child's Name _John Ming_

Introduction:
  Listed below are thirty-five topics and activities generally believed of interest to the parents of exceptional children. Not all parents are interested in any single item, nor is any parent interested in all the items.
  Your response to this questionnaire is used *only* to assist in planning and implementing a parent-teacher involvement program for you. All information is held in strict confidence.

Directions:
  1. Read the entire form carefully.
  2. In Column A check 15 items of interest to you.
  3. In Column B rank 5 of the 15 items you checked in Column A. Number the item of highest priority to you 5, the next highest 4, and so on.
  4. You may write additional comments in the space provided.

A	B	
X		1. Help my child learn.
		2. Build my child's self-confidence.
		3. Select activities to help my child learn (books, games, toys, projects, experiences).
X		4. Teach my child to follow directions.
X		5. Help my child enjoy learning.
		6. Assist my child in language development.
		7. Teach my child problem-solving skills.
		8. Fulfill my role as (father) (mother) to my child.
X		9. Avoid emotional involvement in my child's emotional outbursts.
X		10. Protect my child from getting hurt.
		11. Care for my child when he or she is sick or injured.
X	2	12. Discipline my child.
X	3	13. Deal with my child's misbehavior.
X	4	14. Teach my child respect for people and property.
		15. Teach my child to express feelings in a socially acceptable manner.
		16. Teach my child to show love, affection, and consideration for other family members.
X	5	17. Teach my child to live in harmony with the family (television, bedtime, meals, sharing, responsibilities).
		18. Develop a positive and productive relationship with my child.
X		19. Develop my problem-solving skills.

How can I obtain information on the following topics affecting my child:

A	B	
		20. Art activities
		21. Creative dramatics
		22. Educational games and activities
X		23. Exercise
		24. Health and hygiene
		25. Music
		26. Nutrition and diet
		27. Puppetry
X		28. Recreation
X		29. Sleep
		30. Toys

Other topics and activities of interest to me are:

A	B	
X	1	31. what makes kids' behavior disordered?
		32.
		33.
		34.
		35.

SEPTEMBER

Monday	Tuesday	Wednesday	Thursday	Friday
			1 Meet with principal, nurse, social worker about newsletter "welcome"	**2**
5	**6** Conference: 10:30 AM Mr. & Mrs. Smith	**7**	**8** Conference 6:30 PM Mr. Webster	**9**
12 Conference: 9:00 AM Mrs. Daniels	**13** Conference: 10:30 AM Mr. & Mrs. Smith	**14**	**15** Conference: 4:30 PM Mr. & Mrs. Long	**16** Conference: 8:15 AM Mrs. Ming
19 Conference: 8:00 AM Mr. & Mrs. Pulley 3:30 PM Mr. & Mrs. Ryan	**20**	**21** Conference: 9:30 AM Mr. & Mrs. Holmes 3:30 PM Mr. Webster	**22**	**23** Send Newsletter: a) Welcomes b) Who to call for what c) Children's accomplishments
26 Additional conferences as needed	**27** Follow up calls on needs and activities forms	**28** Parent Meeting: Rights and confidentiality 7:00 PM	**29**	**30**

FIGURE 10A-5
An Example of a
Teacher's Monthly
Schedule for September.

FEBRUARY

Monday	Tuesday	Wednesday	Thursday	Friday
			2	3
	Call Daniels	Behavior Management Group: 10:00 AM	Observation: Mary's sitter 10:00–10:00 AM	
6	7	8	9	10
Fill out periodic report cards this week Call Holmes		Parent Advisory Group Meeting 7:00 PM	Observation: Smith: 10:00–11:00 AM	Check on Parent Partners
13	14	15	16	17
Send periodic report cards to students' homes	Call Long	Behavior Management Group: 10:00 AM	Call Pulley	
20	21	22	23	24
Conference: 4:00 PM Smith	Readings for Mrs. Daniels			
27	28			
Newsletters: Language Accomplishments				

FIGURE 10A-6
*An Example of a
Teacher's Monthly
Schedule for Feburary.*

ASSESSMENT
AND INFORMATION-
GATHERING TECHNIQUES

■ This appendix describes several assessment and information-gathering techniques useful for identifying exceptional children's strengths and weaknesses. Parents can complete most of the instruments described here with minimal assistance from the teacher. In a few cases, the process is collaborative; occasionally, proper administration of the aid requires parent–child interaction or parent observation of the child.

■ 300

*APPENDIX A
ASSESSMENT AND
INFORMATION-
GATHERING
TECHNIQUES*

THE VINELAND ADAPTIVE BEHAVIOR SCALES

The Vineland Adaptive Behavior Scale (Sparrow et al. 1984) is a revision of the original Vineland Social Maturity Scale (Doll 1965). It is available in three versions: the Interview Edition, Survey Form, most similar to the original Vineland and comprised of 297 items; an Interview Edition, Expanded Form, comprised of 577 items; and a Classroom Adaptation, a questionnaire of 244 items for independent completion by teachers. The Survey and Expanded Forms are applicable from birth to eighteen years, eleven months, and low functioning adults, and the classroom edition is applicable for children three years to twelve years, 11 months old. The instrument measures adaptive behavior in four domains and eleven subdomains. The survey and expanded forms also include a maladaptive behavior domain. The communication domain includes receptive, expressive, and written communication skills; the daily living domain contains personal, domestic, and community skills; the socialization domain includes interpersonal relationships, play and leisure time, and coping skills; and the motor skills domain includes both gross and fine motor skills.

A variety of scores are available through this revised instrument. Each adaptive behavior domain and the adaptive behavior compositive can be expressed in a standard score, adaptive level, and age equivalent. Graphic representations of scores may also be drawn. The instrument is normed on samples representative of the population described by the 1980 United States Census.

■

301 ■

APPENDIX A
ASSESSMENT AND
INFORMATION-
GATHERING
TECHNIQUES

BEHAVIOR PROBLEM
CHECKLIST

Quay and Peterson's Behavior Problem Checklist "is a factor analytically derived three-point rating scale for 55 relatively frequently occurring problem behavior traits in children and adolescents. Its development has involved factor analytic studies of problem behaviors in public school children (grades K-8) (Peterson 1961; Quay and Quay 1965), institutionalized juvenile delinquents (Quay 1964; 1966), students in public classes for the emotionally disturbed (Quay, Morse, and Culter 1966), and children seen in a child guidance clinic (Peterson, Becker, Shoemaker, Luria, and Hellmer 1961)" (Quay and Peterson 1967, 1).

The checklist measures four types of problem behaviors: conduct disorders (psychopathy, unsocialized aggression), personality disorders (neuroticism, anxiousness, and/or withdrawal), inadequacy and/or immaturity, and subcultural (socialized) delinquency. Anyone familiar with the child—including parents, teachers, correctional personnel, psychiatric aides, nurses, and clinical professionals—can complete the checklist based on observation. The rating system allows the rater to differentiate between behavior not observed (by checking 0), behavior observed but mild (by checking 1), and behavior observed and severe (by checking 2). Normative data, including studies of reliability and interrater reliability, are available in the manual.

■ 302
APPENDIX A
ASSESSMENT AND
INFORMATION-
GATHERING
TECHNIQUES

DENVER DEVELOPMENTAL SCREENING TEST

The Denver Developmental Screen Test (DDST) (Frankenburg, Dodds, Fandal, Kazuk, and Cohrs 1975) is appropriate for assessing children from birth to six years old. Its designers developed it to meet the need for a simple, standardized, useful tool to help identify developmental problems early. The test administrator requires no specialized training to administer or score the test, and equipment and materials are minimal. The test includes 105 items in four developmental categories:

1. Personal-social: the child's self-care skills and ability to get along with people

2. Fine motor-adaptive: the child's ability to see and to use hands to draw and manipulate objects

3. Language: the child's ability to hear, follow directions, and speak

4. Gross motor: the child's ability to sit, walk, run, and jump.

The test administrator scores items as pass, failure, refusal, or no opportunity. Some items are scored based on parents' reports; the number of items administered to a child varies with age and performance. In scoring, the tester is encouraged to note children's behavior: Are they fearful or shy? Do they manifest other psychic states that could impede performance?

Directions are clear and concise, and test items are generally enjoyable for children. The test's developers standardized the 1970 revised edition on 1,000 children.

WALKER PROBLEM BEHAVIOR IDENTIFICATION CHECKLIST

303 ■

*APPENDIX A
ASSESSMENT AND
INFORMATION-
GATHERING
TECHNIQUES*

Walker's checklist (1976) helps elementary school teachers detect behavior problem children. The checklist is a screening device only, not a diagnostic evaluation instrument.

Walker designed the checklist for use with children in grades 4 and 5. Directions for completing the checklist are clear and concise. Administration of the checklist requires approximately ten minutes.

Composed of fifty statements, the checklist measures five behavior factors: acting out (disruptive, aggressive behaviors), withdrawal (passive and avoidance behaviors), distractibility (inattentiveness, restlessness), disturbed peer relations, and immaturity. Although designed primarily for use by elementary school teachers, parents can also answer most items on the checklist. Interpretation of some items may be necessary for some parents.

■

■ 304

*APPENDIX A
ASSESSMENT AND
INFORMATION-
GATHERING
TECHNIQUES*

DEVEREUX CHILD BEHAVIOR RATING SCALE

The Devereux Child Behavior Rating Scale (Spivack and Spotts 1966) helps describe and evaluate children's manifest behavior disorders. It focuses primarily on patterns of symptomatic behavior observed in real-life situations.

The instrument is for use with children of eight to twelve years old. Some data are available for children six and seven years old. A clinician, child care worker, nurse, recreational person, houseparent, or another person familiar with the child's behavior in a home setting can complete the scale.

The norms for scoring the scale are available in the manual. The instrument includes ninety-seven items rated on scales ranging from five to nine choices; it provides raw and standard scores for seventeen behavior factors: distractibility, poor self-care, pathological use of senses, emotional detachment, social isolation, poor coordination and body tones, incontinence, messiness or sloppiness, inadequate need for independence, unresponsiveness to stimulation, tendency toward emotional upset, need for adult contact, anxious or fearful ideation, impulse ideation, inability to delay, social aggression, and unethical behavior.

Although useful as an information-gathering instrument in a parent-teacher program, "the scale may be employed (a) to assess behavior change as a function of any treatment process or environmental change; (b) as a refinement of current clinical diagnostic labels; (c) as part of intake procedures, wherein information from others (e.g., parents) is required; (d) as an aid in group placement of children in residential treatment; (e) as a research tool when a reliable behavior criterion is required" (Spivack and Spotts 1966, 3).

■

DEVEREUX ADOLESCENT
BEHAVIOR RATING SCALE

305 ■

*APPENDIX A
ASSESSMENT AND
INFORMATION-
GATHERING
TECHNIQUES*

The Devereux Adolescent Behavior Rating Scale (Spivack, Spotts, and Haimes 1967) measures the deviant behaviors of adolescents. A teacher, counselor, child care worker, correctional staff person, or other tester rates eighty-four statements about behavior on either a five-point or eight-point scale. These statements represent twelve behavior factors and three rational clusters, plus eleven additional items. Raw and standard scores can be derived for all factors and clusters, and the manual offers normative data.

The scale measures unethicalness, defiant-resistive behavior, domineering-sadistic behavior, heterosexual interest, hyperactivity and expansiveness, poor emotional control, need for approval and dependency, emotional distance, physical inferiority and timidity, schizoid behavior and withdrawal, bizarre speech and cognition, and bizarre actions. The rational clusters include inability to delay, paranoid thinking, and anxious self-blame. The scale is suitable for screening and treatment evaluation as well as for general information gathering.

■

■ 306

APPENDIX A
ASSESSMENT AND
INFORMATION-
GATHERING
TECHNIQUES

BURKS'S BEHAVIOR
RATING SCALES

Burks's behavior rating scales (Burks 1977) identify behavior problems and patterns of problems in children three through six years old and in children attending grades 1 through 9 (six to fifteen years old). Both scales attempt to measure the severity of negative symptoms, as parents and teacher perceive them.

According to Burks, the scales have the following capability:

1. They distinguish between groups of children with disturbed behaviors.

2. They register changes in behavior over time.

3. They identify personality traits needing further evaluation.

4. They provide information useful in parent-school personnel conferences.

5. They predict success and failure in special education classes.

6. They have practical uses for parents and teachers.

Both scales provide negative measures of eighteen categories of behavior, using a twenty-five–point scale ranging from "not significant" to "very significant." The scale for older children adds a nineteenth category of "academics" to the following list: self-blame, anxiety, withdrawal, dependency, ego strength, physical strength, coordination, intellectuality, attention, impulse control, reality contact, sense of identity, suffering, anger control, sense of persecution, aggressiveness, resistance, and social conformity.

■

THE CHILD BEHAVIOR
RATING SCALE

307 ■
*APPENDIX A
ASSESSMENT AND
INFORMATION-
GATHERING
TECHNIQUES*

The Child Behavior Rating Scale (Cassel 1962) assesses the personality adjustment of kindergarteners through third-grade children. It applies to handicapped children who are unable to read. Anyone who has observed the child or is familiar with the child's behavior can complete the scale; the author recommends it for use by parents and teachers.

The seventy-eight items on the scale represent five areas: self, home, social, school, and physical. The manual contains clear directions for administration and interpretation and provides standardization data.

■ 308

APPENDIX A
ASSESSMENT AND
INFORMATION-
GATHERING
TECHNIQUES

AAMD ADAPTIVE
BEHAVIOR SCALES

The American Association on Mental Deficiency Adaptive Behavior Scales (Nihira, Foster, Shellhaas, and Leland 1975) measure mentally handicapped and emotionally disturbed children's and adults' effectiveness in responding to the natural and social demands of their environment. The scales provide an objective description and assessment of an individual's adaptive behavior.

The first part of the scales assesses behaviors essential "to the maintenance of personal independence in daily living":

1. Independent functioning (eating, toilet use, cleanliness, appearance, care of clothing, dressing and undressing, locomotion, and general functioning)

2. Physical development (sensory and motor)

3. Economic activity (money handling, budgeting, and shopping)

4. Language development (speaking, writing, comprehension, and general language development)

5. Number and time concepts

6. Occupation—domestic (cleaning, kitchen duties, and general domestic)

7. Occupation—general

8. Self-direction (sluggishness in movement, initiative, persistence, planning and organization, and general self-direction)

9. Responsibilities

10. Socialization.

The second part assesses maladaptive behaviors related to individual personality traits and emotional disorders: violent and destructive behavior, antisocial behavior, rebellious behavior, untrustworthy behavior, withdrawal, stereotyped behavior and odd mannerisms, unacceptable or eccentric habits, self-abusive behavior, hyperactive tendencies, sexually aberrant behavior, psychological disturbances, and use of medication.

The authors proposed several uses for the Adaptive Behavior Scales, including the following:

1. Identification of deficiencies to help in programming

2. Rating of behavior over time

3. Comparison of adaptive behaviors in different environments

4. Comparison of raters' perceptions (mother, father, teacher, therapist, child care worker)

5. Use as a common basis for information exchange among individuals and within a group.

Three forms of the AAMD Adaptive Behavior Scales are available: for rating children twelve years old or younger, for rating adolescents and adults thirteen and older, and for use by public school personnel. Extensive research results are available in the contemporary professional literature on the design, application, validity, and reliability of the scales.

309 ■

APPENDIX A
ASSESSMENT AND
INFORMATION-
GATHERING
TECHNIQUES

■ 310
APPENDIX A
ASSESSMENT AND
INFORMATION-
GATHERING
TECHNIQUES

FAMILY INFORMATION AND
BEHAVIOR ANALYSIS FORMS

Blackard (1976) suggested that families of exceptional children are most concerned about developing the child's self-help skills and modifying the child's behavior. To help family members attain these objectives, she recommended that teachers assess the family's counseling, service, and training needs and measure the effectiveness of its existing behavior management techniques and teaching methods before starting a training program.

Blackard developed two forms for this process, the "Family Information Form" and the "Behavior Analysis of Family-Child Interactions Form," both of which are for use in an interview. The "Family Information Form" assesses the frequency and duration of specific child behaviors at home, family members' reactions to these behaviors, and the frequency and duration of contact between the child and specific family members. The interview explores parents' involvement with the child, their teaching methods, possible changes in goals and values, changes in relationships, sources of support, special needs, and behavior management techniques used at home. The teacher can use the resulting information to design family training programs.

The teacher completes the "Behavioral Analysis of Family-Child Interaction Form" in a personal interview with the family as well. The interviewer encourages family members to expand and clarify their concerns about the child's behavior, including self-help skills, discipline, duties and responsibilities, recreation, and others. Questions encourage family members to objectify their concerns as well by describing behaviors in terms easy to define, observe, and measure, and by specifying the antecedents and consequences of behaviors. At the end of the interview, the family ranks the behaviors. The teacher records the information on the form and uses it to guide subsequent training activities.

■

TARGET BEHAVIOR KIT

311 ■

*APPENDIX A
ASSESSMENT AND
INFORMATION-
GATHERING
TECHNIQUES*

Kroth (1972) designed an aid for selecting target behaviors called the Target Behavior Kit. The kit helps parents select and rank specific behaviors. It includes the following materials:

1. A nine-column target behavior board divided into twenty-five squares. The columns vary in length from one to five squares, with the five-square column in the center of the board and the one-square columns on the extreme left and right of the board. Column headings range from "most like me" to "most unlike me," with the "undecided" category in the center of the board. For use with parents, the column designations can change to "most like my child," "least like my child," and so on.

2. Two sets of cards listing twenty-five observable and measurable behaviors. One set lists home behaviors; the other lists classroom behaviors. Several blank cards are available for recording additional observable and measurable behaviors.

3. A manual.

4. Record sheets.

Parents first arrange the cards on the board to reflect the child's real or actual behaviors. In a second ranking, they arrange the cards to reflect ideal behaviors, or "how I want my child to be." As the parents complete the two sortings, the teacher notes discrepancies between their perceptions of their child's real and ideal behaviors. These discrepancies then stimulate discussion on program goals and objectives.

■ 312

*APPENDIX A
ASSESSMENT AND
INFORMATION-
GATHERING
TECHNIQUES*

REFERENCES

Blackard, K. 1976. *Introduction to the family training program: Working paper.* Seattle: Experimental Education Unit, Child Development and Mental Retardation Center, University of Washington.

Burks, H. F. 1977. *Burks' Behavior Rating Scales.* Los Angeles: Western Psychological Services.

Cassel, R. N. 1962. *Child Behavior Rating Scale.* Los Angeles: Western Psychological Services.

Doll, E. 1965. *Vineland Social Maturity Scale.* Circle Pines, Minn.: American Guidance Service.

Frankenburg, W. K., J. B. Dodds, A. W. Fandal, E. Kazuk, and M. Cohrs. 1975. *Denver Developmental Screening Test, References manual.* Rev. ed. Denver: LADOCA Project and Publishing Foundation.

Kroth, R. 1972. *Target Behavior Kit.* Olathe, Kans.: Select-Ed.

Nihira, K., R. Foster, M. Shellhaas, and H. Leland. 1975. *The AAMD Adaptive Behavior Scale manual.* Rev. ed. Washington, D.C.: American Association of Mental Deficiency.

Peterson, D. R. 1961. Behavior problems of middle childhood. *Journal of Consulting Psychology* 25:205 9.

Peterson, D. R., W. C. Becker, J. J. Shoemaker, Z. Luria, and L. A. Hellmer. 1961. Child behavior problems and parental attitudes. *Child Development* 32:151–62.

Quay, H. C. 1964. Personality dimensions in delinquent males as inferred from the factor analysis of behavior ratings. *Journal of Research in Crime and Delinquency* 1:33–37.

Quay, H. C. 1966. Personality patterns in pre-adolescent delinquent boys. *Educational and Psychological Measurement* 26:99–110.

Quay, H. C., and D. R. Peterson. 1967. *Manual for the Behavior Problem Checklist.* Urbana, Ill.: University of Illinois.

Quay, H. C., and L. C. Quay. 1965. Behavior problems in early adolescence. *Child Development* 36:215–20.

Quay, H. C., W. C. Morse, and R. L. Cutler. 1966. Personality patterns of pupils in special classes for the emotionally disturbed. *Exceptional Children* 32:297–301.

Sparrow, S. S., D. A. Balla, and D. V. Cicchetti. 1984. *The Vineland Adaptive Behavior Scales.* Circle Pines, Minn.: American Guidance Service.

Spivack, G., and J. Spotts. 1966. *Devereux Child Behavior Rating Scale.* Devon, Pa.: Devereux Foundation Press.

Spivack, G., J. Spotts, and E. P. Haimes. 1967. *Devereux Adolescent Behavior Rating Scale.* Devon, Pa.: Devereux Foundation Press.

Walker, H. M. 1976. *Walker Problem Behavior Identification Checklist.* Los Angeles: Western Psychological Services.

313 ■

APPENDIX A
ASSESSMENT AND
INFORMATION-
GATHERING
TECHNIQUES

CASES FOR STUDY AND ROLE PLAYING

■ The case studies in this appendix represent a variety of exceptionalities and parent needs. Students with no access to exceptional children or their parents can use these cases to complete the chapter exercises in this book.

MARSHALL P, AGE 8 YEARS, 4 MONTHS

Diagnosis: Educable mentally handicapped.

Academic skills: Marshall's reading and mathematics skills are beginning first-grade level. He functions well with concrete facts and has great difficulty with abstractions. He successfully manipulates objects, pictures, and so on to perform tasks. He is very interested in books and "reads" pictures well.

Language: Marshall is very verbal. His social language is a strength. Marshall does not use conceptual language and cannot demonstrate basic concepts such as "in/out" or "up/down."

Behavior: Marshall tries to do all tasks presented to him. His teachers speak of him as a "good kid." He rarely requests help but sits with a task and continues to work at it (right or wrong) until he completes it or the study period ends. He is passive but cooperates with his peers in play and work tasks.

Parent concerns: Mr. and Mrs. P are upset about Marshall's recent diagnosis of mental retardation. They are angry that the diagnosis came after Marshall repeated kindergarten and first grade and do not understand how their son can suddenly "become retarded." They have hired a tutor to work with Marshall during the summer. They have requested reevaluation of Marshall at a private diagnostic center. Marshall is the only surviving child in this family; a four-year-old sister died in a boating accident when Marshall was an infant. Both parents are still grieving for their daughter and have stated, "First we lost Jessie, and now this."

Diagnosis: Moderately mentally handicapped (Down's syndrome).

Self-help: Louise can dress and undress herself, except that she lacks sufficient fine motor strength and coordination to manipulate small buttons or snaps and to tie shoes. She frequently states "me do" when her parents or older brother or sister try to help her. Louise attempts all tasks without prompting.

Preacademic skills: Louise can complete wooden puzzles of five or fewer pieces. She sings simple songs, finger plays, and works independently. She will busy herself with toys for extended periods. She rote counts to five and understands the concept of "one."

Language: Louise uses two-word statements to express her needs. She frequently sings and babbles to herself while playing. Her articulation is poor. She receives two twenty-minute speech therapy sessions each week.

Social skills: Louise plays well with both exceptional and nonexceptional peers at preschool. She initiates social interaction with adults. She has begun to "tease" adults around her and to display a sense of humor.

Parent concerns: Louise is the youngest of three children. Her older brother is a college freshman, and her sister is a high school junior. Mr. and Mrs. S are concerned that Louise's siblings will become responsible for her care as the parents age. Mr. S is in poor health and is worried about "keeping up" with Louise's needs. Both parents enjoy Louise a great deal. Their only specific concern at this time is Louise's "stubbornness."

HENRY L, AGE 11 YEARS, 3 MONTHS

Diagnosis: Behavior disordered.

Behavior: Henry has great difficulty controlling his behavior in the classroom. He is upset easily and is aggressive verbally and physically. When assigned a task to complete in a specific period, Henry will begin the task, then become distracted. When reminded to return to work, Henry becomes angry and tears up his papers. Henry does not seem aware of the consequences of his actions. Since the beginning of counseling, Henry has gained better control over his impulsiveness.

Academic: Henry is an avid reader of science fiction. His mathematical skills are slightly below grade level. His true ability is difficult to measure because he does not complete tests, worksheets, and other work. His cursive handwriting is barely legible, and his spelling is poor.

Parent concerns: Mr. and Mrs. L were divorced several years ago, and Mr. L has custody of Henry. Henry rarely sees his mother, and his grandmother assumes his primary care. Mr. L is considering remarriage, but Henry has announced that he "hates" his father's fiancée, Ms. J. During a family dinner, Henry threw a plate of food at Ms. J. Mr. L is considering asking his former wife to assume custody or seeking foster home placement. Three-way counseling with Henry, Ms. J, and Mr. L has not resulted in much behavior change.

■

Diagnosis: Profoundly hearing impaired.

Academic skills: Lisa is currently functioning at approximately the 4.5 grade level in reading and written expression and the 6.3 grade level in mathematics.

Language: Lisa uses total communication, signing and speaking simultaneously. Her speech is difficult to understand. She receives three twenty-minute sessions of individual speech therapy weekly. She wears biaural hearing aids but claims these aids do not help her and make her look "ugly." She "forgets" the aids whenever possible.

Social skills: Lisa would like to transfer to the local high school with an interpreter in order to attend school with her neighborhood friends. According to her parents, however, Lisa has little contact with the children in her neighborhood; all her friends attend the special day school for the deaf. Lisa attends Sunday school with nonexceptional peers, but they ignore her. The teacher asked her parents to withdraw her from Sunday school because she was interfering with other students' progress. Several boys in the class called her "doorknob," imitated her signing, talked behind their hands, and otherwise ridiculed her.

Parent concerns: Mr. and Mrs. B want Lisa to develop her speech and language skills to the maximum. They fear Lisa's Sunday school experience represents hearing people's typical reaction to the deaf. They want their daughter to remain in the protected environment of the school for the deaf as long as possible. They are concerned that Lisa is becoming part of the deaf subculture at her school.

∎

EILEEN S, AGE 13 YEARS, 9 MONTHS

Diagnosis: Nonexceptional.

Academic skills: Eileen currently functions at grade level in all subject areas; she reports that her favorite subject is English, and she enjoys writing and illustrating story books for her younger sister.

Extracurricular activities: Though Eileen has taken music lessons (piano) for several years, she is not interested in joining band or choir at her school. She played softball at her elementary school but does not participate in any sports in junior high school.

Parent concerns: Eileen, who was an "A" student throughout elementary school, is earning "Bs" and "Cs" in junior high school. She has only one close friend, a girl who went to elementary school with her. A boisterous leader in elementary school, she has remained outside of extracurricular activities in junior high. Mr. and Mrs. S are concerned that she isn't a "star" any more and that the large junior high may be too competitive for her. Eileen has expressed no concerns, saying only that even though "a lot more kids are around," the larger school does not bother her. Mr. and Mrs. S have decided to begin punishing Eileen for any grade lower than a "B." They have requested a psychological evaluation.

Teacher concerns: Ms. M, Eileen's homeroom and social study teacher, feels that Eileen is adjusting from a small elementary school to junior high school satisfactorily. The teacher believes that Eileen is working to the best of her ability. Ms. M is concerned about Eileen's parents' decision to punish her for grades lower than a "B." She is very hesitant to refer Eileen for testing.

Diagnosis: Autistic.

Self-help: Rebecca cares for her personal hygiene and grooming when reminded. She dresses and undresses herself without help. Though Rebecca's self-feeding skills are good, she eats only four foods (bananas, graham crackers, peanut butter, and marshmallows). Rebecca has a history of eliminating one "favorite" food from her diet and replacing it with another. She will then eat only those few foods for a month or so before eliminating one and substituting another.

Language: Rebecca uses echolalia (repeating others' words) to communicate her needs. When making a request, she answers her own question. ("Do you want a puzzle? Yes.") She receives speech therapy three times a week, and her communication is improving.

Academic skills: Rebecca can word call at the ninth-grade level. She does not demonstrate reading comprehension. She can add and subtract three-digit numbers mentally and is beginning to multiply. She prints carelessly, running words, sentences, and paragraphs together.

Social skills: During free time or recess, Rebecca either walks the perimeter of the room or play area alone or spins an object inappropriately (record player, toy truck wheels). She will use social language if provided a model (please, thank you, hello).

Parent concerns: Mr. and Mrs. H are very concerned about Rebecca's diet. They want to work with the school to increase the number of foods Rebecca will eat. Both parents have completed a behavior modification course and have successfully used behaviorial interventions to control Rebecca's behavior. Rebecca's only sibling, an older brother of fifteen, is embarrassed by his sister's behavior and robotic voice. He spends a great deal of time away from home. The parents are worried about his inability to accept Rebecca.

MICHAEL R, AGE 8 YEARS, 1 MONTH

Diagnosis: Learning disabled.

Academic skills: Michael is reading at the first-grade level; his mathematics skills are at the mid-first-grade level. Michael is very verbal and enjoys making up stories. Michael's poor fine motor skills make his printing very labored and difficult to read.

Language: Michael is very verbal and has a large oral vocabulary. He is quite imaginative and performs well above average in sentence completion tasks.

Social skills: Michael is self-conscious about his poor academic functioning. As a result, he exaggerates his abilities in other areas to his classmates. Michael tells involved stories of imagined experiences. This behavior causes his classmates to label him a liar. He is alone most of the time during recess and free play.

Parent concerns: Michael is the younger of two children. His eleven-year-old brother does well in school, plays saxophone, and is the captain of his soccer team. Mr. and Mrs. R believe that Michael is either lazy, stubborn, or both. Mrs. R states that she has a cousin who had trouble reading and is now an aeronautical engineer. She suggests that if the teachers could get Michael to work, he would achieve. Mr. and Mrs. R are very concerned about Michael's progress. They have tried eye exercises, perceptual motor training, a psychologist, and a counselor for short periods of time, with little success. The counselor advised them that special education held the most promise for Michael, so Mr. and Mrs. R are willing to cooperate with the school in any way.

Diagnosis: Moderately mentally handicapped.

Self-help: Raphael is beginning to dress himself. Until he began school in September, his mother or older sister, who share responsibility for his care, dressed and fed him. Raphael appears able to perform these skills but has not had the opportunity to learn and practice them.

Language: Raphael follows simple commands in both Spanish and English. Though his home is bilingual, Mr. and Mrs. G try to use English with their children. Raphael uses one- or two-word utterances to express his needs. He uses appropriate social language spontaneously (greeting people, please, thank you, and so on). Raphael sings children's songs and makes requests to his mother in Spanish. He uses English in school.

Preacademic skills: Raphael traces his first and last name, names his body parts, and names four colors. He can match letters and order the letters of his first name. He demonstrates one-to-one correspondence and counts to five in English and Spanish.

Parent concerns: Raphael is one of five children. He is the only boy; his sisters are three, nine, fifteen, and seventeen. His oldest sister, Rosa, shares the primary care for Raphael with his mother. Mrs. G works part-time some afternoons and evenings. Mr. G is uncomfortable with the label "mentally retarded." He will not attend parent meetings that include the parents of exceptional children. Both parents belong to the Parent Teacher Organization. Mrs. G is finding it more difficult to deal with Raphael now that he is beginning to perform skills independently. Mr. G is excited about the new things Raphael has learned. However, he has difficulty adjusting to the demands of Raphael's new level of functioning.

Diagnosis: Moderately mentally handicapped.

Academic skills: Mark names eight colors; spells his first name orally; recognizes the first four letters of the alphabet; states his full name, address, and age; and sorts by shape and color. He cannot sort by size, report on the weather, or classify. He has difficulty discriminating letters in sorting, and he reverses letters when printing his first name. In mathematics, Mark rote counts to ten and gives one and two objects when requested. He does not recognize numerals.

Self-help: Mark cannot button small buttons, buckle his belt, or tie his shoes. He needs help toileting because of his inability to fasten clothes.

Language: Mark is very verbal. He uses six-word utterances, has a large vocabulary, and uses "up/down," "out/in," "over/under." Mark has difficulty with directional concepts such as "forward/backward," "away from/toward," "left/right," and "front/back." He also has trouble sequencing when relating his experiences.

Gross and fine motor skills: Mark uses a stencil to produce shapes but cannot hold a pencil correctly and cannot cut along a line. He frequently bumps into objects. Mark cannot ride a large trike, jump on two feet, or balance on one foot.

Behavioral/social skills: Mark becomes frustrated with motor tasks and refuses to attempt them. He interacts well verbally with adults and peers.

Parent concerns: A neurologist has diagnosed Mark as "attention deficit disordered," but his mother feels he is learning disabled and should be placed differently. He is distractible and has difficulty completing tasks. Mark is frequently out of his seat.

Teacher's concerns: The current disagreement between Mark's mother and the school district about his diagnosis is of great concern to Ms. B, Mark's teacher. His difficulties attending to tasks and his out-of-seat behavior are becoming disruptive to her class.

Family description: Mark is the youngest of three children and the only boy. His fifteen- and sixteen-year-old sisters assist him in his self-help skills. Father and mother are both very interested in diagnosis and visited several pediatricians and neurologists before they attained the present diagnosis, which they feel is accurate. Both parents disagree with the school district diagnosis of mental retardation; the mother focuses most on Mark's behaviors and self-help skills, the father on academic progress.

■

Diagnosis: Severely handicapped.

Self-help: Sally can remove her pants and socks herself and can remove her coat with verbal cues. She needs help untying her shoes and needs help with all fasteners. Sally can scoop food independently using a weighted spoon but cannot pierce with a fork. She wipes her mouth with a napkin when reminded. She needs help to carry her tray to her place and to open her milk carton. Sally needs physical assistance to perform basic independent living skills, such as hanging her own coat, using a drinking fountain, and choosing a play activity. She cannot wash her hands without assistance because she cannot turn the water faucets herself. She cannot put toothpaste on her brush but can adequately brush her teeth with a reminder to spit rather than swallow. Sally initiates toileting by using the toilet sign and placing the trainer's hand on the fastener of her pants.

Language: Sally has developed many manipulative skills. When rocked or jostled, she gives the trainer a verbal signal and physical prompt to repeat the activity. "Toilet" remains her only expressive sign. She requests objects by reaching for them or by putting the trainer's hand on the desired object.

Motor skills: Sally can pull herself along a scooter-board obstacle course in ninety seconds. She cannot perform bilateral activities, such as pulling apart popbeads, because she lacks strength on her left side. With her right hand weighted in her lap, she can stack only one of five cones using her left hand.

Preacademic skills: Sally can match three everyday objects. She cannot string beads because of her difficulty using both hands. She responds to her name three out of five times but needs a gesture accompanying the verbal cue to "come here," "pick up," and "give me."

Parent concerns: Sally is the oldest child of a single-parent family. Though Sally is still young, her mother worries about future residential placement. Mrs. G has begun a trust fund for Sally for the placement she prefers, a group home not far from the family's apartment. Sally's five-year-old brother enjoys playing with Sally's wheelchair and adaptive equipment and has begun to ask questions about Sally's not talking, sleeping in diapers, and so on.

Special considerations: This family needs respite care. Mrs. G currently has an excellent sitter for both children, but finding full-time care during the summer remains a problem. Mrs. G is quite supportive of Sally's program and follows through to the best of her ability. At times, however, Mrs. G simply does not have the time or energy to complete home programs for she works full-time and must often work overtime as well.

SUPPORT AND INFORMATIONAL ORGANIZATIONS

The following organizations and agencies provide information and support to parents and teachers of exceptional individuals. Many publish pamphlets, periodicals, and books that can be used as resources in working with parents and their exceptional children. In addition, state and local departments of mental health, local regional offices for developmental disabilities, and family and children service agencies frequently provide publications or conduct groups for families of exceptional children.

Alexander Graham Bell Association for the Deaf
3416 Volta Place, N.W.
Washington, D.C. 20007

Allergy Foundation of America
801 Second Avenue
New York, NY 10017

American Association for Maternal and Child Health
P.O. Box 965
Los Altos, CA 94022

American Association on Mental Deficiency
5201 Connecticut Avenue, N.W.
Washington, D.C. 20015

American Coalition of Citizens with Disabilities
1346 Connecticut Avenue, N.W., Suite 1124
Washington, D.C. 20036

American Council for the Blind
1211 Connecticut Avenue, N.W.
Washington, D.C. 20006

American Diabetes Association
18 East 48th Street
New York, NY 10011

American Printing House for the Blind
1839 Frankfort Avenue
P.O. Box 6085
Louisville, KY 40206

American Speech-Language-Hearing Association
10801 Rockville Pike
Rockville, MD 20852

Arthritis Foundation
1212 Avenue of the Americas
New York, NY 10036

Asociacion de Padres Pro-Bienestar de Ninos Impedidos de
    Puerto Rico
Box Q
Rio Piedras, PR 00928

Association for Children and Adults with Learning Disabilities
5225 Grace Street
Pittsburg, PA 15236

Association for the Education of the Visually Handicapped
919 Walnut, Fourth Floor
Philadelphia, PA 19107

Association for the Gifted
1920 Association Drive
Reston, VA 22091

Association for Persons with Severe Handicaps
7010 Roosevelt Way, N.E.
Seattle, WA 98115

Closer Look Information Center for the Handicapped
P.O. Box 1492
Washington, D.C. 20013

Coordinating Council for Handicapped Children
220 South State Street
Room 412
Chicago, IL 60604

Council for Exceptional Children
1920 Association Drive
Reston, VA 22091

Daycare and Child Development Council of America, Inc.
520 Southern Building
805 Fifteenth Street, N.W.
Washington, D.C. 20005

Epilepsy Foundation of America
1828 L Street, N.W., Suite 405
Washington, D.C. 20036

Federation for Children with Special Needs
312 Stuart Street, 2nd Floor
Boston, MA 02116

La Leche League International
9616 Minneapolis Avenue
Franklin Park, IL 60131

Leukemia Society of America, Inc.
211 East 43rd Street
New York, NY 10017

Muscular Dystrophy Association of America, Inc.
1828 Banking Street, Room 1
Greensboro, NC 27408

National Association for Children with Learning Disabilities
4156 Library Road
Pittsburgh, PA 15234

National Association for Creative Children and Adults
8080 Springvalley Drive
Cincinnati, OH 45236

National Association for the Deaf-Blind
2703 Forest Oak Circle
Norman, OK 73071

National Association for Down's Syndrome
P.O. Box 63
Oak Park, IL 60303

National Association for Retarded Citizens
2709 Avenue E East
P.O. Box 6109
Arlington, TX 76011

National Association for the Visually Handicapped
3201 Balboa Street
San Francisco, CA 94121

National Association of the Deaf
814 Thayer Avenue
Silver Spring, MD 20910

National Black Child Development Institute
1463 Rhode Island Avenue, N.W.
Washington, D.C. 20005

National Downs Syndrome Congress
528 Ashland Avenue
River Forest, IL 60305

National Easter Seal Society for Crippled Children and Adults
2023 W. Ogden Avenue
Chicago, IL 60612

National Federation of the Blind
1346 Connecticut Avenue, N.W.
Dupont Circle Building, Suite 212
Washington, D.C. 20036

National Hemophilia Foundation
25 West 39th Street
New York, NY 10018

National Paraplegia Foundation
333 N. Michigan Avenue
Chicago, IL 60601

National Society for Autistic Children
169 Tampa Avenue
Albany, NY 12208

National Society for the Prevention of Blindness
79 Madison Avenue
New York, NY 10016

National Tay-Sachs and Allied Diseases Association, Inc.
200 Park Avenue
New York, NY 10003

PACER (Parent Advocacy Coalition of Educational Rights)
4701 Chicago Avenue South
Minneapolis, MN 55407

Parent Educational Advocacy Training Center
228 S. Pitt Street, Room 300
Alexandria, VA 22314

PAVE (Parents Advocating Vocational Education)
1010 South I Street
Tacoma, WA 98405

Spina Bifida Association of America
343 S. Dearborn St., Room 319
Chicago, IL 60604

United Cerebral Palsy Association
66 East 34th Street
New York, NY 10016

WORKSHEETS AND FORMS

■ This appendix provides worksheets and forms to help teachers design and implement parent–teacher involvement activities. Readers can use these forms to complete the chapter exercises or to provide models for developing a parent–teacher involvement program responsive to special needs.

FIGURE D-1
Program Development
Form

Parents' Names _____ Teacher _____ Date _____

I	II	III	IV
Assessment	Goals and Objectives	Activities	Evaluation
A. List the assessment techniques used to obtain the data synthesized in IB.	A. List the goals, by priority, derived from the assessment process and mutually agreed on by parents and teacher.	List the activities designed by parents and teacher to meet the objectives in IIB.	A. Process: List the procedures parents and teacher will use to evaluate the processes for carrying out the activities in III.
B. List the needs mutually agreed upon using the assessment techniques in IA.	B. List the objectives derived from the goals in IIA.		B. Content: List the procedures parents and teachers will use to evaluate the content of the activities in III.

336

Parent's Name _____

Child's Name _____

Introduction:

   Listed below are several statements describing concerns common to the parents of exceptional children. The items may or may not concern you at this time. Please complete only those items that currently concern you.

   The information on this form is used *only* to help plan and implement a parent-teacher involvement program. All information is held in strict confidence.

Directions:

1. Read each statement carefully.
2. Circle the number on the 1–5 scale that most closely approximates your current need in each area. Circle *1* to indicate a low priority need and *5* to indicate a high priority need.
3. Below the 1–5 scale are several statements suggesting ways you may prefer to meet your stated needs. Please check only *two* of the four statements listed below each item.
4. You may write additional comments in the space provided.

I. I need the opportunity to discuss my feelings about my exceptional child and myself with someone who understands the problem.

(Circle the appropriate number.)

1	2	3	4	5
Low				High
Priority				Priority

(Check *only* two statements.)

_____ I prefer to talk to a professional.
_____ I prefer to talk to the parent of an exceptional child.
_____ I prefer to be referred to another agency for counseling.
_____ I prefer to read articles and books discussing the reactions of parents of exceptional children.
_____ I prefer _____
_____.

II. I would like to talk with other parents and families who have exceptional children.

(Circle the appropriate number.)

1	2	3	4	5
Low				High
Priority				Priority

(Check *only* two statements.)

_____ I prefer to be in a discussion group.
_____ I prefer to participate in social gatherings (picnics, parties, potluck dinners).
_____ I prefer to meet informally.
_____ I prefer to participate in general meetings, workshops, lectures, demonstrations, and other informational gatherings.
_____ I prefer _____
_____.

FIGURE D-2
Parents' Needs Form

(cont.)

III. I would like to learn more about my child's exceptionality.

(Circle the appropriate number.)

1	2	3	4	5
Low Priority				High Priority

(Check *only* two statements.)

_____ I prefer to obtain information through reading.
_____ I prefer to observe teachers and other professionals working with my child and then discuss my observations.
_____ I prefer individual parent-teacher conferences.
_____ I prefer a parent-teacher discussion group.
_____ I prefer _____

IV. I would like to learn more about how children develop and learn, especially exceptional children.

(Circle the appropriate number.)

1	2	3	4	5
Low Priority				High Priority

(Check *only* two statements.)

_____ I prefer to obtain information through reading.
_____ I prefer to participate in a formal behavior management training course.
_____ I prefer a parent-teacher discussion group.
_____ I prefer individual training in my home by a teacher or other professional.
_____ I prefer to attend meetings at which specialists present information on behavior management.
_____ I prefer _____

VI. I would like to work with a teacher or other professional so that I can use the same instructional methods at home that the school uses.

(Circle the appropriate number.)

1	2	3	4	5
Low Priority				High Priority

(Check *only* two statements.)

_____ I prefer to observe my child in school.
_____ I prefer to attend a training program in observation.
_____ I prefer to attend a course in instructional methods.
_____ I prefer to work with the teacher in my child's classroom.
_____ I prefer in-home training by a teacher or other professional.
_____ I prefer to learn through readings, newsletters, telephone communication, and similar resources.
_____ I prefer _____

*FIGURE D-2
(cont.)*

(cont.)

VII. I would like _____
_____.

(Circle the appropriate number.)

1	2	3	4	5
Low				High
Priority				Priority

(Write the appropriate statements.)

_____ I prefer _____
_____.

_____ I prefer _____
_____.

Comments:

Thank you.

Confidential   Date: _____

Parent's Name _____

Child's Name _____

Introduction:

Listed below are thirty-five topics and activities generally believed of interest to the parents of exceptional children. Not all parents are interested in any single item, nor is any parent interested in all the items.

Your response to this questionnaire is used *only* to assist in planning and implementing a parent-teacher involvement program for you. All information is held in strict confidence.

Directions:

1. Read the entire form carefully.
2. In Column A check 15 items of interest to you.
3. In Column B rank 5 of the 15 items you checked in Column A. Number the item of highest priority to you 5, the next highest 4, and so on.
4. You may write additional comments in the space provided.

A	B	
_____	_____	1. Help my child learn.
_____	_____	2. Build my child's self-confidence.
_____	_____	3. Select activities to help my child learn (books, games, toys, projects, experiences).
_____	_____	4. Teach my child to follow directions.
_____	_____	5. Help my child enjoy learning.
_____	_____	6. Assist my child in language development.
_____	_____	7. Teach my child problem-solving skills.
_____	_____	8. Fulfill my role as (father) (mother) to my child.
_____	_____	9. Avoid emotional involvement in my child's emotional outbursts.
_____	_____	10. Protect my child from getting hurt.
_____	_____	11. Care for my child when he or she is sick or injured.
_____	_____	12. Discipline my child.
_____	_____	13. Deal with my child's misbehavior.
_____	_____	14. Teach my child respect for people and property.
_____	_____	15. Teach my child to express feelings in a socially acceptable manner.
_____	_____	16. Teach my child to show love, affection, and consideration for other family members.
_____	_____	17. Teach my child to live in harmony with the family (television, bedtime, meals, sharing, responsibilities).

*FIGURE D-3
Parents' Activities Form*

(*cont.*)

_____ _____   18. Develop a positive and productive relationship with my child.

_____ _____   19. Develop my problem-solving skills.

How can I obtain information on the following topics affecting my child:

_____ _____   20. Art activities

_____ _____   21. Creative dramatics

_____ _____   22. Educational games and activities

_____ _____   23. Exercise

_____ _____   24. Health and hygiene

_____ _____   25. Music

_____ _____   26. Nutrition and diet

_____ _____   27. Puppetry

_____ _____   28. Recreation

_____ _____   29. Sleep

_____ _____   30. Toys

Other topics and activities of interest to me are:

_____ _____   31. _____

_____ _____   32. _____

_____ _____   33. _____

_____ _____   34. _____

_____ _____   35. _____

Thank you!

342

FIGURE D-4
Behavior Log Form

Target behavior _____

Child observed _____

Observer's name _____

Day or Date	Time		Antecedents	Consequences	Applied Interventions	Comments
	Begins	Ends				

Date: _____

Meeting Subject: _____

Please circle the responses that best reflect your feelings about this meeting.

1. The subject was: Not relevant   Somewhat relevant   Relevant   Very relevant

2. The information was: Not useful   Somewhat useful   Useful   Very useful

3. The manner of presentation was: Poor   Fair   Good   Very good

4. Audio visual materials and handouts were: Poor   Fair   Good   Very good

5. Would you like more information on the subject?   Yes   No

6. Comments:

Thanks! By letting us know how you feel, we can better meet your needs.

Your Advisory Committee

FIGURE D-5
Meeting Evaluation
Form

Date _____
Parents' Names _____
Child's Name _____ Telephone Number _____
Teacher's Name _____

Parents! We need your help. Please consider helping with the activities and projects listed on this questionnaire. Check all those activities for which you can volunteer service. Your participation will help us provide an interesting, stimulating, individualized educational program for your children.

Mother   Father

_____ _____ I would like to assist in the classroom on a regular basis. The times I have available are:

                         Days   Hours
                         _____   _____
                         _____   _____

_____ _____ I would like to assist *occasionally* in the classroom.

                      (check one)
                      a.   Contact me _____
                      b.   I will contact the school _____

_____ _____ I would like to assist from my home.

In-Classroom Activities

_____ _____ Read a story to the children.

_____ _____ Assist children in a learning center.

_____ _____ Assist individual children with learning and remedial tasks.

_____ _____ Assist with the music program.

_____ _____ Assist with the art program.

_____ _____ Assist with the movement activities program.

_____ _____ Work puzzles and play table games with the children.

_____ _____ Help with cooking projects.

_____ _____ Assist with writing activities.

_____ _____ Assist with carpentry projects.

_____ _____ Assist with homemaking projects.

_____ _____ Assist with the care of classroom pets.

_____ _____ Assist with gardening and horticultural projects.

_____ _____ Assist children during recess, snack time, lunch, and free time.

_____ _____ Take a child for a walk.

_____ _____ Assist with field trips.

FIGURE D-6
Parent-Volunteer
Questionnaire

(cont.)

_____ _____ Make instructional materials: games, flash cards, puppets, costumes, charts.

_____ _____ Type.

_____ _____ Help with costumes for dress-up events.

_____ _____ Cut out and catalog pictures from magazines, catalogs, and newspapers for instructional use.

_____ _____ Help repair classroom furnishings and instructional materials and equipment.

_____ _____ Help construct new furnishings and equipment for the classroom.

_____ _____ Organize parties for birthdays and holidays.

_____ _____ Babysit for parents who are volunteering their service to the classroom.

_____ _____ Care for classroom pets during vacations.

_____ _____ Make props and sets for plays, parties, and special events.

_____ _____ Make room and bulletin board decorations.

_____ _____ Make posters.

_____ _____ Assemble and staple materials.

_____ _____ Research and organize field trips.

_____ _____ Help plan and conduct parent activities, such as meetings, educational training programs, and conferences.

_____ _____ Research and contact sources for free instructional supplies (computer cards and paper, wood scraps, boxes, carpet, print shop discards, spools, pencils, paper).

_____ _____ Make items to sell for fund raising.

_____ _____ Assist with fund-raising activities.

_____ _____ Plan and organize social events.

What other activities could you help with?

  A. In the classroom:

  B. At home:

What other family members or friends are interested in volunteering services to the children?

  A. _____

  B. _____

Your comments, concerns, and questions are welcome.

Parent Name(s) _____

Child's Name _____ Birthdate _____

Home Phone Number _____ Work Phone Number _____

Date File Opened _____

Activities	Date

I.   INTAKE AND ASSESSMENT
    A. Intake and Assessment Conference(s) _____

    B. Intake and Assessment Completed _____

II. SELECTION OF GOALS AND OBJECTIVES
    A. Parents' Needs Form Returned _____
    B. Parents' Activities Form Returned _____
    C. Goals and Objectives Conferences _____

    D. Parent-Teacher Involvement Plan Completed _____

III. ACTIVITY ATTENDANCE
    A. Individual Conferences
        1. Home Visit _____
        2. Child Evaluation Conference _____
        3. IEP Conference _____
        4. _____ _____
        5. _____ _____

    A. Group Meetings
        1. Orientation Meeting _____
        2. _____ _____
        3. _____ _____
        4. _____ _____
        5. _____ _____

IV. EVALUATION
    A. Evaluation Form Returned _____
    B. Evaluation Conference _____

Phone Contacts

Date	Reason/Results
_____	_____
_____	_____
_____	_____
_____	_____
_____	_____

FIGURE D-7
Parent Involvement Log

(cont.)

Other Contacts (Letters, notes, and so on)

Date	Description	Reason/Results
_____	_____	_____
_____	_____	_____
_____	_____	_____
_____	_____	_____

May 24, 19__

Dear _____:

The Parent-Teacher Involvement Program is your program, designed with you and for you. We want it to meet your needs and the needs of your child. Thus, it is important to know what you like and dislike about the program and what activities you would and would not participate in next year.

To help in the planning of next year's program and to make it more responsive to your needs, we invite you to complete and return the attached questionnaire. Please be frank. If you wish to remain anonymous, do not sign the form. Anonymous or signed, your responses will be held in the strictest of confidence.

Thank you for your help.

Sincerely,

Sarah Paul
Teacher

FIGURE D-8
Parent Involvement
Program Evaluation
Form

Please make an X in the appropriate columns to the right of each activity listed in the left column. Indicate whether you participated in the activity and how you felt about it. For meetings and workshops, please indicate if you wanted to attend but were unable to. Comments and suggestions are welcome.

ACTIVITY	I was involved in this activity.	I wanted to participate but could not.	I would participate again next year.	My rating of this activity is:			
				Excellent	Good	Fair	Poor
Intake/Assessment Conferences							
Parent Orientation Meeting							
Open House							
Rights and Confidentiality Meeting							
Newsletter							
Passport							
Telephone Calls							
Individual Conferences							
Parent Partners							
Behavior Management Group							
Other:							
Other:							

Use the space below to comment on this year's program and make suggestions for next year.

FIGURE D-8
(cont.)

349

SPANISH WORKSHEETS AND FORMS

■ Today's teachers serve many Spanish-speaking exceptional children and their families, often in bilingual programs. To help develop appropriate programs for these families, this appendix presents Spanish versions of several worksheets and forms used in this text. Readers who serve bilingual children and their parents, or who expect to in the future, can use these forms to complete the chapter exercises or to develop their own programs for Spanish-speaking exceptional children and their families.

FIGURE E-1
Program Development
Form

FORMULARIO DEL PROGRAMA DE DESARROLLO

Nombre y apellido de los padres: _____ Maestro/a _____ Fecha: _____

I Evaluación	II Metas y Objetivos	III Actividades	IV Evaluación
A. Enumere las técnicas de evaluación que se usaron para obtener los datos resumidos en IB.	A. Enumere los objetivos, en orden de prioridad, que han resultado del processo de evaluación y sobre los que se han puesto de acuerdo los padres y los maestros.	Enumere las actividades diseñadas por los padres y el maestro o maestra para lograr los objetivos	A. Haga una lista de los metodos que los padres y maestros van a usar para evaluar los procesos diseñados para implementar las actividades en III.
B. Enumere las necesidades sobre las que se han puesto de acuerdo cuando se han usado las técnicas de evaluación en IA.	B. Enumere los objetivos que se han ido desarrollando a base de las metas u objetivos en IIA.		B. *El Contenido:* Enumere los procedimientos que los padres y los maestros van a usar para evaluar el contenido de las actividades en III.

Confidencial   Fecha: _____

Nombre y apellido de los padres: _____

Nombre del niño/a: _____

Introducción:

A continuación, van a enumerarse una serie de frases que describen temas comunes a los padres de niños excepcionales. Algunos de estos temas pueden no atañer a sus circumstancias en este momento. Por favor complete solamente los párrafos que se apliquen a su situación.

La información en este formulario es estrictamente para propósitos de planeación e implementación de un programa de colaboración entre padres y maestros. Toda la información es estrictamente confidencial.

Instrucciones:

1. Lea cada frase cuidadosamente.
2. En la escala de 1 a 5—el *1* representa baja prioridad y el *5* indica una necesidad de alta prioridad—señale con un circulo la frase que mejor indique su actitud sobre las necesidades descritas.
3. A continuación de la escala de 1 a 5 hay varias sugerencias para cómo llenar sus necesidades. Por favor señale solamente *dos* de las cuatro frases debajo de cada tema.
4. Escriba sus comentarios adicionales en el espacio apropiado.

I. Necesito la oportunidad de discutir mis sentimientos hacia mi niño/a excepcional y hacia mí mismo/a en relación a mi hijo/a con una persona que comprenda el problema.

(Indique el número apropiado con un círculo)

1	2	3	4	5
Baja Prioridad				Alta Prioridad

Señale solamente *dos* reacciones:

_____ Prefiero hablar con un profesional al respecto.
_____ Prefiero hablar con el padre o los padres de niños excepcionales.
_____ Prefiero que me refieran a otra agencia que ofrezca guianza.
_____ Prefiero leer artículos y libros que discutan las reacciones de los padres de niños excepcionales.
_____ Prefiero la siguiente opción _____
_____

II. Quisiera reunirme con otros padres y familias con niños excepcionales.

(Indique el número apropiado con un círculo)

1	2	3	4	5
Baja Prioridad				Alta Prioridad

(Señale solamente *dos* reacciones)

_____ Prefiero participar en un grupo de discusión.
_____ Prefiero participar en reuniones sociales (picnics, comidas informales con otros padres, etc.).
_____ Prefiero que nos reunamos informalmente.
_____ Prefiero participar en reuniones generales, talleres, conferencias, demostraciones, etc.
_____ Prefiero lo siguiente _____
_____

FIGURE E-2
Parents' Needs Forms

(cont.)

III. Quiero informarme más con respecto a las necesidades especiales de mi hijo/a.

(Indique el número apropiado con un círculo)

1	2	3	4	5
Baja				Alta
Prioridad				Prioridad

(Señale solamente *dos* frases)

_____ Prefiero informarme a través de lectura.
_____ Prefiero observar a los maestros y otros profesionales trabajar con mi hijo/a y después discutir mis observaciones.
_____ Prefiero conferencias individuales con el maestro/a.
_____ Prefiero un grupo de discusión que incluya a padres y maestros.
_____ Prefiero lo siguiente _____

_____

IV. Quisiera aprender sobre el desarrollo y el proceso de aprendizaje de los niños, especialmente de los niños excepcionales.

(Indique el número apropiado con un círculo)

1	2	3	4	5
Baja				Alta
Prioridad				Prioridad

(Señale solamente *dos* frases)

_____ Prefiero informarme a través de lectura.
_____ Prefiero participar en un curso formal sobre el manejo de comportamiento.
_____ Prefiero un grupo de discusión entre padres y maestros.
_____ Prefiero recibir entrenamiento individual en mi casa de un maestro/a u otro profesional.
_____ Prefiero atender conferencias en las que varios especialistas presenten información sobre el manejo de comportamiento.
_____ Prefiero lo siguiente _____

_____

VI. Quisiera trabajar con un maestro/a para poder aplicar los mismos métodos de instrucción en mi casa que se aplican en la escuela.

(Indique con un círculo el número apropriado)

1	2	3	4	5
Baja				Alta
Prioridad				Prioridad

(Señale solamente *dos* reacciones de las siguientes)

_____ Prefiero observar al niño en la escuela.
_____ Prefiero atender un programa de entrenamiento en técnicas de observación.
_____ Prefiero atender un curso en métodos de instrucción.
_____ Prefiero trabajar con el maestro/a en el salón de clase.
_____ Prefiero recibir entrenamiento de un maestro u otro profesional en mi casa.
_____ Prefiero informarme a través de lecturas, boletines de noticias, por teléfono, etc.
_____ Prefiero lo siguiente _____

_____

FIGURE E-2
(cont.)

(cont.)

VII. Quisiera lo siguiente _____

_____

(Indique el número apropiado con un círculo)

1	2	3	4	5
Baja Prioridad				Alta Prioridad

(Anote aquí la frase apropriada)

_____ Prefiero lo siguiente _____

_____

_____ Prefiero lo siguiente _____

_____

Comentarios:

Muchas gracias.

<u>Confidencial</u>   Fecha: _____

Nombre y apellido de los padres: _____

Nombre del niño/a: _____

Introducción:

    A continuación van a enumerarse treinta y cinco temas y actividades que generalmente resultan de interés para los padres de niños excepcionales. No todos los padres estarán interesados en un solo tema, ni estarán todos interesados en todos los temas.

    Sus respuestas en este formulario se usarán *únicamente* para la planeación e implementación de un programa colaborativo para ustedes. Toda la información es estrictamente confidencial.

<u>Direcciones</u>

    1. Lea todo el formulario cuidadosamente.
    2. En la columna A señale 15 frases que le parezcan interesantes.
    3. En la columna B enumere en orden de prioridad 5 de las 15 frases que indicó en la columna A. El tema de más alta prioridad debe numerarse 5; el próximo de más alta prioridad debe numerarse 4, y así los 5.
    4. Escriba sus comentarios adicionales en el espacio apropiado.

Columna A	B	Tema
_____	_____	1. Ayudar a mi hijo/a a aprender.
_____	_____	2. Desarrollar la confianza de mi hijo/a en sí mismo.
_____	_____	3. Seleccionar actividades para ayudar a mi hijo/a a aprender (libros, juegos, juguetes, proyectos, experiencias).
_____	_____	4. Enseñar a mi hijo/a a seguir instrucciones.
_____	_____	5. Ayudar a mi hijo/a a gozar del proceso de aprendizaje.
_____	_____	6. Ayudar a mi hijo/a a desarrollar destrezas de lenguaje.
_____	_____	7. Enseñarle destrezas para resolver problemas.
_____	_____	8. Cumplir con mi papel como (padre) (madre).
_____	_____	9. Evitar involucrarme en las crisis emocionales del niño/a.
_____	_____	10. Cuidar de que el niño no se haga daño.
_____	_____	11. Cuidar el niño/a cuando este enfermo o se haya hecho daño.
_____	_____	12. Disciplinar al niño.
_____	_____	13. Manejar el comportamiento inapropiado del niño.
_____	_____	14. Enseñarle a respetar a la gente y a las cosas.
_____	_____	15. Enseñarle a que exprese sus sentimientos de una manera aceptable a la sociedad.
_____	_____	16. Enseñarle a demostrar amor, afecto y consideración con respecto a otros miembros de la familia.
_____	_____	17. Enseñarle a vivir en armonía con la familia (televisión, hora de acostarse, comidas, generosidad, responsabilidades).
_____	_____	18. Desarrollar una actitud positiva y productiva hacia mi hijo/a.
_____	_____	19. Desarrollar destrezas para resolver problemas.

FIGURE E-3
Parents' Activities Forms

(cont.)

Como puedo obtener información sobre los siguientes
temas con relación a mi hijo/a?

_____ _____ 20. Actividades de arte
_____ _____ 21. Drama creativo
_____ _____ 22. Juegos y actividades educacionales
_____ _____ 23. Ejercicio
_____ _____ 24. Salud e higiene
_____ _____ 25. Música
_____ _____ 26. Nutrición y dieta
_____ _____ 27. Títeres
_____ _____ 28. Recreación
_____ _____ 29. Sueño
_____ _____ 30. Juguetes

Otros temas y actividades de interés:

_____ _____ 31. _____
_____ _____ 32. _____
_____ _____ 33. _____
_____ _____ 34. _____
_____ _____ 35. _____

Muchas Gracias!

358

FIGURE E-4
Behavior Log Form

Objetivo de comportamiento: _____

Nombre del observador: _____ Nombre del niño/a: _____

Día o Fecha	Hora		Antecedentes	Consecuencias	Intervención	Comentarios
	Empieza	Acaba				

FORMULARIO DE EVALUACION DE LA REUNION

359 ■

APPENDIX E
SPANISH
WORKSHEETS AND
FORMS

Tema de la reunión: _____   Fecha: _____

Indique con un círculo la respuesta que mejor refleje lo que usted sintió con respecto a esta reunión:

1. El tema fue   no aplicable   algo necesario   importante   muy importante

2. La información que
   se presentó fue: no aplicable   algo práctica   práctica   muy práctica

3. El estilo de
   presentación fue: malo   regular   bueno   muy bueno

4. Los materiales
   audiovisuales
   fueron: malos   regulares   buenos   muy buenos

5. Quiere más información sobre este tema?   sí   no

6. Comentarios

Gracias. Informándonos sobre sus reacciones, podemos servirle mejor.

Comité de Asesoría

FORMULARIO DE PADRES VOLUNTARIOS

Nombre y apellido de los padres _____ Teléfono: _____

Nombre del niño/a _____

Nombre del maestro/a _____

   Padres! Necesitamos su ayuda; por favor considere ayudarnos con las actividades y proyectos que mencionamos en este formulario. Indique en cuales actividades puede ofrecernos sus servicios voluntarios. Para ofrecer un programa educacional interesante, estimulante e individualizado para su hijo/a necesitamos su ayuda.

Padre   Madre

_____   _____   Podría ayudar en el salón de clase con regularidad. Dispongo de las siguientes horas:

                                        Días   Horas
                                        _____   _____
                                        _____   _____

_____   _____   Podría ayudar en el salón de clase ocasionalmente.

                         (indique a o b)

                         a.   Llámeme _____

                         b.   Yo me pondré en contacto con la escuela _____

_____   _____   Quisiera asistir en mi casa.

En las Actividades del Salón de Clase

_____   _____   Leyendo cuentos a los niños.

_____   _____   Ayudando a los niños en el centro de aprendizaje.

_____   _____   Ayudando a los niños individualmente con tareas de aprendizaje y trabajo remedial.

_____   _____   Asistiendo en el programa de música.

_____   _____   Asistiendo en el programa de arte.

_____   _____   Asistiendo en el programa de actividades de movimiento.

_____   _____   Asistiendo en los juegos y actividades de los niños.

_____   _____   Asistiendo en los proyectos de cocina.

_____   _____   Asistiendo en proyectos de redacción.

_____   _____   Asistendo en proyectos de carpintería.

_____   _____   Ayudar en proyectos caseros.

_____   _____   Asistiendo en el cuidado de los animales.

_____   _____   Ayudando en proyectos de jardinería y horticultura.

_____   _____   Ayudando a los niños a las horas de recreo, almuerzo, etc.

_____   _____   Sacando a los niños a caminar.

_____   _____   Asistiendo en excursiones por fuera de la escuela.

FIGURE E-6
Parent-Volunteer
Questionnaire

_____ _____ Trabajando en el diseño y construcción de materiales de instrucción: juegos, tarjetas de instrucción, titeres, disfraces, listas, etc.

_____ _____ Pasando trabajos a máquina.

_____ _____ Ayudando a hacer disfraces para funciones de la escuela.

_____ _____ Recortando y catalogando materiales de revistas, catalogos y diarios para uso en el salón de clase.

_____ _____ Ayudando a arreglar los muebles del salón de clase y los materiales y equipo de instrucción.

_____ _____ Ayudar en la construcción de muebles y materiales para el salón de clase.

_____ _____ Organizar fiestas de cumpleaños y otras fiestas especiales.

_____ _____ Asistir en el cuidado de otros niños cuando los padres estén dando servicios voluntarios en la escuela.

_____ _____ Asistir en el cuidado de los animales que pertenecen a la clase durante las vacaciones de la escuela.

_____ _____ Hacer diseños para funciones de teatro, fiestas y otras ocasiones especiales.

_____ _____ Hacer decoraciones para el salón.

_____ _____ Hacer ficheros.

_____ _____ Ordenar y coser materiales de instrucción.

_____ _____ Investigar y organizar excursiones por fuera de la escuela.

_____ _____ Asistir en la organización de actividades para los padres—por ejemplo reuniones, programas de entrenamiento educacional, conferencias, etc.

_____ _____ Investigar y hacer contacto con gente y organizaciones que puedan donar gratis materiales para uso en el salón: por ejemplo, tarjetas de computadores, pedazos de madera, cajas, retazos de tapetes, desperdicios de imprentas, carretes, lápices, papel, etc.

_____ _____ Hacer cosas para vender en funciones para beneficiar a la escuela.

_____ _____ Asistir en actividades para obtener fondos.

_____ _____ Planear y organizar eventos sociales.

Si hay otras actividades en las que usted pueda participar como voluntario/a, por favor descríbalas aquí.

A. En el salón de clase:

B. En la casa:

■ 362

*APPENDIX E
SPANISH
WORKSHEETS AND
FORMS*

*FIGURE E-6
(cont.)*

Que otros miembros de la familia o amigos estarán interesados en prestar servicio voluntario para los niños?

A. _____

B. _____

Les agradecemos sus comentarios y preguntas.

Nombre y apellido de los padres: _____

Nombre del niño/a: _____ Fecha de nacimiento: _____

Número del teléfono de la casa: _____ Del trabajo: _____

Fecha en que se ha iniciado el archivo: _____

Actividades _____ Fecha _____

I. INGRESO Y EVALUACION
    A. Conferencia de Ingreso y Evaluación   _____
                                                      _____
    B. Ingreso y Evaluación completados   _____
                                                      _____

II. SELECCION DE METAS Y OBJETIVOS
    A. Formulario de Necesidades de los Padres, Devuelto   _____
    B. Formulario de Actividades de los Padres, Devuelto   _____
    C. Conferencias sobre Metas y Objetivos   _____
                                                            _____
    D. Plan de Actividades de Padres-Maestros, devuelto   _____

III. ACTIVIDADES ATENDIDAS
    A. Conferencias Individuales (Descripciones):
        1. Visita a la casa   _____
        2. Conferencia de Evaluación del Niño   _____
        3. Conferencia de IEP   _____
        4. _____   _____
        5. _____   _____

    B. Reuniones de Grupo (Descripciones:)
        1. Reunion de Orientacion   _____
        2. _____   _____
        3. _____   _____
        4. _____   _____
        5. _____   _____

IV. EVALUACION
    A. Formulario de Evaluacion devuelto   _____
    B. Conferencia de Evaluacion   _____

Contactos por Telefono

Fecha   Razon/Resultados

_____   _____

_____   _____

_____   _____

_____   _____

_____   _____

Contactos Adicionales (Cartas, notas, etc.)

Fecha	Descripcion	Razon/Resultados
_____	_____	_____
_____	_____	_____
_____	_____	_____
_____	_____	_____

EVALUACION DEL PROGRAMA PARA PADRES Y MAESTROS

24 de mayo de 19__

Estimado ______________________________:

El Programa para Padres y Maestros es suyo, diseñado para usted y con usted. Este programa se ofrece esencialmente para atender sus necesidades y las de su niño/a. Es importante saber lo que a usted le agrada y le desagrada en el programa y en qué actividades usted podría participar en este proximo año.

Para ayudarnos a planear el programa para el próximo año y hacerlo más apropiado para sus necesidades, le pedimos que complete y devuelva este formulario. Por favor, denos sus opiniones francamente. Si prefiere permanecer anónimo, no firme este formulario. Firmado o anónimo, sus respuestas se mantendrán confidenciales.

Muchas gracias por su ayuda.

Atentamente,

Sarah Paul
Maestra

FIGURE E-8
Parent Involvement Program Evaluation Form

FIGURE E-8
(cont.)

Por favor indique con una X las columnas apropiados a la derecha de cada actividad anotada en la columna izquierda. Señale si usted participó en la actividad y sus reacciones al respecto. En el caso de reuniones y talleres, indique si usted quiso atender pero no pudo. Le agradeceríamos sus comentarios y sugerencias.

ACTIVIDAD	Participé en esta actividad	Quise tomar parte pero no pude	Quisiera participar el año entrante	Mi evaluación de esta actividad fue:			
				Excelente	Bueno	Mediocre	Malo
Conferencia de Ingreso/Evaluación							
Reunión de Orientación para los Padres							
Casa Abierta							
Reunión sobre Derechos y Confidencialidad							
Boletín							
Pasaporte							
Llamadas Telefónicas							
Conferencias Individuales							
Compañero/a a otros padres							
Grupo de Manejo de Comportamiento							
Otra:							
Otra:							

Comentarios sobre el programa de este año y sugerencias para el año entrante:

366

INDEX